Maxwell's Demon and the Golden Apple

Maxwell's Demon and the Golden Apple

Global Discord in the New Millennium

Randall L. Schweller

Johns Hopkins University Press
Baltimore

© 2014 Johns Hopkins University Press
All rights reserved. Published 2014
Printed in the United States of America on acid-free paper
9 8 7 6 5 4 3 2 1

Johns Hopkins University Press
2715 North Charles Street
Baltimore, Maryland 21218-4363
www.press.jhu.edu

Library of Congress Cataloging-in-Publication Data

Schweller, Randall L.
    Maxwell's demon and the golden apple : global discord in the new
millennium / Randall L. Schweller.
        pages cm
    Includes index.
    ISBN 978-1-4214-1277-1 (hardcover : alk. paper) — ISBN 978-1-4214-1278-8
(electronic) — ISBN 1-4214-1277-2 (hardcover : alk. paper) —
ISBN 1-4214-1278-0 (electronic)   1. World politics—21st century—
Forecasting.   2. International relations—Forecasting.   3. International
organization—Forecasting.   4. Twenty-first century—Forecasts.   I. Title.
    JZ1318.S366 2014
    327.1—dc23

                                                        2013025011

A catalog record for this book is available from the British Library.

*Special discounts are available for bulk purchases of this book. For more
information, please contact Special Sales at 410-516-6936 or
specialsales@press.jhu.edu.*

Johns Hopkins University Press uses environmentally friendly book
materials, including recycled text paper that is composed of at least 30
percent post-consumer waste, whenever possible.

For Julie

Contents

Preface

This is a book about how and why international politics is transforming from a system anchored for hundreds of years in enduring principles, which made it relatively constant and predictable, into something far more erratic, unsettled, and devoid of behavioral regularities. In the fall of 2009, I was asked by Justine Rosenthal, then editor of the *National Interest*, to write an essay for their First Draft of History series which posed the question: Twenty-five years from now, what will we be saying about today's international politics? I decided to roll a grenade down the table, so to speak—to write a provocative and theoretically unconventional piece that attempted to capture what is essential and unprecedented about global politics in the new millennium. In that article I argued that contemporary international politics is steadily moving toward a state of chaos and randomness, a change consistent with the universal law of rising entropy.

The present study is an outgrowth of that essay. In a sense, it throws down the gauntlet, challenging the "garden-variety" theoretical treatments of international politics that continue to populate an already crowded field of books—one fueled by the public's "parlor game-like" fascination with what comes after the American century or, in the language of academics, what comes after unipolarity. Most of these works are rooted in concepts, rules, and premises that, tellingly, would be familiar to Napoleon Bonaparte and Otto von Bismarck, both of whom, if they suddenly awoke from their long sleeps and read these books, would mistakenly (but understandably) conclude that little had changed in their absence.

The title, *Maxwell's Demon and the Golden Apple*, is a whimsical play on the book's core theme of global (dis)order. I say *whimsical* because the theme is disguised not only in a fanciful but also a counterintuitive way: a commonsense guess as to which object, the demon or the golden apple, stands for order and which for disorder would most likely prove incorrect. The apple, not the demon, represents disorder and chaos; it is a reference to the mythical Golden Apple of Discord.

According to Greek mythology, Zeus held a banquet among the Olympian gods to celebrate the marriage of Peleus and Thetis. Eris, the goddess of discord (corresponding to the Roman goddess Discordia) was deliberately not invited by Zeus because he feared that she, given her troublesome nature, would make the party unpleasant for everyone. Angered by this snub, Eris showed up at the fête anyhow with a golden apple upon which she had inscribed KALLISTI (THI ΚΑΛΛΙΣΤΗI in ancient Greek), meaning "For the Fairest," and tossed it into the banquet hall, sparking a vanity-driven dispute among the goddesses that eventually led to the Trojan War. The goddesses wanted Zeus to play the role of judge, but he, naturally reluctant to proclaim one of them the most beautiful, decided instead to send the three contestants—Aphrodite, Athena, and Hera—to a mortal but fair-minded Trojan shepherd-prince, Paris, for a decision. Guided by Hermes, the three goddesses appeared naked before Paris at Mount Ida. As he inspected them, each goddess tempted him with a bribe to give her the apple. Hera offered to make him king of Europe and Asia; Athena promised him wisdom and skill in war; Aphrodite said that he could have the most beautiful woman in the world. In what is known as the Judgment of Paris, the prince, being a healthy young lad, gave the apple to Aphrodite, thereby making powerful enemies of Athena and Hera. In Aphrodite's eyes, the most beautiful woman of the world was Helen of Sparta (now known as Helen of Troy), the wife of a Greek king, Menelaus. While the king was away, Paris carried Helen off to Troy, provoking the Greeks to combine their military forces for war on Troy to bring her back. Trojan civilization was destroyed in the process.

The demon, whom you will meet later in the book, is an allegorical creature at the center of a thought experiment by the physicist James Clerk Maxwell to reverse the entropy-rising process inherent in all closed systems. Entropy may be thought of as a measure of disorder in the universe (or, in a purely thermodynamic sense, of the availability of energy in a closed system to do work): the higher the entropy, the higher the disorder. The entropy of an isolated system never decreases because isolated systems spontaneously evolve towards thermodynamic equilibrium—the state of maximum entropy. Maxwell's demon defies the Second Law of Thermodynamics by means of a superhuman sorting of molecules according to their differing kinetic energies. Guarding a frictionless door between two rooms filled with gas, the demon opens the door for particularly fast-moving molecules, allowing them to pass into a room that becomes progressively hotter. Likewise, the demon allows particularly slow-moving molecules to pass out of the warmer room into the cooler one. By segregating the fast particles from the slow ones, the demon creates a growing temperature difference within the system that violates the Second Law, restoring the potential energy available for work and, thereby, increasing order in the universe.

One of the core ideas of the book will strike most readers as counterintuitive. Large, destructive wars are not always or in all ways bad; they serve the function of providing world order. Indeed, the time-honored solution for rising global disorder—as well as for rising discord among nations and what political scientists refer to as system disequilibrium—is a large and total war fought among all the great powers. These so-called hegemonic wars have regularly ensued every hundred years or so. The destructiveness of modern weaponry, however, precludes any rational thought of another hegemonic war, and if rationality did not prevent another one being fought, a twenty-first-century hegemonic war would eliminate not only global disorder but everything else on the planet. That major-power war is unthinkable is a good thing, to be sure. The downside, however, is that there is no other known remedy for rising entropy in international politics. Also, today's rising disorder is not confined to the international politics conducted solely by nation-states but to a global system composed of many different types of actors exerting various kinds of power. Add to this the accelerated pace of technological change and we have a world that is dauntingly complex and driven by the certainty of unpredictable change. Is there a Maxwell's demon in our future? Can the allegory become a reality? Candidates abound, but only time will tell if one will step forward. If not, that's fine too. International politics will be messier than ever, but life will carry on as it always does.

Acknowledgments

My deepest thanks go to Daniel Drezner and Andrew Moravcsik for their immeasurably helpful advice and criticism on the initial proposal and later drafts of the manuscript. I am also indebted to Justine Rosenthal for her insightful suggestions and queries that were incorporated in the *National Interest* article, which spawned the present work.

Some of the talks I gave about the book generated probing questions and useful suggestions from the audiences. I want to especially thank my hosts, Michael Reese and Charles Lipson, at the University of Chicago's Program on International Politics, Economics, and Security (PIPES); Charles Glaser, Director of the Institute for Security and Conflict Studies at George Washington University's Elliott School of International Affairs; and Barry Posen, Director of the Security Studies Program Seminars at the Massachusetts Institute of Technology. I am also grateful to A. Burcu Bayram, Bear Braumoeller, Julie Clemens, Eric Grynaviski, Ted Hopf, Robert Jervis, Jennifer Mitzen, Xiaoyu Pu, Gideon Rose, David Schweller, Jack Snyder, Alex Thompson, Alexander Wendt, the audience at the Research in International Politics (RIP) Seminar at Ohio State University, John Ikenberry and the distinguished participants at the National Intelligence Council workshops in Washington, DC, and three anonymous reviewers for their comments on an early incarnation of the project: "Entropy and the Trajectory of World Politics: Why Polarity Has Become Less Meaningful," *Cambridge Review of International Affairs*, vol. 23, no. 1 (March 2010), pp. 145–63.

At my academic home, the Department of Political Science at the Ohio State University, I benefit from a group of first-rate international relations theorists whom I am thankful to call "colleagues" and from whom I continue to learn. I am grateful for the support I received from the Mershon Center for International Security Studies at Ohio State University and from the Center's two directors, Richard Herrmann and J. Craig Jenkins. I am also indebted to the College of Arts and Sciences at Ohio State University for awarding me a Joan N. Huber Faculty Fellowship in 2012, which provided vital research support for the project.

This is my first project entrusted to Suzanne Flinchbaugh. She confirmed her reputation as an editor who cares deeply about the books she works with and makes them better with her detailed analysis, generous enthusiasm, and sensible and informed counsel. She also takes care to select expert reviewers who provide challenging and constructive criticisms that refine and tighten the logic of the arguments. Finally, I thank Glenn Perkins for his superb copy-editing of the manuscript.

The book is dedicated to my beloved wife, Julie Clemens, who not only improved the manuscript's substance and style but encouraged me with her belief in the value of the project and my ability to bring it to life. Last but not least, I want to acknowledge the warmth and inspiration that Street Kitty lovingly provided during many long, dark nights of thinking and typing. The world was a far better place with him in it.

Maxwell's Demon and the Golden Apple

Navigating the Chaos of Contemporary World Politics

Network versus No-work

The world is undergoing transformation. We are entering the age of entropy, a chaotic period where most anything can happen and little can be predicted; where yesterday's rule takers become tomorrow's rule makers, but no one follows rules anymore; where competing global visions collide with each other; where remnants of the past, present, and future coexist simultaneously. In this world, global interdependence is increasing, power is diffusing, and multilateral cooperation is dwindling; capabilities to block, disable, damage, and destroy prevail over those to adopt, enable, repair, and build; where geography no longer distinguishes friends from enemies, and no one can be trusted. The once impenetrable "hard shell" of the territorial state gives way to a permeability that undermines sovereignty and independence.[1] The future hinges on what the present anticipates, on how established and emerging powers portray the coming world and how they intend to act on their present understandings.

The Old Order constructed by the United States after World War II—an order that provided roughly sixty years of global stability, development, and prosperity—is under serious strain, and the status quo cannot hold much longer.[2] While the United States remains the lone superpower, it is no longer a hyperpower towering over all contenders. The rest of the world is catching up. America's strength and influence have markedly diminished from what they were only a decade ago. The United States has lost 30 percent of its relative economic power since 2000, and its annual growth rates are down almost 50 percent from what they were during the years 1993–2000.[3]

Statistics like these have prompted a new wave of Chicken Little declinists, who—having spent the past twenty years in the wilderness—are once again sounding the alarm: "Help! America is in unprecedented decline! China is rising! India too! I think I see Brazilians as well! Help!" I say "Chicken Little" because, by the scholar Josef Joffe's count, this is the fifth wave of declinism in the last six decades.[4] But unlike its last appearance two decades ago, when "Decline 4.0" claimed that Japan was winning back commercially what it lost at Pearl Harbor and predicted that the twenty-first century would see Pax Nipponica replace Pax Americana, the sky may indeed be falling this time.[5] We should not automatically dismiss Decline 5.0 because past surges of pessimism turned out to be unfounded. As Wall Street likes to warn, "past performance is no guarantee of future results."[6]

Whether the extent and rate of U.S. decline are unique in history, the crisis of a major downward trajectory in future power—most likely an irreversible one—is not a uniquely American problem; it extends to Washington's traditional partners and allies, whose collective fall is comparatively deeper and more rapid than America's. Across the Atlantic, a double-dip recession is now a very real possibility, as the Eurozone stumbles from one crisis to the next. The problems of the heavily indebted PIIGS (Portugal, Ireland, Italy, Greece, and Spain)—confronted with the toxic mixture of falling revenues and soaring bond yields—are the stuff of nightmares, from which the world's bankers who own much of the debt wish they could awaken. Driven by deleveraging, massive unemployment (24% in Spain, 22% in Greece, with youth unemployment over 50% in both countries), and contracting growth (in 2012, by 4.7% in Greece, 3.3% in Portugal, 1.9% in Italy, and 1.8% in Spain), the gathering Eurostorm threatens, at best, a prolonged global economic slump that experts expect will last a decade or more (economic data covering a span of eight centuries convincingly show that financial crises led to slumps that were longer and deeper than other recessions).[7] At worst, further financial crises could tear asunder the social and political fabric of many Western countries.[8]

For Europe and Japan, the long-run challenge is to reduce debt and clear the way for sustained economic growth in the face of rapidly aging populations.[9] Their labor forces will be shrinking at a time when their social entitlement payments are set to grow, making it more difficult for them to pay down their accumulated debt. What little growth they can reasonably hope to achieve will need to come from increased labor productivity, which means boosting automation, developing and adopting innovative products and services, and shedding low-skilled workers. But here's the rub: while the size of the developed world's working-age population is expected to contract by one million people over the next two decades, developing countries will be adding 932 million new workers to the global labor pool.[10] Pitted against this external competition, even the shrinking labor forces of Europe and Japan may not be fully employed.

The Rise of Non-Western Countries

The world seen from a bird's-eye view is undergoing a massive shift in power from the developed to the developing countries, roughly from West to East and South.[11] According to the latest report by the U.S. National Intelligence Council on long-range global trends: "By 2030, Asia will have surpassed North America and Europe combined in terms of global power based on GDP, population size, military spending, and technological investment."[12] The World Bank similarly predicts that, by 2025, (1) China and India together will be twice the engine for global growth as the United States and Eurozone, (2) six major emerging economies will account for more than half of all global growth, and (3) the international monetary system will no longer be dominated by a single currency.[13] In addition, the International Institute for Strategic Studies predicts that for the first time in modern history, Asia's defense spending is set to exceed Europe's in 2012.[14]

Like the BRICS (Brazil, Russia, India, China, and South Africa, which became a member in 2011), the so-called Next Eleven, or N-11, countries (Bangladesh, Egypt, Indonesia, Iran, South Korea, Mexico, Nigeria, Pakistan, Philippines, Turkey, and Vietnam) are rising as well—so much so that the aggregate power of the non-Western emerging market and developing nations is projected to overtake that of the developed countries before 2030.[15] We already see evidence in support of this massive power shift. By 2010, emerging and developing countries held three-quarters of all official foreign exchange reserves (a reversal of the prior decade, when advanced countries held two-thirds of all reserves), and their share of international trade flows rose from 26 percent in 1995 to 42 percent in 2010, mostly due to expansion in trade not between advanced and developing economies but rather among the developing countries themselves.[16] And the future looks just as bright.[17] As long as they maintain these stable conditions for growth, all of the N-11 states have the capacity to grow at 4 percent or more over the next twenty years. Indeed, N-11 gross domestic product (GDP) alone could reach two-thirds the size of the G-7 by 2050, predicts Goldman Sachs.[18]

Growth in these emerging-market countries over the next fifteen to twenty years will trigger a 50 percent increase in global demand for food and a 45 percent increase in the demand for energy. More important, it will enormously complicate the global economic and geopolitical landscape. Power is being dispersed more evenly across the globe; the world is leveling out. This will make working together to get things done more difficult. At a time when the "diffusion of global growth and economic power raises the imperative of collective management . . . for addressing the challenges of a multipolar world economy,"[19] the very existence of these new power centers will render cooperation of any sort that much harder to pull off. Simply put, international cooperation will be least feasible when most needed.

The rate of change in the global power structure is also off the charts by historical standards. From the start of its industrial revolution, Britain took 154 years (1700–1854) for GDP per person measured at purchasing-power parity to double from $1,300 to $2,600. One hundred and twenty years later, the United States, with roughly the same size population (in the tens of millions), took a third of the time to double its GDP per person (53 years, from 1822 to 1875). Both India and China, with roughly a hundred times the population of Britain during its heyday, achieved the same feat in a tenth of the time: China did it in just twelve years; India, in sixteen. Looking ahead, GDP per person in both China and India (using the International Monetary Fund average of growth forecasts for 2011–16) could double from 2011 levels by the end of this decade. People in the developed economies, in contrast, will have to wait another quarter century to see their incomes double.[20]

If, as forecasted, the parallel rise of China and India continues over the coming decades, the United States will have to struggle mightily just to preserve its demoted position of primus inter pares—first among equals. For China, the last decade under the leadership of President Hu Jintao has been a "Glorious Decade," as the *People's Daily* calls it.[21] China rose from a middle-ranking power to one viewed as second only to the United States in its capacity to shape global affairs. From climate change to financial crises, from African countries that supply China with minerals to European ones that depend on China's spending power and mountain of foreign currency as bulwarks against their own economic ruin, Beijing's influence is felt in places it did not affect a decade ago.

Moreover, the past few years have witnessed a striking change in the global perception of the balance of power. According to the Pew Research Center's twenty-three-nation *Global Attitudes Survey* conducted in 2011, "the balance of opinion is that China either will replace or already has replaced the United States as the world's leading superpower. This view is especially widespread in Western Europe, where at least six out of ten people polled in France (72%), Spain (67%), Britain (65%) and Germany (61%) see China overtaking the U.S. Majorities in Pakistan, the Palestinian territories, Mexico and China itself also foresee China supplanting the U.S. as the world's dominant power."[22] Notably, the percentage of West Europeans naming China as the top economic power has increased by double digits in Spain (49%), Germany (48%), Britain (47%), and France (47%) since 2009.[23]

Of course, China is not without its own troubles. Even the official media describes the next ten years as unusually tough ones, both economically and politically. China's ruling Communist Party confronts a growing crisis of legitimacy fueled by, among other things, a wealth gap, law-flouting officials, and instability at the grassroots level. In August 2012, the official media republished an article that had previously circulated in a secret journal, warning of a "latent crisis" of public mistrust: "There are so many problems now, interlocked like dogs' teeth," with frequent "mass disturbances" (protests) that, if mishandled by the party, could engender "a chain reaction that results in social turmoil or violent revolution."[24]

With the heady days of double-digit growth rates in China's rearview mirror, the coming decade will be the last chance for the party to implement economic reforms—such as loosening the state's grip on vital industries, especially the financial sector—that might prevent the country from sliding into a "middle-income trap" of fast growth followed by prolonged stagnation. Moreover, the introduction of its "one child" policy thirty years ago means that China will be facing the most severe aging process in human history. Going forward, China confronts a falling workforce and sharply rising dependency ratios, as the number of pensioners increases to 300 million over the coming two decades. China's ratio of workers per retiree will plummet from eight-to-one today to two-to-one by 2040; the fiscal cost of this swing in dependency ratios may exceed 80 to 100 percent of China's GDP.[25] A report written by Jonathan Anderson for UBS Investment Research notes, "With the exception of eastern Europe, this makes China virtually unique among emerging markets. The aging process closely resembles that in developed economies such as Japan, Korea or Europe—but at a level of income many times lower. Meanwhile, China's emerging Asian, Latin and African neighbors are still growing their populations at a fast clip."[26]

To be sure, this demographic trend presents a problem for China, but not an insurmountable one. The same UBS report concludes, "The surprising fact is that the government has a number of feasible financing tools in its arsenal which taken together could easily cover the net pension debt, including adjustments to the pension system itself, diversion of other tax revenues, issuing new debt and selling state assets."[27] Meanwhile, most analysts expect China's economy to grow at strong single-digit rates for the rest of the decade—a growth rate that the advanced economies can merely envy.

It is not just the West's dominance in material capabilities that is winding down, however. America's motivation to bear the costs of world leadership is fading as well. Leadership is a choice. No matter how much stronger the preeminent power is compared with its nearest peer competitor, it cannot be called a world hegemonic leader until it demonstrates that it is willing to accept the burdens of global management.[28] Otherwise, like it was between the two world wars, America is merely an elephant on the sidelines, a potential but reluctant hegemon unwilling to lead.[29] It is worth recalling just how unenthusiastic Americans were about the role of global leader and the obligations associated with that lofty position. It took the horrific destruction and chaos that followed World War II and the very real threat that the Red Army would waltz in and take over a defenseless Western Europe for America to finally accept Europe's "invitation to empire." Its acceptance came grudgingly and only after Truman's plan to turn Europe into a "third force" capable of standing up to the Soviets by itself—a plan designed to divest the United States of any further responsibility for the security of Europe—had proved hopeless.

In the coming decade, America must decide whether it is time, given the Great Recession and the nation's ballooning debt, to abandon its hegemonic strategy and replace it with one of restraint, narrowing its foreign policy to a few large and vital objectives.[30] Or, more drastic still, should the country retreat into isolationism? Will the longtime sheriff, having shot many a feared gunslinger at high noon, finally decide to throw his badge in the dirt and leave town for good? Consider who gained the most the last time the United States removed the leader of an outlaw country, Iraq. Not the United States or its allies. No, the biggest beneficiary of the "post-Saddam" oil boom in Iraq is none other than America's main rival, China, whose state-owned companies have poured over $2 billion a year and hundreds of workers into Iraq to secure a supply of energy for China's growing economy and increasingly energy-hungry population. Already Iraq's largest customer, buying almost half the oil it produces (nearly 1.5 million barrels a day), China desires an even larger share of the market. In late 2012, therefore, the China National Petroleum Corporation began bidding for a 60 percent stake now owned by ExxonMobil in one of Iraq's largest oil fields, the lucrative West Qurna I. "We lost out," said Michael Makovsky, a former Defense Department official in the Bush administration. "The Chinese had nothing to do with the war, but from an economic standpoint they are benefiting from it, and our Fifth Fleet and air forces are helping to assure their supply."[31]

A More Selective Superpower

Unlike the Cold War days, the current world is no longer a zero-sum contest, where a gain for them is a corresponding loss for us and vice versa. It's not that simple anymore. There is no "us" and "them," no existential threat to America's security that warrants bloated defense budgets, and nothing much to be gained (and a lot to lose) from Washington's continued pursuit of unrestrained foreign policies, like spreading democracy, defending human rights, building nations, ridding the world of terror, and preventing nuclear proliferation. The dearth of serious threats in the United States' security environment is good enough reason for Americans to cease paying the lion's share of the costs of running the world. But even if Uncle Sam were nonetheless inclined to continue bankrolling international order, his checks would be returned to him marked "insufficient funds." The problem is that the nation is saddled with a fiscal crisis that will take decades to remedy. A recent report by a Washington-based think tank lobbying for entitlement reform calculates that by 2029, Social Security, Medicare, Medicaid, and interest on the debt combined will amount to 18 percent of GDP, which is exactly what the government has averaged in tax collections over the past forty years. This means that the growth in entitlements alone, which currently account for two-thirds of the entire federal budget, will soon "crowd out all other government spending, including on defense and the investments needed to spur the next wave of economic growth."[32]

It is a sad state of affairs that one would think would compel both Democrats and Republicans to abandon America's post–World War II internationalist mindset and turn the nation's energies inward. At least, logic tells us that there should be a convergence toward a more introverted, anti-interventionist American foreign policy. In the age of entropy, however, logic is an extremely unreliable signpost. As Richard Burt and Dimitri K. Simes point out, the convergence appears to be in the opposite direction:

> Strangely, it is precisely in [the area of America's interventionist foreign policy] that the two leading foreign-policy schools—liberal interventionism and neoconservative unilateralism—converge. For example, Princeton professor Ann-Marie Slaughter and *Washington Post* columnist Charles Krauthammer often agree on the need for U.S. intervention abroad. . . . Some voices have challenged the American elite's foreign-policy groupthink . . . but they have not significantly influenced U.S. political discourse. As a result, a dangerous disconnect has emerged between academic discussions and the policy process in which foreign-policy realists have been marginalized.[33]

Like old habits, entrenched mindsets die hard. Nevertheless, the ever-widening gap between America's means and ends will, sooner than later, repair the severed connection between reality and U.S. foreign policy. It won't be long before the American people—encumbered by federal debt that will reach 70 percent of GDP in 2012 and a debt-to-revenue ratio approaching 262 percent—demand significant retrenchment from their government's far-flung global commitments.[34]

Evidence of Americans' world-weariness is already apparent. According to a survey conducted by the Pew Research Center in May 2011, the percentage of U.S. respondents who favored "reducing U.S. military commitments overseas" rose from 26 percent in September 2001 to 46 percent in May 2011; "promoting democracy abroad" was supported by just 13 percent of respondents; and nearly 50 percent said America "should mind its own business internationally."[35] Similarly, the 2012 Chicago Council Survey of American Public Opinion and Foreign Policy concluded, "Americans have a strong desire to move on from a decade of war, to scale back spending, and avoid major new military entanglements." Most dramatically, the survey found that support among independents for an active foreign policy has declined by 15 percentage points in the past decade.[36] It appears that after the sorry experiences of Iraq and Afghanistan and with a national balance sheet soaked in red ink, American voters have lost enthusiasm for foreign adventurism. With no fire-breathing dragons left to slay, the United States, tired and broke, may be tempted to beat a hasty retreat back to the womb of the Western Hemisphere.

A wholesale return to nineteenth-century isolationism is out of the realm of possibility, however. The United States is too big, too strong, and too influential to ever be isolationist again. America will, instead, become a more selective superpower—its role as permanent guarantor of the global commons replaced by a sharper assessment of its national interests.[37] Thus, in its latest quadrennial report, the U.S. National Intelligence Council posits "a world in which the slow dissolution of the existing postwar order gives way to the return of great power competition, albeit probably framed by patchwork multilateralism."[38]

In the absence of America's preponderant power, international politics will shift from order to disorder. The emerging international system will have neither a single designer nor an overall, coherent design. Instead, its arrangement will be the product of many diverse rule-making groups and institutions pursuing their own parochial interests and visions. This atomized structure of global governance will yield multiple sources of competing and contradictory international organizing principles, rules, and decision-making processes. As these disorganizing processes develop, enduring patterns of political relations will crumble, old schools of thought will become obsolete, and time-honored solutions will no longer work. The past can no longer be relied on for guidance. The new norm is increasingly the lack of a norm.

Profound dislocations throughout the global system are causing the narrative of world politics to become an increasingly fragmented and disjointed story. Like a postmodern novel, the plot features a menagerie of wildly incongruent themes and unlikely protagonists, as if divinely plucked from different historical ages and placed in a time machine set for the third millennium. Chaos and randomness abound as history enters the age of entropy. It will be a world defined by a considerable breakdown of order, covering a wide range of social and political relations.

What Is Entropy?

Invented in the field of thermodynamics, the term *entropy* measures the ability of a system to perform work or activity in the future. A system with no entropy has a lot of potential; a system with high entropy has little. The Second Law of Thermodynamics states that as work is performed, entropy increases—that is, energy becomes less and less available to do work, and so the potential to perform further work declines. As the capacity for activity gets used up, the system eventually comes to a point of equilibrium at which time no further activity can take place. Thus, water at the top of a hill performs work, turning mills and turbines, by flowing downhill. Once the water is at the bottom of the hill, however, it has exhausted its capacity for further work. Likewise, aging in a biological system can be seen as a process of rising entropy that uses up potential: a fertilized egg has enormous biological potential compared with an old person. Social systems and institutions, too, exhibit a tendency to originate with an outburst of potential energy that runs down over time. Thus, corporations, churches, and empires arise from the energetic activities of gifted entrepreneurs, prophets, and conquerors. They may flourish for a time, but all will eventually decline and sometimes disintegrate altogether as the initial energy that created them dissipates.[39] In short, the performance of work diminishes the system's ability for future activity. As the system runs down, it eventually reaches a point of maximum entropy when no more work can be done.

Entropy can also be thought of as a measure of chaos, which is, oddly enough, the most probable state of a system. There are many ways that a system can become disordered, messed up, chaotic, and unpredictable. There are very few ways that a system can exhibit order, especially complex arrangements, structures, and patterns designed to perform tasks. Accordingly, negative entropy—the opposite of entropy—measures a system's order, that is, the organization, structuring, or improbability of a system. The inexorable rise of entropy suggests the coming of an all-pervasive uniformity: a cosmic "end state" as a uniform soup that lacks any type of differentiation or dominance, making it impossible to do anything. In this ultra-stable equilibrium, all energy is used up and all matter is evenly distributed in its most probable pattern. Nothing more can happen.

What Is Order?

Order is a necessary condition for any human activity, for anything the human mind is to understand—whether the layout of a house, the proper table setting for a formal dinner, a merchant's display of wares, a story's narrative, or the shape of a painting or musical composition. Order makes possible our ability to focus on what is different and what is alike, what belongs together and what needs to be separated. One might go so far as to say that order is a prerequisite for survival, that the impulse to produce orderly arrangements is inbred by evolution. As disorder increases and entropy rises, people become more disoriented and disconnected from each other and the world around them.[40] They become depressed, have problems concentrating, and tend to exhibit, among other things, something known as high "flow duration entropy"—meaning they frequently switch among Internet applications like e-mail, chat rooms, music players, browsers, and games.[41] What, then, is order?

When we say that several discrete objects taken together display some kind of order, we mean that they are related to one another according to some pattern, that their relationship is not miscellaneous or haphazard but accords with some discernible principle. Order prevails when things display a high degree of predictability, when there are regularities, when there are patterns that follow some understandable and consistent logic. Disorder is a condition of randomness—of unpredictable developments lacking regularities and following no known principle or logic.

When we speak of order and disorder in social life we tend to have something more in mind, however, than methodical arrangements or recurrent patterns. Order serves some function or purpose in our daily lives; order is "a pattern that leads to a particular result, an arrangement of social life such that it promotes certain goals or values."[42] We call things orderly when the observer can grasp their overall structures and the meanings and purposes of those structures. Books arranged on a shelf according to author or subject—as opposed to size or color or merely heaped in a random pile on the floor—serve the functional purpose of selection. This is what Augustine meant when he defined order as "a good disposition of discrepant parts, each in its fittest place."[43]

We address elements of disorder all the time in our everyday lives. We bring home miscellaneously bagged groceries and, within minutes of placing them on the kitchen counter, have put everything away in its special place. We collect the mail six times a week, sorting it in all our "fittest places": bills in the filing cabinet, greeting cards on the refrigerator door, junk mail tossed in the garbage. For reasons of efficiency and psychological well-being, we are all experts at imposing order on disorder.[44]

The degree of order exhibited by social and political systems is partly a function of stability. Stability is the property of a system that causes it to return to its original condition after it has been disturbed from a state of equilibrium. Stable systems respond to perturbations in ways that nullify or reduce their disequilibriating effects by means of "negative feedback." An example from engineering makes clear the meaning of this term.

The temperature of a room is kept constant by the combined operation of a furnace and a thermostat. A rise in the room's temperature distorts a bimetallic strip in the thermostat to the point where it breaks an electric contact, thus turning off the furnace and lowering the room's temperature. Conversely, a drop in the room's temperature re-establishes the electric contact, turning the furnace back on and so raising the room's temperature. When we say that the room's temperature is kept constant, therefore, we mean that the temperature fluctuates about the thermostat's "set point" within certain limits. Negative feedback assures that variations within the system do not exceed these limits—we call this region the *homeostatic plateau*.[45]

Systems are said to be unstable when slight disturbances produce large disruptions that not only prevent the original condition from being restored but also amplify the effect of the perturbation. This process is called "positive feedback" because it pushes the system increasingly farther away from its initial steady state. Money put out on compound interest and the unimpeded reproduction of any species of living organism are both examples of systems with positive feedback. Money that is initially interest becomes principal (money), earning more interest (money); children become parents and produce more children. Hence, the term feedback: the system's output feeds back as input.[46]

The classic example of positive feedback is a bank run caused by self-fulfilling prophecies: people believe something is true (there will be a run on the bank), so their behavior makes it true (they all withdraw their money from the bank); others' observations of this behavior increases the belief that it is true, so they behave accordingly (they, too, withdraw their money from the bank), which makes the prophecy even more true, and so on.

Some systems are characterized by robust and durable orders. Others are extremely unstable, such that their orders can quickly and without warning collapse into chaos. Like an avalanche, or peaks of sand in an hourglass that suddenly collapse and cascade, or a spider's web that takes on an entirely new pattern when a single strand is cut, complex and delicately balanced systems are unpredictable: they may appear calm and orderly at one moment only to become wildly turbulent and disorderly the next. This inherent instability of complex, tightly coupled systems is captured by the popular phrase, "the butterfly effect," coined by Edward Lorenz, an MIT meteorologist, to explain how a massive storm can be caused (or prevented) by the faraway flapping of a tiny butterfly's wings.[47] The principal lesson of the butterfly effect is that when incalculably small differences in the initial conditions of a system matter greatly, the world becomes radically unpredictable. Indeed, we can seldom predict what will happen when a new element is added to a system composed of many parts connected in complex ways. Such systems undergo frequent discontinuous changes from shocking impacts that create radical departures from the past.

History has always been written in this way, large effects arising from small causes: the Sons of Liberty tossed tea into Boston Harbor; Archduke Franz Ferdinand was assassinated; Rosa Parks "got tired of giving in"; a wave of labor strikes hit Poland in 1988. But today, the unregulated space of the Internet accelerates and amplifies both the intended and unintended consequences of viral media. As we have learned, sometimes painfully, "virtual reality" has real-world effects. Most recently, the posting of a fourteen-minute trailer on YouTube of the fifth-rate film, *Innocence of Muslims*—"a video so comically amateurish it might have passed for a *Saturday Night Live* skit"[48]—resulted in a wave of radical Islamist mobs storming U.S. embassies and waging violent protests in more than twenty countries. The producer of the film who posted the trailer probably didn't see any of this backlash coming. But does it really matter?[49]

Of course, the analogy of the "butterfly effect" can be taken too far, turning cause-and-effect arguments into laughable caricatures. Consider the following causal chain that connects the health of the British Empire to the existence of old maids: old maids keep cats, cats eat field mice, field mice destroy bumblebee nests, bumblebees fertilize red clover, red clover is eaten by cattle, roast beef keeps British soldiers fed, British soldiers defend the British Empire. Ergo the continuance of the British Empire depends on an abundant supply of old maids. Now that is a caricature.[50]

Careful to avoid arguments that slide down these kinds of slippery slopes, we must nevertheless acknowledge that social and political systems exemplify organized complexity. Principles developed in the natural sciences should, therefore, apply to the international system. We should also recognize that the international system, like all complex systems composed of a large number of interacting parts—whether they be physical, biological, economic, political, or social systems—operates somewhere between order and randomness; it exists on "the edge of chaos," in the phrase of computer scientist Christopher Langton.[51]

The Age of Entropy

In the coming age, disorder will reign supreme as the world succumbs to forces akin to rising entropy, an irreversible process of disorganization that governs the direction of all physical changes taking place in the universe. It is a world in which one senses a compulsive, purposeless dynamism to its operations. Its rising entropy is observed in the diametrically opposed but strangely intertwined forces that drive its confused state. Consider, for instance, the essential question of whether humankind is becoming more or less united.

Through one end of the telescope, we see the digital revolution, unprecedented worldwide information and capital flows, global production, marketing, and supply chains, outsourcing, open-source technology, private and public transnational interdependence that continues to grow in scale and complexity, and, in the view of many, the triumph of democracy and market-based approaches to economic growth—the so-called Washington Consensus. We also see the decline of war and political violence to record low levels, far lower than in recent decades and centuries, and a world becoming wealthier, with its riches spread more broadly than ever. The planet is shrinking at warp speed, and we all seem to be playing the same game. Transnational organization is near universal, as the world constitutes a single economic system, within which private and public transnational actors allocate resources with a global calculus. Gone are the days of huge ideological battles among communism, fascism, and liberal democracy. Even the Arabs, who seemed resigned to tyranny, have not let liberty bypass them. Since December 2010, the revolutionary wave of demonstrations and protests known as the Arab Spring (or Arab Awakening) has spread like a contagion across the Arab world, deposing long-standing dictators. Can we be far from the dreaded "global monoculture"—that final state of sameness captured by the term *Westoxification*? Perhaps. But looks are deceiving, especially at a glance.

Viewed through the other end of the telescope, the world appears very different. We see the return of powerful autocratic-capitalist states, of a new Great Game in Central Asia, of imperialism in the Middle East, piracy on the high seas, rivalry in the Indian Ocean, a 1929-like market crash, 1914-style hypernationalism and ethnic conflict, warlords and failed states, a Maoist insurgency in India, genocides in Bosnia, Rwanda, and Darfur, and a new Holy War waged by radical Islamists complete with calls for a restored Caliphate and beheadings reminiscent of medieval times. Remnants from the past continue to encode the present. We have entered a formless world that is in many ways outside of time. All eras coexist and none dominates in the post-era era that we now live in.[52]

In this atemporal sense of an aura-free universe where anything goes and nothing brands the times, history is, indeed, ending. This is a far cry, however, from the original notion of history's end in the triumph of liberal democracy, a prediction that seems far less plausible now than it did during the euphoric days of 1989, when Francis Fukuyama first trumpeted it. Today, the only consensus about the Washington Consensus is that it is dead. The excessive market fundamentalism that led to the 2008 financial meltdown—a witches' brew of liberalization, privatization, and deregulation—damaged the brand name beyond repair. And the future for postindustrial liberal democracy appears gloomier still. Advances in technology and globalization will, as they have in the past, disproportionately benefit a small number of people in high technology and finance while undermining the middle classes, whose median incomes have been stagnating in real terms since the 1970s. Indeed, the world's advanced democracies confront nothing less than a crisis of governability—an inability to respond to the decline in living standards and the growing inequality caused by unprecedented global goods, services, and capital.[53]

While the West suffers from a mismatch between the demand for effective governance and its shrinking supply, from deindustrialization and outsourcing, from global trade and fiscal imbalances, excess capital and credit and asset bubbles, America's most likely peer competitors in the coming decades, China and India, became economic juggernauts by following policies that ran exactly opposite to the main recommendations of the Washington Consensus. Both had high levels of protectionism, no privatization, extensive industrial policies planning, and lax fiscal and financial policies through the 1990s. In the eyes of many of the developing world's dictators, the so-called Beijing Consensus of authoritarian state capitalism offers an appealing alternative economic development model to the Washington Consensus of market-friendly policies, which—as Chinese leaders, including new president Xi Jinping, like to remind the West—were responsible for the global financial crisis.[54] Perhaps the bigger threat to U.S. competitiveness, however, comes from what Rob Atkinson, founder and president of the Information Technology and Innovation Foundation, calls China's "innovation mercantilism." Launched seven years ago, China's drive for "indigenous" innovation has triggered massive government subsidies to state-owned enterprises to generate technological innovations without regard to intellectual property rights and other rules of fair play.[55]

The current malaise in Europe, the United States, and Japan has catapulted Asia's emerging economies to new heights as vital engines of global growth. From their intensifying voices in the IMF to their mounting footprints in global development assistance to their exchange-rate valuations, energy pricing, fiscal policies, and investment decisions, Asia's big economies, along with those of other emerging powers such as Brazil and Turkey, now have global impact, and this presents new and complex challenges for world order. Most obviously, there is a fundamental divide between the developed and emerging powers regarding core aspects of regional and global order, including "the composition and scope of international and regional institutions, the competing imperatives of sovereignty and intervention, and the operation of global markets."[56] As Michael

Wesley observes, "The gap in economic perceptions and preferences between the United States and the major Asian economies is wider than ever; what has changed is the significance of these disagreements for the global economy and their new prominence in shaping U.S.–Asian relations."[57]

Adding fuel to the fire, China has been frequently vilified in the American presidential campaign, and Xi Jinping has not taken kindly to these attacks. "There are a few foreigners with full bellies, who have nothing better to do than try to point fingers at our country," Mr. Xi said. "China does not export revolution, hunger, poverty nor does China cause you any headaches. Just what else do you want?"[58]

As for the Arab Spring, few pundits predicted it, and fewer still know where it's heading. All that can be said with relative certainty is that the Middle East is in for a long and potentially perilous transformation—one that former Secretary of State Henry Kissinger fears could lead to a "war of all against all."[59]

Observed from both ends of the telescope, the emerging world appears schizophrenic and, in many ways, indecipherable. Forget quaint notions about the West versus the Rest. We are entering a jumbled world run by and for no one, in which the nature of power itself is changing, an ungovernable place in search of a workable ideology to guide it.[60]

How Did We Get Here?

The post–Cold War era was a brief and uncertain period with a fittingly backward-looking moniker. As Condoleezza Rice observed in *Foreign Affairs*, "We knew better where we had been than where we were going."[61] For the United States, the 1980s was a decade that ended in triumph but began with self-doubt. The majority opinion was that American economic competitiveness— defined as America's ability to produce goods and services that meet the test of international markets while its citizens enjoy a standard of living that is both rising and sustainable—was in slow but steady decline.[62] Japan had emerged as an economic powerhouse destined to eat America's lunch. Its economic planning agency, MITI (now defunct), was then the envy of "competitiveness" gurus, who were urging Washington to wake up to the realities of the "new international economic environment." This meant abandoning its outmoded mindset of laissez-faire free trade in favor of strategic (or managed) trade policies—that is, the same government policies that were creating huge competitive advantages for Japan's exporters.[63] It was as if Japanese companies were on steroids and American firms, absent similar assistance from the U.S. government, could not compete, especially in light of Japan's nontariff barriers that traditionally impeded access to its home markets.

For competitiveness experts, the solution to America's ills was straightforward: keeping pace with the land of the Rising Sun required the United States to emulate Japan's use of export subsidies, import tariffs, and subsidies to R&D investment—policy instruments that shift profits from foreign to domestically based firms facing global competition and, thereby, boost national economic welfare at the expense of other countries. In addition, Americans had to become more Japanese in terms of their thriftiness, dedication to the workplace, and academic diligence. For Americans, the key to prosperity and economic competitiveness was, as the Vapors sang in 1980, "Turning Japanese."

Looking back, we see that Japan reached the peak of its prosperity in 1990. Since then, it has suffered two lost decades of economic recession, during which time the Japanese government has barely managed to keep the economy afloat with massive pork-barrel spending that has raised public debt to world-record levels. And the future looks bleaker still. The most serious crisis confronting Japan is not its recovery from the March 11, 2011, earthquake and tsunami and the resulting meltdowns of three of the six reactors at Fukushima Daiichi nuclear power plant, though these are certainly major setbacks. Rather, Japan confronts a seemingly insurmountable demographic problem: it is the "grayest" country in the history of the earth. Japan's workforce is barely over 50 percent of its population, and these workers must not only support themselves and their children but also Japan's retirees, who comprise a whopping 40 percent of the country's population. The author Bill Emmott got it right way back in 1989, when he correctly noted of Japanese economic power: the sun also sets.[64]

The year 1990 was not only the high-water mark of Japan's rise but, more importantly, year 1 A.W. (After Wall). The Berlin Wall fell on November 9, 1989 (actually, it was opened by the East German government, which announced ten new border crossings the following weekend), signaling the eventual end of the Cold War, which came in 1991. While there was little doubt that history had reached a turning point, there was nothing inevitable or inevitably peaceful about the nature of the transition out of bipolarity. As the Cold War historian Mary Sarotte recalls, the Berlin Wall's "opening had yielded not only joy but also some extremely frightening questions. Would Germans demand rapid unification in a massive nationalistic surge that would revive old animosities? Would Soviet troops in East Germany stay in their barracks? Would Gorbachev stay in power or would hard-liners oust him for watching the wall fall while failing to get anything in return? Would Communist countries in the rest of Central Europe subsequently expire violently and leave bloody scars?"[65]

To most everyone's surprise, the Soviet Union simply rolled over and went belly-up. The mighty superpower died on the operating table at the hands of its own physician, Mikhail Gorbachev. As *Nezavisimaya Gazeta* wrote shortly after the country's demise, "His choice of cures was commendable—glasnost, democratization, and all—but in the end, even a small dose of these proved fatal to the patient."[66] Cadavers are notoriously poor bargainers, and so the Cold War's endgame was a dramatically one-sided affair with the West pocketing one costly Soviet concession after another. Indeed, no Kremlinologist, Sovietologist, or merely informed (sane) person would have predicted in the early 1980s that Moscow, in the throes of losing two layers of empire less than a decade later (who would have guessed that?), would become so distracted by internal problems that it not only agreed to German reunification but, in a testament to Russia's utter emasculation, allowed this new entity—its most potent European rival, against whom it had fought for its life a mere generation earlier—to reside within NATO. Such are the perils of forecasting. Thus, the United States, having spent the 1980s fretting over its imminent decline vis-à-vis Japan, found itself at the end of the decade a lone hyperpower sitting on top of the world.

While the peace that broke out—one historically unparalleled in terms of its size and scope—was largely unexpected, the exuberant idealism that followed was all too predictable. The sudden collapse of the Soviet Union, the absence of rival ideologies, and the successful restructuring of the American economy catapulted the United States to a position of unrivaled power. America's formidable advantages in military, economic, political, technological, and cultural capabilities were not only unprecedented in modern history but between 1990 and 1998, the gap in power between it and the rest of the world widened, as the American economy grew at 27 percent (twice that of the European Union and three times that of Japan) and its federal budget was in surplus. Convinced of the longevity of Pax Americana and a one-superpower world, American strategists confidently predicted that the spread of liberal democracy and triumph of capitalism were culminating in "the end of history," the obsolescence of major war, and a world in which satisfied nations would learn to live happily alongside each other. A lasting era of global bounty and great-power peace had finally arrived.

What a difference a decade makes. Since the events of September 11, 2001, the world does not appear so easily transformed, nor history so easily escaped. Even American unipolarity, which seemed strangely durable only a few years ago, appears today as a "passing moment." By any measure, the U.S. macro-statistical picture is a bleak one. America's personal saving rate is close to zero.[67] Its currency is sliding to new depths; it runs huge current-account, trade, and budget deficits.[68] Its medium income is flat; its entitlement commitments (Medi-care, Medicaid, and Social Security) are unsustainable, consuming about 40 per-cent of the federal budget; its once-unrivaled capital markets are now struggling to compete with Hong Kong and London.

A major cause of U.S. troubles, both in the short and long term, is debt.[69] Since the 1980s, Americans have been consuming more than they have been producing, and they have borrowed to make up the difference. To finance cur-rent consumption, America borrows $4 billion per day, nearly half of that from China—a rising peer competitor, with whom the United States is running huge trade deficits and which, if current projections hold, will become the world's largest economy by 2040. Some pundits predict that today's creditors in China and the Middle East will set the global agenda and the rules of international order, just as Britain did in the nineteenth century and the United States did in the twentieth century.[70]

If these predictions of America's demise and the impending downfall of its Old Order prove correct, it will not be cause for celebration. As the world's reign-ing liberal hegemon since 1945, the United States has provided vital global public goods that no other major power could or would supply. America is home to the world's richest and most open market; it supplies the world's leading currency; and most of its defense budget goes to support missions that benefit the world as much as, and sometimes more than, they do the United States itself. America's military power is essential to the global economy; its navy safeguards the world's most important trade routes, helping to assure the free flow of oil from the Per-sian Gulf. Indeed, the United States is not just Europe's pacifier; it is the world's pacifier.[71] America's overseas military presences and its extension of security umbrellas in Europe and East Asia signal that Uncle Sam will act as an effective watchman—one who will not tolerate fighting among the states of these regions and who will be on hand to deal with any serious threats to peace with over-whelming power.[72] By any measure, the American system has been an unqual-ified success, engendering unparalleled global prosperity. Between 1950 and 2000, annual GDP growth for the entire world was 3.9 percent (with growth rates in Asia matching or exceeding those in Europe and the United States), as compared with 1.6 percent between 1820 and 1950. Between 1980 and 2002 alone, world trade more than tripled.[73]

All this is about to change, however. In June 2011, the nonpartisan Congressional Budget Office (CBO) predicted that U.S. government debt will reach 76 percent of gross domestic product (GDP) by 2021; a more dire—and more likely—scenario shows public debt at 101 percent of GDP ten years from now, well into the economic danger zone of 90 percent or more, and then soaring to 187 percent of the economy in 2035. This depressing fiscal outlook means that America will be able to afford to do less in the world in the future than it has in the past. To be sure, spending on foreign and security policy will be major casualties of deficit reduction. And as U.S. defense budgets contract, American global retrenchment will become larger and more inevitable.

This trend toward global downsizing was evident in the contentious negotiation that produced the Budget Control Act of 2011 signed by President Barack Obama on August 2, 2011, to raise the American debt ceiling while cutting the federal budget deficit—the first of many imminent brawls in the battle to bring deficits under control. That legislation called for $1 trillion in spending cuts over a ten-year period, roughly $350 billion of which would likely be reductions in the defense budget. It also mandated a further $1.5 trillion cut in expenditures in the next decade. If Congress could not agree on where those reductions should come from, an automatic trigger would impose across-the-board cuts that would slash the Defense Department's budget by an estimated $500 billion.

Not surprisingly, Congress couldn't agree, and sequestration cuts went into effect in March 2013, reducing the Defense budget by $37 billion in 2013. A report issued by Democrats on the House Appropriations committee calculated that U.S. defense spending would drop by 11.5 percent in the first quarter of 2013, after having fallen by 22.1 percent in the fourth quarter of 2012. "This is the biggest back-to-back reduction in defense spending since the post-Korea drawdown in 1954," according to the report.[74] What these sobering numbers indicate is that, for politicians on both sides of the aisle, the perceived scale of deficit reduction required to put the country on solid fiscal footing is so large that the projection of American power around the world must be downgraded.

The Current Debate

Most observers agree that the American-led international order is eroding and giving way to something new. A "return to multipolarity" is one way of describing this shift. It tells us that several great powers will emerge to challenge U.S. supremacy. That is all. The more important question is what sort or international order will emerge on the other side of this transition from unipolarity to multipolarity. Will it be one of peace and plenty or conflict and scarcity? On this issue, experts are divided into two camps, Pessimists and Optimists, those who think we are headed back to the future and those who believe that we are headed forward to the future.

"Back to the future" realists, a.k.a. Pessimists, believe that the coming multipolar world will closely resemble the one that held sway over international politics from 1648 until 1945, which was permeated by problems of insecurity, rivalry, arms races, nationalism, and fierce competition for scarce resources.[75] Embedding their arguments in examinations of historical power shifts, such as those provoked by Napoleonic France or the unification of Germany in 1871, they predict that the United States and China will soon engage in an intense security competition with considerable potential for war. This forecast is grounded in the assumption that history unfolds in repeating cycles of global war that destroy the old international order and replace it with a new one. According to this cyclical view of history, time has no direction; the world is not going anywhere it has not already been. The future, therefore, will resemble the past.

In contrast, liberals, a.k.a. Optimists, reject the notion of a competitive, multipolar world. They see, instead, a smooth evolutionary transition from unipolarity to multipolarity, as the world's major powers (old and new) find ways to build an architecture to jointly manage and preserve the existing international system.[76] They believe in a Kantian "triangulating peace"; that democracy, economic interdependence, and a strong system of international organizations reinforce one another to promote a peaceful, just, and prosperous global community. Embracing principles and practices of restraint, accommodation, reciprocity, and cooperation, the great powers will work in concert to establish mutually acknowledged and agreed-upon roles and responsibilities to co-manage an evolving but stable international order that benefits all of them. The return of multipolarity will usher in a new age of Liberal peace, prosperity, and progress built on the rule of law. Swords will be beaten into ploughshares, and a harmony of interests will reign among the states and peoples of the world. In short, multipolarity begets cooperative multilateralism.

This is the essence of Secretary of State Hillary Clinton's vision of a "multipartner," as opposed to a multipolar, world. "It does not make sense to adapt a nineteenth-century concert of powers or a twentieth-century balance-of-power strategy. We cannot go back to Cold War containment or to unilateralism," Clinton said in a speech at the Council on Foreign Relations in July 2009. "We will lead by inducing greater cooperation among a greater number of actors and reducing competition, tilting the balance away from a multipolar world and toward a multipartner world."[77] It is a view based on the assumption that history moves forward in a progressive direction—one consistent with the metaphor of time's arrow.[78]

As is often the case, reality lies somewhere between these two extremes—there is too much gloom and doom among Realists; too much dewy-eyed optimism among Liberals. Realists' fears that China's rise will provoke war with the United States are unwarranted. The destructiveness of nuclear weapons and the benefits of economic globalization have made war among the great powers unthinkable. The cycle of war among the great powers has been replaced by a perpetual peace, just as Liberals claim. Ironically, this is precisely why Liberals are too sanguine about the future. International order—particularly one that is legitimate, efficient, and dynamic—requires periodic global wars, one roughly every hundred years or so, that crown a new king, clever and powerful enough to organize the world. Otherwise, inertia and decay set in.

Of course, to say anything nice about war—an enterprise designed to kill people and destroy things—much less large and destructive world wars seems ludicrous. And yet one need not be mad as a hatter to recognize something inherently indispensable about war. Great thinkers from Alexis de Tocqueville to Emile Zola, Heinrich von Treitschke to Georg Hegel, Thomas Mann and Igor Stravinsky have sung its praises. Even those who opposed war, such as Kant, Ralph Waldo Emerson, Oliver Wendell Holmes, H.G. Wells, and William James, conceded its healthful properties.[79] Thus, on the eve of the Great War, Arthur Conan Doyle had Sherlock Holmes conjecture: "There's an east wind coming . . . such a wind as never blew on England yet. It will be cold and bitter, Watson, and a good many of us may wither before its blast. But it's God's own wind none the less, and a cleaner, better, stronger land will lie in the sunshine when the storm has cleared."[80] The sweeping broom, the bracing wind, the cleansing storm, the purifying fire, whatever the metaphor, there remains a kernel of truth in the doctrine of romantic militarism: a world undisturbed by war cannot cleanse and renew itself; like still seas, it becomes foul.

In other words, the evolution of international order can never be a purely linear process. It must combine aspects of both time's arrow and time's cycle. Like a wheel rolling on a track up a hill, international order progresses through upwardly moving cycles—advancing as they turn—of order creation, erosion, destruction, and renewal. Before a new order can be created, the old order must be destroyed and the institutional slate wiped clean. Otherwise, new governance structures will simply be piled on top of old, moribund ones—a recipe for chaos, not order. The perpetual peace among the great powers means that there will be no future hegemonic war—the only known engine of wholesale international change and order creation. Unless and until the world finds a new mechanism— one other than hegemonic war—for the rebirth of international order, the anti- quated global architecture constructed by the United States in the aftermath of World War II will simply become increasingly creaky and resistant to overhaul. Entropy will increase. No one will know where international authority resides because it will not reside anywhere; and without authority, there can be no governance. The already overcrowded and chaotic landscape will continue to be filled with more and more meaningless junk; the specter of international cooperation, if it was ever anything more than an apparition, will die a slow but certain death.

Information Entropy

Rising entropy is not only a structural problem that affects states at the macro- or global level of world politics. It is also engulfing the system's processes at both the macro-level (e.g., the diffusion of power; the increase in the number and variety of influential transnational actors) and the micro-level—the level of individual agency and human social interactions—with enormous implications for regular people in their everyday lives. Consider the relentless phenomenon of information overload. The digital world is saturated with over 555 million Web sites (300 million were added in 2011!), nine thousand TV channels worldwide, innumerable online newspapers constantly updated, over one million new books published every year, 160 million blogs, one trillion video playbacks a year on YouTube alone, and a gazillion podcasts, mp3s, and video downloads. The stu- pendous amounts of data set in motion each day by the worldwide explosion of digital information require tens of thousands of data centers, each with rows and rows of servers spread over hundreds of thousands of square feet, that use about 30 billion watts of electricity, equivalent to the output of roughly thirty nuclear power plants.[81] In our efforts to adapt to, push back against, sort through, and manipulate this information blitzkrieg, we have turned to Adderall, Ambien, power browsing, multitasking, slacktivism, and hacktivism, among other things.

More basically, some scientists believe that the Internet threatens to turn us into scatter-brained, shallow thinkers, flitting among bits of online information but incapable of profound thought. Neuroscience has recently shown that virtu- ally all our neural circuits are subject to change. The old assumption—one that had held sway among biologists and neurologists for hundreds of years—that the structure of the adult brain never changes turns out to be demonstrably false. The human brain is immensely plastic: it constantly reprograms itself, destroying old neural connections and forming new ones. Thus, it is not surprising but no less disturbing to discover that the Internet is rewiring our brains, reprograming how we think, and changing the way we process information. As Nicholas Carr puts it, "Calm, focused, undistracted, the linear mind is being pushed aside by a new kind of mind that wants and needs to take in and dole out information in short, disjointed, often overlapping bursts—the faster, the better."[82]

Information entropy affects the international system at the level of process— the density and complexity of its interconnections. As societies become more dependent on globally networked information systems and communications infrastructure, power will diffuse along multifaceted and amorphous global networks. Nonstate actors of all kinds—whether average citizens, celebrities, nongovernmental organizations (NGOs), multinational corporations, terrorists, religious movements, shadowy transnational criminal groups, and so on—will be empowered. This is because, as the world becomes more tightly coupled and interconnected, "sensitivity interdependence" among all actors increases; that is, the ripple effects of a disturbance originating in one area of the system quickly spreads throughout the entire system and affects everyone. Those actors that best understand how to operate within and exploit networks will exert disproportionate influence (relative to their actual power capabilities) on state and global policies: they will punch above their weights, so to speak.

Network power, however, differs from conventional power in the way it can be used. It is more about veto power than positive power. By exaggerating, amplifying, and thereby overstating an actor's actual capabilities, network power is unlike power in the typical sense of getting others to do things they otherwise wouldn't do; it does not require a large and sophisticated toolbox of power bases and assets of the sort that undergirds the statecraft of the most influential great powers, past and present. Instead, network power is mostly about negative power, about disrupting and blocking policies, about constraining leaders' choices and frustrating compromise. Paralysis rather than action is, and will continue to be, the name of the political game.

The universe of influential nonstate actors is moving beyond the usual suspects. The most important new player is Big Data, which continues expanding exponentially, spawning its own ecosystem. It is a world populated by an assortment of voraciously feeding organisms—consumer database marketing firms,

Internet service providers (ISPs), Web-hosting companies, cloud and mobile providers, financial and telecommunications companies—each processing and digesting massive quantities of information about every one of us, which they then sell to companies seeking to target their advertisements more accurately. It's not only a lucrative business but an increasingly political one.[83]

In June 2012, for instance, Google upped the ante in its long-running dispute with the People's Republic of China over censorship. A new feature on Google's popular search engine now warns users in China attempting to search banned keywords that this might cause their Google connection to be interrupted and suggests alternative spellings and phrases that will ensure access to the desired content. This latest circumvention of China's censorship of the Internet will no doubt further irritate Chinese authorities, who have already implemented an array of techniques to punish Google. But unlike the search results of Baidu, China's own popular service, Google searches cannot be fine-tuned by Chinese censors because "they are produced by servers outside mainland China, and thus are out of the censors' reach. So the government resorts instead to blocking any search or page that includes an offending term."[84]

Google's ongoing sparring match with the Chinese government has inspired the term "corporate sovereignty" to describe the power of social media companies like Google, Apple, Microsoft, and Facebook over so-called Netizens, digital networks, and online speech and expression. Well-known Web activist and author Rebecca MacKinnon views these companies as mythical nation-states, which she calls "Googledom" and "Facebookistan," equating their private power with the political power of actual governments:

> Companies like Apple, Facebook, Google, and many other digital platforms and services have created a new, virtual public sphere that is largely shaped, built, owned, and operated by private companies. These companies now mediate human relationships of all kinds, including the relationship between citizens and governments. They exercise a new layer of sovereignty over what we can and cannot do with our digital lives, on top of and across the sovereignty of governments.[85]

Here, MacKinnon, like many cyberlaw and Internet policy scholars, employs a very loose and misleading definition of sovereignty, which allows her to overstate the "corporate sovereignty" case and, in the process, miss the larger point.

The term *sovereignty* has both an internal and external dimension. *Internal sovereignty* means supreme, independent authority over a defined geographic territory. *External sovereignty* (also called *international legal sovereignty*) means that the state is recognized by other sovereign states as acting independently on the international scene.[86] At its core, sovereignty is about power: the supreme coercive power of the state over the body politic. A sovereign state can imprison, tax, and confiscate the property of anyone living within its borders; it has the power to, among other things, coin money, regulate various forms of commerce, form standing armies, make treaties with foreign sovereigns, and declare war on other states or external groups.[87] By simple virtue of their location within the state's geographic borders, people find themselves belonging to a state and falling under the authority of its rule. And though once upon a time millions of people were able to live outside the jurisdiction of sovereign states, that is no longer possible. There is no outside left; the sovereign states system went global in the twentieth century. The entire population of the world now lives inside one sovereign state or another.[88]

Corporations, in contrast, exercise no such powers; and they are not recognized as sovereigns by other sovereign actors. Neither Facebook nor Google possess anything like the coercive power of sovereign states. They "rule" over no one. We can escape their virtual "territories" whenever we decide to leave, or we can simply not join them in the first place.[89]

The corporate sovereignty argument obscures the larger, more fundamental, point: private actors, though incapable themselves of exercising sovereign power, can thwart, impinge, frustrate, and deny the sovereignty of other actors (most notably, nation-states) within certain circumscribed but nonetheless important areas—ones that in theory, but not practice, remain under the control of sovereign states. In other words, what is noteworthy is not corporations exercising a new form of sovereignty—sometimes partnering with governments and sometimes challenging their authority—but rather the facility of private actors operating in cyberspace to undermine state sovereignty. This portends a global trend of control, authority, and effective governance being increasingly replaced by incapacity, powerlessness, and vulnerability.

The central point—one consistent with the theme of rising entropy—is that power is diffusing and dissipating at the same time: more actors have power but only enough to thwart the effective rule of others—far too little to exercise political authority themselves. Like all forms and aspects of power in the age of entropy, sovereignty is on the wane; coercive control over others, much less absolute rule, is becoming increasingly difficult to exert. As the power to thwart authority continues to diffuse throughout the system, we are fast approaching a point where no actor or group of actors will be able or disposed to rule.

Driven by the forces of entropy, we are neither going to Hell nor being delivered to the Promised Land. We are, instead, heading for a place more akin to a perpetual state of Purgatory—a chaotic realm of unknowable complexity. The increasing disorder of our world will lead eventually to a sort of global ennui mixed with a disturbingly large dose of individual extremism and dogmatic posturing by states. It is a world subsumed by the inexorable forces of randomness, tipped off its axis, swirling in a cloud of information overload. Amid all this blooming confusion, we must turn to physics for a conceptual metaphor that captures the core dynamics of contemporary international politics and, accordingly, can be used to navigate the choppy seas of a changing world order.

Understanding the Language of Energy
Why Entropy Does Not Herald Doomsday

The story of entropy begins in Victorian Britain in the early 1850s, in the city of Glasgow, where academic and religious debates seethed against the backdrop of striking poverty, spectacular economic growth, and dramatic political upheaval. It is here that the University of Glasgow professor of natural philosophy William Thomson (later known as Lord Kelvin), who invented the new word *energy* as a science term but never took credit for it, and his partner in engineering science, Macquorn Rankine, began replacing the older language of Newtonian mechanical force—the tendency of a body to pass from one place to another—with terms such as "actual and potential energy." They were soon joined by like-minded "North British" scientific reformers and natural philosophers: James Prescott Joule, Peter Guthrie Tait, Fleeming Jenkin, and James Clerk Maxwell. Their quest, which they pursued with missionary zeal, was to raise the modern physical concept of energy to the level of a grand unifying principle that would integrate all natural processes and cultural activities.[1]

When the nineteenth century began, there were few signs that the rock-solid stability of the Scottish Enlightenment and aristocratic establishment would soon prove illusory; that a coming cultural transformation would splinter Scottish society, ultimately provoking the 1843 "Disruption," when Reverend Thomas Chalmers led his followers out of the established church to the Free Church of Scotland that he founded. None of this coming disorder was discernible in 1800, as Scotland enjoyed one of the longest periods of tranquility in its turbulent history.

Although its culture had been grounded in Presbyterianism since the Reformation, Scotland's natural theology still embodied the values of liberal Anglicanism as articulated south of the border by the Archdeacon of Carlisle, William Paley. It was a theology firmly rooted in the Enlightenment idea of nature's stability and perfection. Just as a watch required a watchmaker, nature had been created by a designer, whose wisdom, power, and goodness were evidenced in all manner of plants and animals and by the sum total of happiness and harmony in nature, which far outweighed any corresponding quantity of pain and misery. Designed by the hand of the Almighty, nature's beautiful dispositions exhibit eternal perfection and unchanging stability.[2]

By the 1820s and 1830s, such assumptions about the fixed and permanent order of nature were being undermined by the new science of geology, with its fossil findings of species that no longer roamed the earth. Nature had not proven so permanent for them. Speculation grew that the planet had originated as a molten mass that had subsequently cooled over many millions of years, allowing for the progressive introduction of various species suited to different climactic epochs.[3] Astronomers were also discovering that the solar system might not be as eternally stable and enduring as Enlightenment models suggested. Then, at midcentury, came the great thunderclap of the Second Law of Thermodynamics and its extrapolative nightmare of the eventual death of the sun and all humankind. The picture physics painted of the universe was of a clock running down; of an ultimate extinction of all becoming; of universal physical death.[4]

As a consequence of these scientific revelations, natural theology would need revisions that embraced change and decay more so than immanence and stability. And so it was that Thomas Chalmers began preaching that God's justice, truth, and goodness did not easily flow from nature; that there is no divine utilitarian weighing of nature in favor of happiness and pleasure over pain and misery. Stressing the principles of destruction at work in the visible creation, Chalmers pronounced the absolute and universal truth of 2 Corinthians 4:18: "the things that are seen are transient, but the things that are unseen are eternal." All the visible world is transitory and finite—subject to the processes of decay, disease, derangement, and death: "Nature contains within itself the rudiments of decay . . . unless renewed by the hand of the Almighty, the earth on which we are now treading must disappear in the mighty roll of the ages and of centuries . . . we may be prepared to believe that the principles of destruction are also at work in other provinces of the visible creation—and that though of old God laid the foundation of the earth, and the heavens are the work of his hands, yet they shall perish; yea, all of them shall wax old like a garment, and as a vesture shall He change them, and they shall be changed."[5] According to this Calvinist-inspired natural philosophy, the universe itself was cursed by depravity, imperfect in its parts, and destined for inevitable decay. Only "uncreated God" was absolutely eternal and enduring.

Chalmers's preachings about the transitory nature of visible things not only heralded the new age of classical thermodynamics but also—like Joseph William Turner's magnificent pictorial combinations of sun, ocean, and steamships—deftly rendered into allegorical tales and pictures the industrial shift from a world of pulleys and harnesses to one consumed in the chaotic fury of heat engines. A new order of energy was thereby impressed within the public consciousness, transforming nineteenth-century Western culture and society.

The New Science of Energy

Thermodynamics emerged simultaneously with steam engines in 1822; indeed, it began as little more than "the theoretical study of the steam engine."[6] It is "the science of the power of heat to do work and of the dissipation of that power."[7] From the Greek word, *energeia* ("activity," "working"), energy in physics means "the power a thing has of doing work arising from its own motion or from the 'tension' subsisting between it and other things."[8] Long before its modern scientific meaning, however, *energy* was a common literary and philosophical term, connoting "emotional and textual as well as physical intensity, intellectual as well as bodily vigor, and in particular, rhetorical force."[9]

Energy comes in many forms but all are equivalent; one form can disappear but the same amount of energy will appear in another form. This is the principle of the conservation of energy, also known as the First Law of Thermodynamics—numerous energies are constantly being converted from one form to another, altering quality without loss of absolute quantity. The importance of the First Law as a grand unifying principle of the cosmos cannot be exaggerated. In Maxwell's words, the principle of energy conservation "gives us a scheme by which we may arrange the facts of any physical science as instances of the transformation of energy from one form to another. It also indicates that in the study of any new phenomenon our first inquiry must be, How can this phenomenon be explained as a transformation of energy? What is the original form of the energy? What is its final form? And what are the conditions of transformation?"[10]

With thermal energy, however, there are limits to the efficiency of this conversion to other forms of energy due to the effects of the Second Law of Thermodynamics, or entropy. Coined by the German scientist Rudolf Clausius in 1865, the term *entropy*, formed from the Greek to mean "transformational content," denotes the increment of disorder in a thermodynamic system. The Second Law of Thermodynamics asserts that a system's total energy consists of two separate parts: energy available for work (useful or free energy) and energy unavailable for work (useless or bound energy). Entropy is the rate at which useful energy is converted into irrecoverable forms (useless energy); that is, the rate at which energy is forever lost in an isolated system.[11] As collisions over time cause bodies to exchange heat, the energy contained in a closed system becomes distributed in the most probable pattern—one of equal energy among particles—with all individual particles engaged in random, disordered motion.[12]

Heat itself does not produce work in a thermodynamic system. Rather, as pointed out by Sadi Carnot (1796–1832), who formulated the basic ideas that later led to the discovery of entropy, work is generated by the difference in temperature between hot and cold bodies; *the equivalent of the work done by heat is found in the mere transfer of heat from a hotter to a colder body.*[13] When everything reaches the same temperature, no work can be done. In Clausius's well-known formulation of the Second Law, known as the Clausius statement: "Heat can never pass from a colder to a warmer body without some other change, connected therewith, occurring at the same time."[14]

In summary, the First Law of Thermodynamics states that energy can neither be created nor destroyed. The Second Law states that it is not possible to convert all heat (or thermal energy) to work in a continuous process, with the consequence that, in a closed system, you cannot finish any real physical process with as much useful energy as you had to start with—some energy is always wasted.[15] The Second Law can be stated very succinctly: within a closed system, entropy can never decrease—it can only remain the same or increase. And because the Second Law governs the direction of all physical changes taking place in the universe, the entropy of the universe is always increasing. Once again, Clausius elegantly expressed the fundamental laws of the universe that correspond with the First and Second Laws:

1. The energy of the universe remains a constant.
2. The entropy of the universe tends to a maximum.[16]

The Cosmological Consequences of Nature's Arrow of Time

The Second Law recast the whole seventeenth- and eighteenth-century framework of scientific thought by introducing the direction of time in the form of "irreversible processes." As David Hawkins puts it: "The second law had one peculiarity that distinguished it from all previous formulations of physical law since the time of Galileo: it took account of time direction, and they did not. . . . The second law implied that physics, by its own means, was finally moved to acknowledge one of the most pervasive features of experience, the difference between 'before' and 'after.'" Once a state of maximum entropy has been reached, there is no going back. In the words of Léon Brillouin, "Time flows on, it never comes back."[17]

Within the scientific community, the credibility and legitimacy of the science of energy was resisted by members of the elite Royal Society and the British Association for the Advancement of Science (BAAS), who admired the preeminence of French mathematical physics exemplified by Pierre-Simon Laplace's pivotal, five-volume *Mécanique Céleste* (Celestial Mechanics). The North British physicists and engineers countered this resistance to the science of energy by means of a Whiggish rhetorical strategy, stressing the inexorable march of human progress from darkness to light, from error to truth.

Public credibility for the new science of thermodynamics was gained in a different setting, Glasgow's marine engineering works on the River Clyde, through the heat engine, steam power, and the great commercial expectations for ocean steam navigation. The scientists of energy, most notably Rankine, promoted the discipline of thermodynamics as a core tool in the hands of Glasgow's Clydeside marine engine-builders for the production of the most efficient and compact heat engines for long-distance navigation.[18] They succeeded. By the 1860s, the bustling shipbuilding and engineering works on the south bank of the River Clyde—where compound engines were being produced that powered ocean-going iron steamers, making them "economical," and therefore profitable for investors—had elevated the status of Glasgow to maritime legend: Clydeside steamships challenged the sail's supremacy for the privilege and profits of carrying the trade of empires, and they won.

The science of energy and entropy changed everything from commerce to religion to culture. The new language of energy was a scientific revolution—a profound conceptual shift—unlike anything that preceded it. The universe would now be understood neither in terms of "action-at-a-distance" forces nor in terms of discrete particles moving through void space. Rather, it was a universe of continuous matter possessed of kinetic energy—a cosmos, in contrast to Laplace's deterministic astronomy, that ensured a role for human free will in directing energy during its transformation from states of intensity to diffusion. As Sir Joseph Larmor, heir to the Lucasian Chair of Mathematics at Cambridge once occupied by Newton, observed in 1908: "This doctrine [of energy] has not only furnished a standard of industrial values which has enabled mechanical power . . . to be measured with scientific precision as a commercial asset; it has also, in its other aspect of the continual dissipation of mechanical energy, created the doctrine of inorganic evolution and changed our conceptions of the material universe."[19]

By the mid-nineteenth century, the cosmological consequences of the mysterious concept of entropy had gone so far as to rob the sun of its mythic status as the fountain of life and renewal and, from a religious perspective, as the limitless source of power linking nature's goodness to the infinite providence of God. If, as the concept of entropy claimed, there is a universal tendency in the material world for energy to be dissipated, then there must have been a time when the earth was too hot for man's habitation, and there must also come a time when the earth will be too cold for human life. This was the thesis of William Thomson's controversial paper of 1852, "On a Universal Tendency in Nature to the Dissipation of Mechanical Energy," which alerted the world to the grim fact that the solar system is fated some thirty million years from now to exhaust its resources and enter a terminal state of "heat death"—at which point no further mechanical work can ever be extracted from the universe. The popularization of this chilling doomsday vision signaled the cultural arrival and resonance of classical thermodynamics.

The cosmological picture drawn by Thomson's "heat death" theory was bracketed by the moment of creation and the moment when all activity ceased. Between these two points lay the vast span of time when natural law operated. This "time's arrow" or linear view of natural history placed Thompson and his fellow energy scientists in opposition to the standard "uniformitarian" geological view expressed by Charles Lyell's publication, *Principles of Geology*, which assumed a constancy of the forces of nature—they being no more or less violent in antiquity than in the present. Lyell argued that all past events could be explained by the action of causes now in operation. No old ones are extinct; no new ones have been introduced. A barrister skilled in verbal persuasion, Lyell defended his uniformity dogma in Manichean terms: those who, like Thomson, view the past as different from the present, represent the forces of darkness, impeding scientific progress; those who adhere to the scientific practices of uniformity are the source of light and truth.

Seeking to contain the professional and popular firestorm ignited by his dire predictions, Thomson published an article, "On the Age of the Sun's Heat," in *Macmillan Magazine* in 1862. True, entropy implied "a certain principle of *irreversible action in nature*" leading to an inevitable state of universal rest and death; and, true, "we may say, with equal certainty, that the inhabitants of the earth cannot continue to enjoy the light and heat essential to their life, for many million years longer, unless sources now unknown to us are prepared in the great storehouse of creation." But, on the bright side, "it is also impossible to conceive either the beginning or the continuance of life, without an overruling creative power," and so "no conclusions of dynamical science regarding the future condition of the earth can be held to give dispiriting views as to the destiny of the race of intelligent beings by which it is at present inhabited." Thus, in the final moments of darkness and freezing cold, God will suddenly appear to provide what He has prepared in the "great storehouse of creation" and save the human race from extinction.[20] This quirky article on solar physics inspired no less than Edward Bulwer-Lytton's popular novel of 1871, *The Coming Race*, and H. G. Wells's famous novella *The Time Machine*, of 1895. And, in an ironic twist, because Thomson estimated the sun's age at less than 100 million years, he became embroiled in a controversy with Darwinians that put him on the "side of the angels" in a scientific debate closely followed by the Victorian public.[21]

With this brief historical review serving as back story, we can now move on to examine how the concept of entropy works as a root metaphor for a theory of contemporary world politics.[22]

Entropy as Metaphor

Pattern Recognition, Time's Arrow, and the Big Chill

The use of entropy as a metaphor has much to offer, but it is not without problems. Entropy only applies to isolated (or closed) systems, and there are no observable isolated systems. The earth itself is part of the solar system, which receives energy from—and radiates it back out to the rest of—the universe. Only the universe as a whole qualifies as a truly closed system. There is also the problem of entropy's conceptualization. More than any other concept in the natural sciences, entropy has engendered diverse and sometimes contradictory interpretations. As James Johnstone, put it in his *Philosophy of Biology* (1914): "Entropy is a shadowy kind of concept, difficult to grasp. But the reader who would extend the notion of mechanism into life simply *must* grasp it."[1] I suspect if Johnstone were writing today, he would have added that the reader who seeks to understand modernity *must* come to terms with it.

Pervasive in many fields within both the arts and sciences, entropy is widely acknowledged to be one of the most mysterious and elusive concepts ever created.[2] The physicist-philosopher Percy Williams Bridgman complained, "There are almost as many formulations of the second law as there have been discussions of it."[3] Similarly, John von Neumann, the brilliant mathematician, pioneer of the computer age, and father of game theory, advised the communication theorist Claude E. Shannon to use the term *entropy* when discussing information because "no one knows what entropy really is, so in a debate you will always have the advantage."[4] Whether entropy's indefinable quality—its inherently ambiguous nature—is the source of its greatest strength or greatest weakness or both, it probably explains why the concept has proven to be such a seductive and persistent metaphor. (I say *metaphor* because entropy only applies to closed or isolated systems.)

To be specific, entropy has been variously associated with: (1) disorganization, disorder, or what the nineteenth-century American theoretical physicist J. Willard Gibbs called "mixedupness"; (2) nature's "arrow of time"; (3) positive information, that is, information that makes a difference; (4) ignorance or lack of information; (5) uncertainty, randomness, and indefiniteness; (6) information overload and distortion; (7) unbounded freedom and the absence of constraints; (8) homogeneity and a flattening effect; (9) the dissipation of mechanical energy, enervation, and ennui; and (10) the universe's inevitable heat death (the Big Chill).[5]

Further complicating matters, recent computer simulations by University of Michigan scientists and engineers trying to herd tiny particles into useful ordered formations have found entropy to be an unlikely ally. Incredible but true. Under certain conditions, the property of entropy actually induces order from disorder—in the computer simulations, it nudged tightly packed particles to form organized structures. Professor of chemical engineering Sharon Glotzer cautions, however, that this is not really about disorder creating order. Rather, entropy needs its image updated: it is a measure of possibilities rather than disorder. "It's all about options. In this case, ordered arrangements produce the most possibilities, the most options. It's counterintuitive, to be sure," Glotzer explains.[6] This conceptualization of entropy as possibilities is important and relevant to global politics in the age of entropy. I return to this subject in chapter 3.

Entropy as a Statistical Law of Probability

As discussed, the property of entropy within the domain of physics arises from the Second Law of Thermodynamics, which tells us that there is (1) available energy that we can direct into most any desired channel and (2) dissipated energy that we cannot lay hold of and direct at our pleasure. It further captures nature's basic tendency toward the dissipation of available energy and order. By extrapolation, the Second Law suggests the eventual "heat death" of the universe, as mechanical motion and the energy used to create that motion continually run down.[7]

Outside the domain of physics, entropy appears as a commonsense statistical law of probability, which posits that high-frequency events occur more often than low-frequency ones. Grounded in this truism, entropy tells us that closed systems proceed from initial states of low probability (order) to end states of highest probability (disorder).[8] Here, let us consider the work of Josiah Willard Gibbs and Ludwig Edward Boltzmann, who brought the methods of statistical mechanics to Rudolf Clausius's theorem that the entropy of an isolated system always continually increases. Gibbs and Boltzmann explained that the isolated system—galaxy, engine, human being, culture, or whatever—must evolve spontaneously toward the Condition of the More Probable. As Boltzmann put it: "There is no difference for the universe as a whole between 'forward' and 'backward' directions of time. But for those worlds on which life exists—and which are therefore in a relatively improbable state—the direction of time is determined by the direction of growing entropy, which points from less probable states to more probable ones."[9] Given the improbability of order arranging itself from disorder (without help from elsewhere), it follows that, statistically, everything tends toward maximum entropy. Once maximum entropy is reached, the system stays there forever, never returning to its initial state.[10] The system has achieved final equilibrium.

To illustrate the process of rising entropy, consider the act of shuffling a deck of cards with a well-defined initial order.[11] For simplicity's sake, shuffling consists of removing the top card and randomly placing it back in the deck. After one shuffle, the deck has changed to one of fifty-two alternatives, each strongly resembling the original order. But after many repetitions, the original sequence will have been completely destroyed.[12] The order will never come back no matter how long you shuffle. Something has been done that cannot be undone: a random element has been introduced in place of arrangement. To explain how the introduction of a randomizer induces disorder, Peter Landsberg uses the example of a child's playroom: "Tidy away all your children's toys in a toy cupboard, and the probability of finding part of a toy in a cubic centimeter is highly peaked in the region of the cupboard. Release a randomizing influence in the form of an untidy child, and the distribution of the system will soon spread."[13] Returning to our shuffling example, for the cards to return to their original order is not physically impossible; it is just improbable in the extreme. As Maxwell put it, "The 2nd law of Thermodynamics has the same degree of truth as the statement that if you throw a tumbler of water into the sea, you cannot get the same tumbler of water out again."[14]

The process of increasing disorder in a deck of playing cards after each shuffle is a statistical example of rising entropy, wherein the decrease of free (useful) energy refers to lost order or missing information as the system moves toward its final or mean distribution.[15] What does it mean to say that the final distribution is one with minimum information? To answer this question, physicists began speaking of microstates and macrostates.

A macrostate might be the number seven as the outcome of throwing a pair of dice. The corresponding microstates would be all the possible configurations of the thrown pair of dice—(3,4), (4,3), (2,5), (5,2), (1,6), or (6,1). Technically speaking, the entropy of a given macrostate is the logarithm of the number of its possible microstates. When presented a given macrostate, entropy measures our degree of uncertainty or ignorance about its specific microstate—in our example, the specific configuration for a pair of dice that totals seven—by counting the number of bits of additional information needed to specify it. Sometimes there is no uncertainty whatsoever. For instance, if told that the macrostate of a pair of dice is 12, we know that the microstate is 6,6. Similarly, if told that the macrostate is 2, we know that the particular die arrangement (microstate) must be 1,1. These "least probable" macrostates of a pair of dice provide the *most* information and, therefore, represent the least entropy. The "most probable" macrostate, 7, provides the *least* information because it has the largest number of corresponding microstates, so it represents the most entropy. Entropy measures this change in the amount of missing information, whereby a gain in entropy means a loss of information.

Entropy is often associated with disorder and chaos because random configurations have a higher probability than more ordered ones of occurring. Randomness can be found in virtually unlimited combinations of specific configurations, whereas order implies a specific combination of a relatively small number of configurations. Consider an egg rolling off a table. The splattered egg represents a condition of maximum entropy; the pristine egg signifies the absence of entropy (or neg-entropy). The former macrostate does not tell us much about the specific configuration, whereas the latter one does. As entropy increases, the macrostate can be composed of a greater number of specific configurations, and accordingly it reveals less information about the particular microstate.

Entropy and Purposive Direction

From the perspective of the natural sciences, however, the idea that information and order perform work (analogous to available energy) is a rather strange one. How can this be so? The answer lies in a tradition of cause and effect originating with Anaxagoras (c. 500-428 BCE), in whose cosmology Order (Cosmos) is born from Chaos by the sorting action of Mind (Nous).[16] It is a cosmology that associates cause with reason and the order of nature with the order of thought. Here, the performance of useful work means providing or transferring some order or information to a system to produce a situation having a certain order.[17] In other words, free energy capable of doing useful work rests on purposive behavior, which means not just having goals but acting in such a way as to realize them—to bring about the initial thought or description of purposive activity.

Advancing just such an argument, Sir Oliver Lodge (1851–1940) explained why mechanical operations and physical energy must be guided by purposive intelligence to perform useful work. It is of no consequence to "energy," he pointed out, whether a stone rolling over a cliff falls on point A or point B of a beach.

> But at A it shall merely dent the sand, whereas at B it shall strike a detonator and explode a mine. Scribbling on a piece of paper results in a certain distribution of fluid and production of a modicum of heat: so far as energy is concerned it is the same whether we sign Andrew Carnegie or Alexander Coppersmith, yet the one effort may land us in twelve months' imprisonment or may build a library, according to circumstances, while the other achieves no result at all. . . . [It is intelligence that liberates energy with some resultant effect] that determined whether the stone from the cliff should fall on point A or point B—the same sort of process that guided the pen to make legible and effective writing instead of illegible and ineffective scrawls—the same kind of control that determines when and where a trigger shall be pulled so as to secure the anticipated slaughter of a bird. So far as energy is concerned, the explosion and the trigger-pulling are the same identical operations whether the aim be exact or random. It is intelligence which directs; it is physical energy which is directed and controlled and produces the result in time and space.[18]

If purposive intelligence to direct available energy is required for useful work, then it follows that entropy increases in the absence of such guidance. This is the general intuition that things tend to go to pot unless someone intervenes; that willful intelligence circumvents the natural tendency for disorder to increase in the world. It is an intuition rooted in the principle of the thermodynamic arrow of time, often described in terms of the "irreversibility" of many common processes, particularly decay, disorder, and disorganization.[19] Within Nature, time's arrow is the property of entropy alone: it points in the direction of increasing randomness, with improbable order succumbing to more probable chaos.[20]

At its simplest level, the law of entropy is disconcertingly familiar, decreeing that things never fix themselves, that things are easier to break than to fix, that order is more difficult to achieve than disorder.[21] We intuitively understand that when the Titanic hits an iceberg, it tears a hole in its hull; the iceberg does not repair a hole in its hull. Cars do not get newer over time but instead grow older and more rust-eaten until their structural integrity is lost. Batteries do not recharge themselves; they drain their charge and lose their effectiveness. Water does not run out of a submarine when a torpedo opens a hole in it; it rushes into the submarine. The odor of perfume flows from the bottle and dissipates throughout the room. One cannot enter a room enveloped in the odor of a perfume, open a bottle, and observe the perfume concentrating itself back into the container.

Less obviously, entropy tells us that closed systems initially containing a variety of elements will, as time passes, move toward greater homogeneity. Imagine two separate containers of the colors blue and yellow with a valve connecting the two closed systems. When the valve is opened, molecules of each color advance to the other side. Over time, the two colors will blend together to form a uniform color of green. Because "you cannot stir things apart," as the precocious young Thomasina says in Tom Stoppard's *Arcadia*, the mixing process becomes, statistically, a one-way street.[22] Once the system reaches an equilibrium of greenness, there is no going back to the initial states of separate yellow and blue; these colors have become lost information. In this way, rising entropy results in less variety as equilibrium averages out to the literally mediocre.

In its most hardcore version, the entropy metaphor suggests that we live in a universe of mounting chaos marching toward heat death; that we, the embattled residents of this doomed universe, can only accomplish a temporary reversal of this ineluctable driving force by sorting through confusing and profuse information, by pattern recognition, by attempting to discover the hidden order of things, the meanings or codes that may or may not have been purposely put there. Despite our best efforts, however, we merely forestall the natural disorder that awaits us, which is as near at hand as the closest rusty nail, as the nearest ramshackle house.

Entropy and Contemporary International Politics

At this point the reader may be wondering how the two entropies (thermodynamic and information) fit together to tell a story about today's global affairs. The answer is straightforward. All systems, including the international system, are composed of attributes associated with both their *structure* (how the units are arranged) and *processes* (how the units interact with one another). The two forms of entropy map onto these two dimensions (structure and process) of the international system. The metaphor of thermodynamic entropy suggests how changes at the structural level of the emerging international system cause entropy to rise; while information entropy explains how changes in the system's processes increase entropy. The story goes like this.

The metaphor of thermodynamic entropy describes the absence of international structural constraints that produce behavioral regularities among states and keep international outcomes within limited ranges. By constraint, I mean "restrict[ing] freedom of action by forbidding, or raising the costs of, certain kinds of actions, or compelling other kinds of actions."[23] By loosening structural constraints, rising structural entropy generates random behaviors and events. More specifically, just as maximum entropy in a thermodynamic sense yields particles of equal weight, a condition of rising structural entropy will be one in which power diffuses throughout the system. This process of power deconcentration results in a system-wide leveling effect, such that the number of power centers increases but traditional bases of power become less useful than they were in the past (analogous to rising entropy's by-product of useless energy). The concept of system structure also encompasses social structures that affect individual behavior at the micro level. Here again, the absence of structural constraints on individual behavior, given the virtual nature of reality in cyberspace and its conduciveness to personal anonymity, facilitates transgressions of traditional morality and social and cultural norms. Individual behavior is less constrained and, therefore, more random and unpredictable. Most important for international politics, decision-makers will increasingly commit the error of misplaced certainty, imposing unwarranted certainty on inherently uncertain situations.

The metaphor of information entropy relates not to international structure but rather to international processes: the system's dynamic density; its level of interconnectedness; the nature and volume of its various flows; how the units interact over a range of activities—political, military-strategic, economic, social—with each other and their environment. Information entropy measures the distortions created by the increased volume, density, and speed of interactions and information flows on the behaviors of the units comprising the system.

Table 2.1   Micro and Macro Manifestations of Rising Entropy

	Rising entropy within the system's structure	Rising entropy within the system's processes
Micro-level indices	The virtual nature of reality and the anonymity of cyberspace results in transgressions of norms and moral codes and a heightened pleasure principle. In response to a random world, decision-makers become increasingly susceptible to misplaced certainty.	The digital world changes how the brain processes information. Humankind transitions from linear to nonlinear thinking. Information overload causes ennui, loneliness, apathy, alienation. The infosphere facilitates the formation of fact-resistant personal worlds, which inhibit the building of consensual knowledge bases. In a post-fact world, political polarization becomes the norm.
Macro-level indices	International structure no longer constrains actors. Actor behaviors become more random and international outcomes less predictable. Global power is diffusing and is less usable. The number of global actors with negative power to disrupt, negate, and frustrate cooperation rather than to create, shape, and construct solutions to global problems increases. Dysfunctional global governance is systemic. World runs on automatic pilot.	Globalization reduces the importance of geography and borders in choosing friends and enemies and in determining identity. Networked power rises. Global culture becomes more homogeneous. Nonmilitary warfare (cyber, economic, resource, psychological, and information-based forms of conflict) becomse more prevalent among state and nonstate actors.

These processes along with international structure determine the characteristic dynamics of an international system, distinguishing one era from another. Structural and process variables exert their effects at both the macro level (geopolitics) and micro level (the actors: states, nongovernmental organizations, corporations, individuals, etc.).

It is no mere coincidence that both structural and process entropy are rising at the same time. These are not two separate stories: reciprocal causation is at work. Dense global interconnections—the free flow of goods, information, and capital—allow for the rapid diffusion of knowledge and technology, spreading power among nation-states more evenly throughout the world. These multifaceted information networks and material flows also empower nonstate actors—such as energy exporters, drug cartels and mercenaries, terrorists, militias (e.g., Hamas, MS-13, FARC, Hezbollah, the Mahdi Army, the Taliban), private military companies, warlords, pirates, religious movements, nongovernmental organizations (NGOs), large corporations, and so on—to challenge state authority and legitimacy in unique and various ways.

Cause-and-effect is not unidirectional, however; it runs both ways. Rising entropy at the structural level causes entropy to rise within the system's processes. Specifically, the more influential actors that emerge on the international scene, the more connections among them will increase. Consequently, global processes become thicker and more complex, resulting in the rise of entropy at the level of system process.

That said, it is important to point out that my use of the entropy metaphor is less as a causal variable than as an effect. Global entropy is a condition or environment within which action takes place. The key questions are: What kind of things should we see in an environment of high and increasing entropy? (In other words, how does rising entropy manifest itself at the macro and micro levels?) And what are the contributing factors that are causing entropy to rise in global politics? This part of the present argument is more a descriptive exercise than an explanatory one.

Table 2.1 combines the four dimensions—system structure and process with the micro and macro levels—to provide a graphic representation of the most salient features of the age of entropy. Chapter 6 focuses on manifestations of rising entropy at the macro level (listed in the bottom two cells of the table). Chapter 7 discusses indices of rising entropy at the micro level (the top two cells of the table).

The Multidimensions of Disorder

Thermodynamics and World Politics

Presumably, the Second Law of Thermodynamics is valid always and everywhere. One might suppose, therefore, that it must have existed at the time of early civilizations; of the Roman Empire and the Han dynasty in China; and preceding the First World War, when the British Empire reigned over the globe and competed with other European great powers. So why invoke the metaphor of entropy now to explain international politics?

There are five main reasons why entropy is an especially appealing and useful metaphor for contemporary world politics: (1) because decolonization made virtually every inch of Earth's territory part of a sovereign state, such that international politics only became a closed system by the mid-1960s; (2) because the unipolar structure of international politics doesn't constrain actors within the system, so they have endless behavioral options and possibilities; (3) because the emerging post-unipolar era will not be ushered in by a hegemonic war; (4) because it will contain many more power centers than normal multipolar systems; and (5) because globalization and the digital revolution dissipate power and exert homogenizing pressures. How each of these factors contributes to rising entropy will be discussed in turn.

Decolonization

Entropy arises in systems where no new information is yet to be discovered, all actors are known, and the space is clearly defined. International politics became a closed system susceptible to increasing entropy when it subsumed the entire earth, such that nothing remained outside of it. This process began roughly one hundred years ago, after the Age of Discovery that witnessed European expansion across the oceans to new lands. It was then that English geographer Sir Halford Mackinder proclaimed the birth of a "closed political system" of "world-wide scope."[1] Yet the modern state system did not become fully defined until the completion of decolonization in the mid-1960s. It was only then that the world system—almost every territorial inch of it—was composed of states and nothing but states.[2] The process of increasing entropy in international politics, therefore, commenced a mere fifty years ago—a short time period in the larger scheme of things.

It was only after decolonization that the trend toward increasing globalization appeared in earnest, and it has picked up speed with each successive decade. Many of the phenomena that characterize globalization fit the "entropy" metaphor. For instance, global consumerism (powered by Madison Avenue) exhibits tendencies similar to rising entropy from the least to the most probable, from differentiation to sameness, from ordered individuality to a kind of chaos. Postmodern novelist Thomas Pynchon made this observation in his short story "Entropy," wherein the main character, Callisto, finds himself "restating Gibbs' prediction in social terms, and envisioned a heat-death for his culture in which ideas, like heat-energy, would no longer be transferred, since each point in it would ultimately have the same quantity of energy; and intellectual motion would, accordingly, cease."[3] I return to this notion of globalization's homogenizing effects at the end of the chapter.

Unipolarity and the Absence of Constraints

In terms of the structure of international politics, entropy measures change in the degree of constraint the international system exerts on the behavior of states. Constraint is a property of the international system that restricts the freedom of action of states by forbidding or raising the costs of certain kinds of actions or by compelling other kinds of actions. The more entropy increases, the less the international system constrains the behaviors of states.

Returning to our prior discussion of entropy as possibilities (recall Professor Sharon Glotzer's image makeover of entropy from chapter 2), when international structure exerts only weak or no constraints on the behavior of the units (or actors) within the system, actors are free to do whatever they choose. This constraint-free structural environment is the opposite of one in which system structure determines actor behavior—what is known as a "single-exit" or "strait-jacket" structural environment, wherein intense structural pressure forces actors to choose one and only one option or behavior (for instance, when the theater is on fire, we all run for the exits). Under the most intense structural constraints, actor behavior becomes entirely predictable. In contrast, the absence of structural constraints creates a situation in which actors have limitless policy options from which to choose. Unconstrained, they can behave in random and chaotic ways. Anything and everything becomes possible; nothing is predictable or stable.

This absence of system constraints on the behavior of states is a recent phenomenon associated with the onset of unipolarity in 1991. Prior to the end of the Cold War, states behaved in predictable ways, and we could speak of enduring patterns of international politics. Indeed, during the first three hundred years following its birth, in 1648, the modern states system was nothing if not predictable. Several great powers (also called poles) of roughly equal strength fiercely competed with each other for ever more power, prestige, and security. The multipolar structure of the international system—composed of France, Spain, Sweden, Portugal, Russia, Prussia, Austria-Hungary, Britain, and later Japan, Italy, Germany, and the United States—bred classic balance-of-power politics, which constrained all the major players to behave in similar ways: they built arms, formed alliances based on power calculations, sought opportunistic territorial conquest and expansion, and so forth. Predictable behaviors of this kind were determined by the structure of the system (multipolarity). Thus, we say that the system constrained great powers to behave in ways that conformed with the pressures of their environment. Non-great powers, whether weak states or middle powers, were to be seen, and sometimes conquered, but rarely heard. They were mere voiceless pawns (ask Poland) in the realpolitik game of Great Power politics.

International systems composed of two great powers are even easier than multipolar ones to understand and predict. All the action centers on the two poles or superpowers, as they were known during the Cold War when a bipolar system existed. The rest of the world, though viewed by the superpowers in highly competitive terms, becomes largely superfluous to the stability of the global system. Under bipolarity, international politics boils down to a feud between the Hatfields and the McCoys. The behavior of the two poles, the rigidity of their alliance systems (or blocs), and the flexibility of their foreign policies is, for the most part, structurally determined.

The primary feature of both multipolar and bipolar systems—what made them predictable and kept state behaviors within certain ranges—was constant insecurity and the struggle for power that this induced. In international politics, there is no higher authority, no 911 or night watchman, that states can call when their survival is threatened. This condition is referred to as anarchy. Anarchy does not mean disorder per se but rather the absence of a world government or sovereign arbiter to make and enforce agreements among states. Given the condition of anarchy, a central aspect of life in the international system is that great powers fear each other. It is a fear derived from two facts: (1) all great powers have some offensive military power that they can use to attack each other and (2) states can ever be certain that others do not intend to use that power against them. Accordingly, it is said that war always lurks in the background of international politics as a final resort.

Living in a world of constant insecurity, of uncertainty about others' intentions, and with no 911 to call, great powers were compelled (constrained, if you will) by an irreducible level of fear to maximize their share of world power. Bad things happened to those states that ignored power realities. And so foreign policy decisions were invariably rooted in calculations of power. The logic of anarchy and the drive to maximize power generated very predictable state behaviors.

Under today's unipolar structure, in contrast, systemic constraints are weak or nonexistent. Consequently, much of our current state of global randomness can be laid at the doorstep of unipolarity, which has shown itself to be an "anything goes" international structure. Consistent with increasing entropy, unipolar dynamics are random because the structure constrains the choices of neither the unipole nor anyone else. With no great-power rivals, the dominant state makes choices relatively unfettered by the imperatives and constraints of its external environment. The United States enjoys the luxury of choosing with whom to align based on non-power considerations, such as ideological affinity, economic needs, or the vagaries of domestic politics. And when it so chooses, the United States can simply go it alone, cobbling together ad hoc "coalitions of the willing." The idiosyncratic beliefs and capricious choices of unconstrained American leaders tell us more about recent U.S. foreign policy than does international structure. Boundless freedom breeds randomness.

One can reasonably argue that the very concept of polarity has become virtually meaningless. The appearance of power (that is, conspicuous possession of the standard accoutrements of power) is not the same thing as being powerful. History is replete with cases of David beating Goliath, when large advantages in fighting power did not translate into victory on the battlefield. In the early 1960s, for instance, France lost to its colony Algeria. A few years later, the northern half of tiny Vietnam—one of the poorest countries in the world—defeated the United States. Ten years later, the USSR was beaten and bloodied by "backward" Afghanistan.

The fact that the United States currently spends more on defense than all the world's countries combined begs the question: What do its huge military advantages provide in terms of usable American power and influence?[4] Not as much as one might expect. True, the United States is and will long remain the only state capable of projecting considerable global firepower. Unique among all "post-seventeenth century" major powers, America possesses what Barry Posen calls "command of the commons," that is, invincible military dominance over the sea, air, and space—areas that provide access to much of the globe and, though they belong to no one state, that the United States gets vastly more military use from and can credibly threaten to deny their use to others.[5]

Far from ruling the world, however, the United States cannot even count on its allies to follow its lead. The United States is king, but the world beneath it does not behave in the predictable ways of traditional international politics. Of course, with no great-power rivals, the United States makes foreign-policy choices unfettered by structural imperatives and constraints; it enjoys enormous freedom of choice in terms of its national security policies.[6] Freedom is a good thing, to be sure. But the rest of the world is free too. No longer is it a world of the Cold War threat über alles. No longer must states scurry to find patrons and allies for fear of war. States rely less on the security services of a superpower patron, like the United States, than they did when balance of power ruled the day. They are now free to choose to align with the United States, against it, or not align at all. Structure doesn't constrain anyone anymore.[7]

Consider the behavior of Russia. Under the previous bipolar structure, the Soviet Union was an implacable foe of the Western bloc. As such, it could not align with the United States or its allies. Today, Russia can align *with* or *against* the United States and its allies. It could side with the United States, for instance, against China, or with China against the United States. Likewise, it could side with India against China or China against India. Or it could join an alliance with

India and China against the United States or vice versa. The point being that Russia, like everyone else, can form or join any alliance it so chooses because, under unipolarity, anything and everything is possible.

For the United States, the paradox of power under unipolarity is that it cannot convert its enormous military and economic capability advantages into power and influence over others. America's impotence is largely a product of its prior success: there is no longer a common threat (aside from the hegemon itself) to bind others to its policies. The demise of the Soviet Union diminished America's bargaining power vis-à-vis its Cold-War allies. Consequently, the United States has less influence today than it did during the Cold War, when it had to share the stage with a peer competitor.

None of this is to suggest that unipolarity constrains the use of American military force or that it is an especially "peaceful" international structure. To the contrary, unipolarity is a system of weak structural constraints. Little wonder, then, that the United States, and to a lesser extent Britain and France, have used force more often than they did prior to the demise of the Soviet Union in 1991.[8] The succession of American deployments in Panama, the Gulf War, Haiti, Bosnia, Kosovo, Afghanistan, Iraq, and Libya is unmatched during the Cold War era. Of course, these conflicts are small by comparison with wars fought among the great powers or even those waged by the United States during the Cold War (e.g., Korea and Vietnam). Nevertheless, they call for an explanation.

The international structure of unipolarity largely explains the increase in American military activity. As the sole superpower, the United States is no longer deterred from entering local conflicts by the fear of a confrontation with a peer. Its power is unchecked (and unconstrained by international structure) and so can be exercised in reckless and capricious ways.[9] In addition, others have come to rely on America as the global policeman: when states get in trouble, they call 911 expecting to get the U.S. president on the phone. Unipolarity means that the United States can now elevate to greater salience nonsecurity values that were previously trumped by the bipolar superpower rivalry. Under bipolarity, the security challenges posed by the Soviet Union required the United States to focus on military dangers. Every U.S. administration understood that resolute efforts to spread democracy would have entailed enormous risks, including the roll-back of Soviet control. As a state's security increases, however, so too does its leeway to divert substantial military forces from protecting its vital interests toward the pursuit of nonsecurity objectives and values.[10] Thus, America's relatively benign security environment under unipolarity—in addition to the lack of constraints on the use of its power—have afforded it the luxury of pursuing interests in human rights and liberal-democratic ideology. Indeed, its post–Cold War humanitarian interventions and efforts to spread liberal democracy appear excessive to some. As Robert Jervis puts it, "Having done well, states can seek to do good. This is particularly true for the U.S. because of its liberal ideology, the difficulties it has in understanding barriers to democracy, and its resistance to seeing limits to the possibilities for material and spiritual improvement."[11]

The problem is that America is expected to lead but doing so makes it all the more difficult to attract and keep followers. On the one hand, if the United States acts boldly and unilaterally, it risks being perceived as a hyperpower—a Tyrannosaurus Rex that provokes the rest of the world to band together and balance against it. On the other hand, if it acts indecisively or in ways that materially harm the rest of the world, it risks being perceived as a clumsy elephant whose leadership is unneeded and unwanted. Nobody wants to follow a dangerous or incompetent leader. What is new and noteworthy about unipolarity is that subordinate states now have fewer compelling reasons to do so than in the past. In other words, weak powers not only have fewer reasons to follow and obey the hegemon but also enjoy unlimited freedom and autonomy to decide for themselves how to respond to the hegemon's demands. In this respect, contemporary unipolarity is an exemplar of unusable power and influence: America's large power advantages are akin to rising entropy's "useless" energy. Leadership requires followers, after all.

Hegemonic War: The Broken Cycle of Destruction and Renewal

If the current historically unique structural condition of unipolarity has caused entropy to rise, then the onset of multipolarity should fix the situation, right? Not quite. The problem is that deconcentration of power itself induces rising entropy in the form of system disorder and disequilibrium. As power diffuses, relations among established and ascending powers tend to be troubled and often violent. The onset of war between the dominant and rising powers grows more likely as the gap in relative strength between them narrows and as their grievances with the existing order—grievances that expand in lockstep with their mounting capabilities—move beyond any hope of peaceful resolution.[12] Little wonder, then, that rising powers have been portrayed in both theory and practice as "troublemakers" that "feel constrained, even cheated, by the status quo and struggle against it to take what they think is rightfully theirs."[13] And because status demands are usually at the forefront of their dissatisfaction with the established order, rising powers are expected to act assertively to signal their increased strength and preferred higher status.[14]

In the past, entropy arising from this process of uneven growth among the major powers—and the status inconsistencies it causes—was remedied, strangely enough, by global wars fought among all the great powers, sometimes lasting decades. These so-called hegemonic wars performed three essential tasks that replenished the depleted international system with a new flow of energy that was put to work to restore world order and lasting peace. First, akin to Joseph Schumpeter's notion of "creative destruction," hegemonic wars obliterate the old order, wiping the institutional slate clean so that a new efficient global architecture can be rebuilt. Second, they concentrate power in the hands of one dominant state that towers over a world in ruins. Pocketing the majority of the spoils of victory, the newly crowned hegemon possesses the power, will, and legitimacy to transform the world and enforce its new order. Third, these wars clarify the bargaining situation among the great powers—confusion over which is the root cause of war in the first place.[15] The logic here is not obvious; let me explain.

States decide to fight rather than settle their differences by peaceful means when they disagree about their relative military strengths. If, prior to war, they had agreed on the issue of who is militarily stronger than whom, then they would have struck a mutually acceptable prewar bargain that reflected the power realities and avoided the costs of war. By the same logic, wars end when states, having tested their competing estimates of each other's military power on the battlefield, come to agree about their actual strengths. In short, wars are the result of one side misestimating its bargaining power prior to the outbreak of war: the eventual loser must have exaggerated its own military strength relative to that of the eventual victor; otherwise, it would not have fought in the first place. The battlefield determines which side was correct in its prewar estimates. Wars end, therefore, when both sides finally agree about who has power and who does not.

By performing these three tasks—destroying the old order, crowning a new king, and clarifying the bargaining situation among the great powers—hegemonic wars are followed by long periods of peace. The Pax Romana (27 BC–180 AD) rose from the ashes of the republican civil wars; the Pax Britannica (1815–1914) from the French Revolutionary and Napoleonic wars; and Pax Americana (1945–present) from the First and Second World Wars. Just as computers periodically need to be shut down and restarted to reload the operating system, the international system sometimes needs a reboot. In international politics, hegemonic wars have been the surest way to hit the reset button.

Rocked by dramatic and accelerating shifts in power, the international system will soon reach a point in the cycle where another hegemonic war will be needed to remedy the global crisis of legitimacy. After the system crashes this time, however, there will be no required reboot to start the process over again with fresh ideas and replenished energy. The problem is that nuclear weapons have rendered war among the great powers unthinkable. It is a "problem" that the world is thankful to have, of course. Nevertheless, the absence of hegemonic war is as much a cause of entropy as the proliferation of actors and information. With the historic cycle of destruction and renewal permanently broken, how can a new international order be forged—one that is both efficient and accurately reflects the tectonic shifts in power? Can additional deterioration of global institutions be prevented?

Further complicating matters, there is no reason to expect a smooth transition from unipolarity to multipolarity. Although the decline of a hegemonic power may, in theory, be gradual, it is most often abrupt, punctuated by wholly unexpected instances of dramatic change. This is because states with the power to dominate world politics must, of necessity, be complex systems. And like an avalanche, complex and delicate systems may appear calm at one moment only to become wildly turbulent the next. Order can quickly and without warning collapse into chaos. This is why great powers often fail to see their own decline coming until it's too late to properly manage and prepare for it.

Such was the case with Britain roughly a century ago. During the late nineteenth century, the British were comforted by the belief that "history is something unpleasant that happens to other people." A mere fifteen years later, Britain was a second-rate power. Unanticipated declines of this kind are driven by wildly uneven rates of growth among the great powers. Figure 3.1 illustrates the sudden and dramatic nature of decline when a rising country is bigger and grows at a much faster rate than a declining one. Looking at the graph, one easily understands how the British were entirely blindsided by their precipitous downfall a century ago.

To understand the graph, suppose that State A has one hundred units of power and grows at 5 percent per year, while State B has ten units of power and grows at 10 percent per year. During years 1 through 36, A's *absolute* advantage in power increases over B, even as B's power increases as a portion of A's power (that is, even though B grows at a faster rate than A). This occurs because A starts out with a much larger economy than B. Thus, A can grow at half the rate of B and still, year after year, significantly increase its absolute advantage over

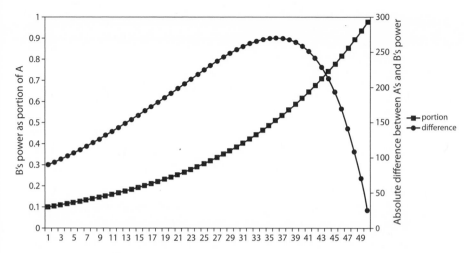

Figure 3.1. The Difference between Relative and Absolute Indicators of Power. B's power as a portion of A vs. the absolute difference between A's and B's power.

Source: Adapted from Alastair I. Johnston and Sheena Chestnut, "Is China Rising?" in Eva Paus, Penelope B. Prime, and Jon Western, eds., *Global Giant: Is China Changing the Rules of the Game?* (New York: Palgrave Macmillan, 2009), p. 243. Used with permission of Palgrave Macmillan.

the rising challenger. By year 37, however, a tipping effect appears as a result of the differential growth rates between the two states. Once the size of B's economy catches up with that of A, then B swiftly and dramatically overtakes A.[16] Indeed, A sinks like a stone relative to B.

This kind of process is precisely what happened to Britain vis-à-vis the United States (and Germany) at the turn of the last century. The average Brit living in the midst of this rapid and discontinuous change might be excused for thinking that "history would never happen to them"—totally unaware that the end of British hegemony was little more than a decade away. The more general point is that complex systems, such as states, often succumb to precipitous and unexpected changes; the process of decline, therefore, may not be gradual and predictable. For a declining hegemon, "the future is uncertain and the end is often near," as Jim Morrison of the Doors sang many years ago.[17]

At present, the United States is the lone superpower with unrivaled command of land, air, sea, and space. The situation can change in hurry, however. The American economy, which sustains the nation's military and political power, might not decline gently and predictably; along with U.S. power, it may fall off a cliff. In any large-scale complex system, collapse may be the result of a small unexpected input that produces enormous, unexpected changes—what scientists call "the amplifier effect." The source of great change may be insignificant; it may completely confound our expectations about appropriate movers of big history.[18] In the words of the historian Niall Ferguson, "A defective brake of a sleeping driver can be all it takes to go over the edge of chaos."[19]

The major cause of U.S. troubles, both in the short and long term, is debt: the nation is borrowing massively to finance current consumption. The United States continues to run unprecedented trade deficits with its leading peer competitor, China, which, based on current trajectories, is predicted to become the world's largest economy by 2040. As of July 2009, the United States owed China over $800 billion, meaning that every person in the "rich" United States has, in effect, borrowed about $3,000 from someone in the "poor" People's Republic of China over the past decade.

The 2008 economic crisis exposed the highly leveraged nature of the U.S. economy. For years, economists warned that U.S. control over the world's growth cycle and its ever-rising current account imbalance rendered global economic growth vulnerable to an abrupt end. What is needed, they claim, is a more balanced global economy—something that analysts argued could only be achieved through meaningful improvements in Japan and Germany, the world's second- and third-largest economies. The analysts were wrong. Global rebalancing is happening even without the contributions of Japan and Germany. Robust domestic demand growth in emerging market economies has reached substantial levels. This shift in global demand trends is historic in the way it has redefined the relationship between advanced and developing economies. Growth projections indicate that the BRICS countries alone will collectively match the original G-7's share of global GDP by 2040–2050, heralding the arrival of a new age of multiple power centers.

The Emergence of Multiple Power Centers

The diffusion of power throughout the international system is causing entropy to rise. The term *power diffusion* has been used to mean several things. First, the gap in power between the United States and its nearest competitor is closing. Here, power diffusion is a dynamic, long-run view of the power trajectories of the two strongest states in the system. Second, the world is becoming more multipolar. America is seeing its power decline while others are seeing their power rise. This version of power diffusion provides a more encompassing picture than the "two-nation" view, but it is far from complete. Indeed, to say that we are witnessing a return to multipolarity—the consensus opinion among experts—is to trivialize the tectonic shift currently under way.

International relations will no longer be dominated by one or two or even several great powers. New actors—regional and global organizations, local militias, global crime and terrorist networks, nongovernmental organizations (NGOs), and large corporations—are emerging to compete with states, each possessing and exerting a different kind of power. As the Cold War ended and central and East European countries began dumping their stocks of weapons, governments across much of the developing world weakened relative to their societies.[20] Unlike the 1960s, when the state had all the guns, domestic challengers to weak governments in Africa and elsewhere were able to procure weapons on the international market. Many of these weakened governments currently find themselves at war with internal political foes or as willing or unwilling hosts to violent nonstate actors (VNSAs). Nuclear-capable Pakistan is only the most terrifying example.[21]

Indeed, in the twenty-first century, relatively few sovereign states represented in the United Nations can truly claim a monopoly of force within their territorial borders. VNSAs are no longer minor players in a world dominated by states; they now pose a pervasive challenge to the sovereignty of nation-states. According to a recent study by the Federation of American Scientists, there are 385 "parastate" organizations, defined as entities that challenge the state's monopoly on the use of violence within a specified geographical territory.[22] As a global phenomenon, this fundamental change has been underappreciated largely because the VNSAs have taken different forms in different parts of the world, including tribal and ethnic groups, warlords, drug-trafficking organizations, youth gangs, terrorists, militias, insurgents, and transnational criminal organizations. These subnational challenges to the dominance of the Westphalian state will become ever more prevalent as states become increasingly deficient providers of basic governance functions.[23]

Entropy dictates that systems composed of large numbers of actors tend toward greater randomness and disorder. A world populated by dozens of power centers will prove difficult to navigate and control. Herding a few cats is no simple task; herding dozens of them is an impossible one. In the new global disorder, those in possession of a large advantage in traditional power capabilities (military, economic, and diplomatic) are no longer guaranteed that they can get others to do what they want them to do. Indeed, it is essentially impossible for modern states, no matter how militarily and politically powerful they may be, to use diplomacy or deterrence (the threat of force to gain compliance from the target) to influence violent nonstate groups that are detached from territorial concerns and that prosper in the ungoverned spaces of failed states or within virtual communities. The problem for modern states is not only that a nonterritorial actor does not offer a clear target that can be threatened and, if necessary, destroyed (the "no-return address" problem) but that many of these violent groups are motivated by non-negotiable religious rather than secular concerns. Worse still, violence is not a deterrent but rather a source of social cohesion for them. All of these factors weaken the ability of states to gain influence with these groups by threatening to impose clear costs on them.[24]

As power and influence become less and less linked, global order and cooperation will be in short supply. Instead, international relations in the twenty-first century will consist of messy ad hoc arrangements cobbled together by means of "à la carte multilateralism" and networked interactions among state and nonstate actors.[25] One wonders what order and concerted action mean in a world that lacks fixed and predictable structures and relationships.[26] Given the haphazard and incomplete manner by which the vacuum of lost state power is being filled, why expect order at all?

The main issue here is not about the oft-mentioned distinction between "hard" and "soft" power: the former being about wielding carrots and sticks to get others to do things we want and not do things we don't want, the latter being about the persuasive effects (lure) of, among other things, a nation's culture, political values, ideas, economic and educational systems, personal contacts and exchanges, and overall success. The distinction between these two forms of power—though it has prompted much ink to be spilled in the past decade—does not seem any more important today than it has been in the past. After all, was not the Cold War both a global military and ideological contest waged equally with weapons (hard power) and ideas (soft power)?

Nor is the sea change in power today primarily about the skillful combination of both hard and soft power within an integrated strategy, resource base, or tool kit to achieve national objectives—what has been recently termed "smart" power and variously defined as: (1) "an approach that underscores the necessity of a strong military, but also invests heavily in alliances, partnerships, and institutions of all levels to expand American influence and establish legitimacy of American action"; (2) the "strategic use of diplomacy, persuasion, capacity building, and the projection of power and influence in ways that are cost-effective and have political and social legitimacy"; and (3) the "enlisting of others on behalf of U.S. goals, through alliances, international institutions, careful diplomacy, and the power of ideals."[27] Secretary of State Hillary Clinton offered a more literal definition of smart power: "The intelligent use of all means at our disposal, including our ability to convene and connect. It means our economic and military strength; our capacity for entrepreneurship and innovation; and the ability and credibility of our new President and his team. It also means the application of old-fashioned common sense in policymaking. It's a blend of principle and pragmatism."[28] As these various definitions attest, the problem with the concept of "smart power" is that—just as a theory that explains everything explains nothing—the concept means so many things to so many different people that it is virtually meaningless.

What is different about power today is its increasingly limited and conditional nature. Moreover, the emergence of new and varied kinds of globally influential actors means that power, whether hard, soft, or smart, is becoming more about the ability to disrupt, block, disable, and destroy than to adopt, enable, repair, and build. We see this trend not only among nonstate actors in their relations with states but in the military strategies of traditional nation-states vis-à-vis each other. For example, China is aggressively pursuing "anti-access/area-denial" (A2/AD) capabilities (mainly cyberwarfare and antisatellite) that target the U.S military's information and communications systems, with the goal of significantly increasing the risks to U.S. forces operating in the western Pacific. Similarly, Iran is pursuing A2/AD capabilities, such as submarines and antiship cruise missiles and sophisticated mines, with the objective of transforming the Persian Gulf into a "no-go-zone" for the U.S. Navy. As Andrew F. Krepinevich Jr., president of the Center for Strategic and Budgetary Assessments, avers, "The current and future challenge to stability in the western Pacific and the Persian Gulf is not a cross-border invasion but the spread of A2/AD capabilities, which will make it increasingly difficult for the United States to operate freely in those areas."[29] Power today hinges on the capability to deny.

When power is used for constructive purposes, it is becoming increasingly issue-specific and is, in many cases, best wielded by partnerships among governments, public and private actors, and individuals. The issue is fundamentally about the bases of power (what types of capabilities will be best suited for gaining influence over whom in what situations) and the need for networked, as opposed to hierarchically based, power.[30] Regarding the former, just as nuclear weapons are effective tools for deterring attacks on one's soil but are of no use in stemming the flow of illegal aliens across one's borders, certain types of power assets will be of great use in some areas and of little use in others. That is to say, national power assets (such as population, resource endowments, wealth, political skill, and military power) are never completely fungible; economic wealth is of highest fungibility because it is easiest to convert into the most liquid asset of all, money.

What is new and noteworthy in the age of entropy is not that political power resources will be much less liquid than economic ones; this has always been the case. Rather, traditional power assets will become even less fungible and more circumscribed by specific domains than they were in the past, when military power seemed to purchase all kinds of influence over nonmilitary issues.[31] Related to this point, the power of most international actors will be limited, such that a given actor will be able to exert influence over certain issues but not others.

Globalization and the Digital Revolution

Entropy is associated with the dissipation of useable energy, enervation, homogenization, and diffused or deconcentrated power. Globalization reinforces these entropic effects in four fundamental ways. First, globalization dissipates useable national power. While globalization has been going on for centuries, it is thicker, quicker, cheaper, and deeper than ever before. It now amplifies "up to eleven"—to borrow Nigel Tufnel's memorable phrase from *This Is Spinal Tap*—the volume, velocity and importance of contemporary cross-border flows of just about everything, from capital, manufactured goods, e-mails, greenhouse gases, weapons, drugs, information, and viruses. These cross-border flows are largely beyond the control of governments or any other authority, for that matter. In addition, the exponential growth of transnational channels of contact—in the number and variety of multi-continental participants in global networks—"means that more issues are up for grabs internationally, including regulations and practices (ranging from pharmaceutical testing to accounting and product standards to banking regulation) that were formally regarded as the prerogatives of national governments."[32]

Second, globalization's rapid diffusion of knowledge and technology is dramatically shifting power among nation-states, driving down America's edge in productive capacity and overall power position. And because rising powers inevitably seek enhanced prestige, status, and authority commensurate with their actual power, this leveling process will beget a crisis of international legitimacy. The stronger emerging powers become, the more determined they will be to revise their standing and voice within international institutions, the current division of territory and spheres of influence, and the rules of the game.[33]

Third, the free flow of goods, information, and capital has strengthened the capacities of nonstate actors, such as energy exporters, drug cartels, terrorists, hacktivists, and Fortune 500 companies. Strong states no longer have a monopoly on power. Multifaceted networks make it easier than ever for individuals and groups to accumulate and project power, to interfere with the workings of, and penetrate the once impenetrable regions within, governments. Private information held by states, corporations, and individuals becomes more difficult to keep private; secrets cannot be kept undisclosed; confidentiality is more easily breached. Thus, for example, in September 2012, the hacking group known as AntiSec—a subset of the loose hacking collective known as Anonymous—say they obtained 12 million identification numbers for iPhone, iPad, and iPod Touch devices by hacking into the computer of an FBI agent, proving, they claim, that the FBI used device information to track people.[34] The more actors in the system, the more power centers there exist, the weaker and more diffuse power becomes within the system.

Fourth and finally, the processes that drive the global economy and information society tend to push in the direction of uniformity. We live within an increasingly homogenized global culture; "cultures have become so intermixed that there is no longer any pure or authentic culture distinct from others."[35] This is the rather benign "hybridization" or "convergence" form of the "cultural colonization" argument.[36] The less subtle, more malevolent version claims that globalization is the latest incarnation of Western imperialism. The birth of the global consumer, so the argument goes, was not merely the result of "the utilitarian convenience of global products" but was deliberately coaxed by "the sale of dreams of affluence, personal success, and erotic gratification evoked through advertising and the culture industry of Hollywood."[37] Through the force of its ubiquitous and irresistibly seductive "soft" power, the West continues to subjugate the "periphery"—a logic captured by the phrases "Coca-colonization," "McDonaldization," and "Westoxification."

Claims that globalization is imperial and works to the hegemonic advantage of the United States and its western allies are rooted in two basic observations: (1) many important choices (individual and national) seem to have been decided already due to the "coordinating" effects of globalization, and (2) privileged countries seem to benefit disproportionately from the processes of globalization. In contrast, many observers portray globalization in precisely opposite terms, as an astonishing advance in human freedom to be celebrated. In their eyes, transnational flows of goods, money, and ideas are engendering an increasingly liberal international order, wherein individuals are freer than ever before to participate in a global economy and culture.

These two competing views are reconcilable when we come to understand just what globalization means. As David Singh Grewal argues, globalization is a game of social coordination to decide on the languages, laws, technologies, and frames of reference (or standards) by which we can best facilitate our now global activities; it is the uneven process by which some standards of social coordination become prominent and prevail over alternative ones.[38] While we share these global standards and conventions, we have little influence in their adoption. Instead, convergence on global standards is driven by an accretion of individual choices that can be considered both free and unfree.

To participate in globalization processes, we are all "forced," if only indirectly, to adopt the standard of dominant networks or else face isolation. Indirect coercion of this kind resides at the core of so-called network power—a faceless (agentless) structural-institutional form of coercive power; it is "the pressure to adopt a standard that comes from the threat of losing access to others, the social isolation from people who use a different standard."[39] Those who see globalization as "an agent-less process in which standards spread like free-floating viruses across the planet" are not far from the truth.[40] Neither are those who see nefarious, self-interested agency behind network power—a privileged group of elites driving the world anonymously but purposively to places of their advantage. It would seem that globalization cannot help but create "an international in-group that welcomes the entire globe on settled terms: a new world order in which we clamor for connection to one another using standards that are offered up for universal use."[41]

In conclusion, the massive increase of information flows generated by the information economy has significantly increased entropy at the level of system process. For reasons discussed in chapter 7, the digital age serves as a quintessential engine of rising information entropy.

The Role of Emerging Powers in the Age of Entropy

Or, What Happens When the Sheriff Leaves Town and Anonymous Moves In

In the contemporary debate over the future of international politics, both Pessimists and Optimists expect unipolarity to give way to a multipolar system. Likewise, the age of entropy alternative expects concentrated power to diffuse over time. Disagreement among the competing models is over the likely future consequences of de-concentrated power. The Great Power Conflict model championed by Pessimists sees power diffusion triggering a system-wide war among the established and newly emergent great powers. The Great Power Concert scenario advanced by Optimists expects the current order to be preserved by means of multilateral bargains and common understandings among the great powers. In contrast, the age of entropy suggests a dysfunctional world of disorder, a world muddling through on automatic pilot—as new rules and arrangements get piled on top of old ones with no locus of international authority to adjudicate among competing claims or decide which rules, norms, and principles should predominate. Conflict short of war abounds, and without war to resolve conflicts, rivalries endure.

The Roles of Emerging Powers: Spoilers, Supporters, or Shirkers

The reason why the models disagree over the consequences of power diffusion is that they make very different assumptions about the interests and roles of emerging powers. In theory, a rising power may choose to be (1) *a supporter*, which shoulders its fair share of the responsibilities associated with co-managing an evolving but essentially unchanged global order; (2) *a spoiler*, which seeks to destroy the existing order and replace it with something entirely different, or, less dramatically, to raise the costs of maintaining and managing the existing order; or (3) *a shirker*, which desires the privileges of status and prestige but is unwilling to pay for them by contributing to global governance.[1] Great Power Conflict assumes that emerging powers will be spoilers; whereas Great Power Concert sees them as supporters. In the age of entropy, emerging powers are, instead, conflicted states that can play all three roles—spoiler, supporter, and shirker—depending on the issue and the targeted audience (for instance, domestic, regional, South-South, global, etc.). Over the near term, however, their behavior will approximate the role of shirker more so than either the spoiler or supporter roles.

GREAT POWER CONFLICT: EMERGING POWERS AS SPOILERS

According to the Great Power Conflict model, rising powers are invariably spoilers, hell-bent on revising the international order. It is an assumption rooted in power transition theory, the core logic behind Hegemonic-War Cycle notions of system change.[2] In brief, the theory goes as follows: Given the law of uneven growth among states, a gap emerges over time between the actual distribution of power in the system and its distribution of prestige (or reputation for power), throwing the system into disequilibrium and causing persistent instability. To peacefully restore system equilibrium, the waning hegemon must cede influence to the rising challenger to the point where the latter's prestige matches its actual power.[3] In theory, this process of appeasement should solve the problem without resort to war. In practice, it rarely works because (1) satisfying a rising power's legitimate demands often means compromising the stability of the existing international order, as well as the security and vital interests of the declining hegemon and its allies; (2) the rising power advances illegitimate grievances; and (3) concessions increase the rising challenger's actual power, which encourages it to demand more concessions. For the declining hegemon, such a process of granting one concession after another to its rival and peer competitor amounts to little more than death on the installment plan.

When bargaining fails to resolve the system crisis, hegemonic war breaks out because either the rising challenger perceives that its demands have not been met and, given its newfound relative power, the benefits of war now outweigh the costs or the declining hegemon believes that war is inevitable and better fought now than later, so it initiates a preventive war against the rising challenger. Regardless of who initiates it, the war will be one of unlimited means and scope to decide who designs and controls the postwar order.[4]

The main driver of the theory is the emergence of a rising challenger—one dissatisfied not only with its place in the established order but with the legitimacy of the order itself. The insatiable revisionism of the rising challenger triggers persistent crises that eventually ignite a hegemonic war. Yet, the logic behind this "spoiler" assumption is quite murky and, frankly, somewhat illogical. By definition, rising powers are doing better than everyone else under the current order. It is not obvious, therefore, why they (of all states) would seek to spoil the established order; why they would choose an enormously costly global war of uncertain outcome to overthrow an order that has demonstrably worked for them, only to replace it with an untested one that they (and no one else) must pay the costs to start up and manage. What are they so dissatisfied about that they are willing to risk all the gains that they have made to this point and will make in the future? The theory attributes their revisionist aims and general dissatisfaction with the status quo to the disjuncture between actual power and prestige. But prestige matters most when powerful states have serious material conflicts of interests, disagreements over the rules of the game, and expectations that their differences will be settled by fighting. Such conflicts and expectations are largely absent today and do not appear fated to emerge in the future.

Moreover, with prestige comes international responsibilities and obligations. Yet the Great Power Conflict model does not recognize this tradeoff. Consequently, it expects all rising powers to demand prestige commensurate with their relative growth in capabilities. After all, if gains in prestige come without a price, as the model assumes, rising powers have nothing to lose by demanding more of it.

Consider the last time hegemonic leadership changed hands. A declining Britain—one gravely imperiled by threats in Europe and elsewhere and too weak to both defend its interests and manage the international system—grudgingly decided that it was time to pass the baton of global leadership to the United States. The handoff was dropped, however, because the United States demanded unparalleled prestige but was unwilling to pay the price of increased global responsibilities and obligations associated with an exalted position in the international pecking order. It took the attack by Japan at Pearl Harbor to bring the United States out of its isolationist shell. In the immediate postwar period (1945–52), the United States emerged as a reluctant hegemon, grudgingly assuming leadership because it was the only victor able to construct a new global order. Even then, the United States dreamed of creating a third pole in Europe so it could return to the Western Hemisphere. It was the failure of this plan and the emergence of a powerful nonliberal enemy, not an appetite for prestige, that finally drove America to manage its half of the international order.

Roughly the same problem exists today. The United States complains that China wants the privileges of power but not the responsibilities that top dogs are obligated to perform. To many Western observers, China appears as a shirker that must be coerced into taking appropriate actions when global crises arise. But the United States only assumed global responsibilities many years after it became the most powerful state on earth, when it produced almost half of the world's total economic output—a relative power position that China is not even close to achieving at this stage in its development. Why, then, should Washington or anyone else expect China, which produces roughly 8 percent of the world's total economic output, to make substantial contributions to global governance?

Great Power Concert: Emerging Powers as Supporters

Liberals believe that the transition from unipolarity to multipolarity will unfold smoothly because the world is primed for peace: great-power security is plentiful, territory is devalued, and a robust liberal consensus exists among the established powers—one ensconced in a thick ensemble of global institutions that put strict limits on the returns to power. Operating within this benign international setting, the emerging poles will be driven more by the prospect of maximizing their own absolute gains than by fear of relative losses or the temptation to make gains at each others' expense. A restored global balance will arise, therefore, without traditional "hard" balancing in the system's core. Consistent with these propositions, the Great Power Concert model assumes that emerging powers will be supporters—so-called responsible stakeholders—of the Western liberal order. There are two problems with this assumption.

First, integrating new powers within existing international institutions is trickier than the model assumes. Rising non-Western powers do not always share the United States' view on global governance; it is unreasonable to expect them to adopt wholesale the principles, norms, and rules of an inherited Western order. And even when the basic interests of the established and emerging powers align, their priorities may differ. For example, both China and the United States would like to see North Korea's nuclear program dismantled. But Washington places a high priority on this objective, whereas Beijing desires first and foremost to maintain good relations with Pyongyang. The bottom line is that principled differences and mismatched priorities between established and emerging powers, and between emerging power themselves, suggest that multipolarity does not necessarily imply cooperative and successful multilateralism.[5]

Second, "catching up" requires the rising state to focus most of its energies on internal matters, such as promoting sustainable economic and social development, redressing the domestic imbalances caused by dramatic and sudden economic growth, and managing the often dangerous socioeconomic dislocations associated with rapid urbanization of the population. Because accepting costly international commitments can jeopardize these domestic plans and demands, rising powers are reluctant to actively support the established order. They would prefer, instead, that the declining hegemon pay the costs of order while they ride free. To the extent that free-riding incentives prevail, the established and emerging powers are less likely to co-manage the international system than to clash over the questions: Who has responsibilities for what? What is a fair contribution to the collective good? Who decides whether a global initiative is a collective good? Tensions can be expected to mount in the system's core, as the declining hegemon cajoles rising powers to accept more of the responsibilities for meeting global challenges; while they, in turn, demand greater voice and representation but shirk their fair share of global burdens. Meanwhile, the process of power diffusion will continue to flatten the world, producing a more balanced multipolarity with no single dominant power capable of providing global order. Frustrated by the shirking of its peer competitors and seeking to arrest its own decline, the hegemon will eventually retrench from its global commitments, leaving no state or group of states in charge of the international order or whatever remains of it.

The Age of Entropy: Emerging Powers as Conflicted States

Unlike the other models, the age of entropy sees rising powers as conflicted states with multiple identities, variously adopting all three roles—supporters, spoilers, and shirkers. What role the state plays largely depends on the particular issue and, most important, the targeted audience, whether domestic, regional, South-South, North-South, or global.

CHINA: A CONFLICTED ECONOMIC SUPERPOWER

As a military power, China is transitioning from a country whose strategic priorities have been limited to defense of its borders to a regional power able to project force within East Asia and a bit farther to secure sea lanes of communication in the South China Seas. In 2011, Beijing's official defense expenditure was more than two-and-a half times its 2001 level. Moreover, the People's Liberation Army (PLA) is steadily developing antisatellite capacities, antiship ballistic missiles, cruise missiles, and cyber-warfare capabilities, and it has test-launched the J-20 stealth fighter plane. Despite these accomplishments, China still does not have the capability to operate fixed-wing aircraft from a carrier.[6]

Even as China's military achievements are altering the strategic balance of power across the Taiwan Strait, it has barely put a dent in the global balance of power. According to the International Institute for Strategic Studies, the U.S. defense budget still accounts for 45 percent of global defense spending—a far larger share than the next nine largest spenders combined; and the U.S. military enjoys an exponentially growing lead in advanced technologies, such as precision weapons and drones. Meanwhile, the PLA has only just begun to construct a next-generation guided-missile destroyer, which, in terms of both quality and quantity, will be no match for those of the U.S. Aegis-class destroyer fleet. As for Beijing's first aircraft carrier, launched in August 2011, it was an old and relatively small ship purchased from the Russians. As Robert Ross observes, "China's main tool to counter the U.S. Navy and deter an American intervention in Asian conflicts remains a fleet of diesel submarines that has been in service since the mid-1990s."[7] For the foreseeable future, therefore, the United States will remain the only country capable of sustaining large air-sea operations and of projecting substantial ground forces on a global scale for a prolonged period of time.[8] Little wonder, then, that an independent task force comprised of more than thirty experts recently found "no evidence to support the notion that China will become a peer military competitor of the United States."[9]

Compared with America's muscle-bound military capabilities and given its lack of world-class force projection capabilities, China is still many years away from becoming a full-fledged superpower in the sense of the term that described the United States and the former Soviet Union. There are, however, partial forms of "superpowerdomness" that are issue-specific (economic, political, military, cultural, and, perhaps, energy). China, which boasts the world's second largest economy and whose trade surplus surged to about $155 billion in 2011, currently lays claim to the status of economic superpower.

To qualify as an economic superpower, a country must be sufficiently large, dynamic, and globally integrated to the point where it exerts a significant impact on the world economy. Given these criteria, China, the United States, and the European Union—if we treat the EU as a single unit loosely equivalent to a country (which it certainly is not)—are the only entities holding dominant enough positions within the international economic system to be called economic super-powers. That noted, the aggregate economic numbers remain somewhat misleading. Per capita income in China remains under $4,000, roughly one-tenth of the level of the United States and Japan. As Minxin Pei points out, "More than half of the Chinese population still live in villages, most without access to safe drinking water, basic healthcare, or decent education. With urbanization growing at about 1 percent a year, it will take another three decades for China to reduce the size of its peasantry to a quarter of the population." Thus, "it may be too soon to regard China as the world's next superpower."[10]

Nevertheless, given the enormous size of China's economy, the United States and the EU would like to see China integrated within the existing economic institutions that they built and have defended over the past six or so decades. Co-opting China to become a responsible stakeholder within the West's global economic system presents unique challenges, however. China remains poor, relatively non-marketized, and authoritarian—characteristics that make it unlikely to accept the responsibilities that come with "economic superpower" status.[11]

In many areas, China has pursued economic strategies that diverge from well-established institutional norms and rules. China has refused to play a constructive role in the Doha Round of international trade negotiations. It is in the process of creating its own free-trade area in East Asia (one that it seeks to dominate). It alone among the world's major economies has rejected the adoption of a flexible exchange-rate policy, enabling it to maintain an immensely undervalued yuan and a current account surplus that reached a whopping 11–12 percent of its GDP in 2008—unprecedented for a major trading nation.[12] And as the world's largest donor of foreign aid, it rejects the social and economic standards of conditionality on aid that virtually all bilateral and multilateral agencies have required as a matter of course over the past quarter century (e.g., human rights, labor conditions, the environment, poverty alleviation, and good governance).[13]

Some observers attribute China's rule-breaking behavior to little more than "the usual free-riding and skirting of responsibility by a powerful newcomer cleverly exploiting he loopholes and weak enforcement of existing international rules to pursue its perceived national interests."[14] But as C. Fred Bergsten observes, "The situation is worrisome [because] China actually has a profound interest in seeing that the international rules and institutions function effectively. It should be trying to strengthen the system, whether the present version or an alternative version more to its liking." Yet "China continues to act like a small country with little impact on the global system at large and therefore little responsibility for it."[15]

Consistent with a "developing country" international mindset, many Chinese analysts argue that China is still a relatively poor nation, lacking the capabilities to become fully engaged in global governance. Others are downright suspicious of global governance, viewing it as a trap laid by the West to retard and restrain China's growth by tying it down with overseas commitments and bleeding it white with foreign entanglements unrelated to its national interests. If this view gains ascendance, it means we will soon see a different Chinese policy—one signaling that China is starting to embrace the role of spoiler. The official view, delivered by Foreign Minister Yang Jiechi in a 2010 speech before three hundred leading diplomats and several senior US officials, is that a "more developed China will undertake more international responsibilities and will never pursue interests at the expense of others. We know full well that in this interdependent world, China's future is closely linked to that of the world. Our own interests and those of others are best served when we work together to expand common interests, share responsibilities, and seek win-win outcomes. This is why focusing on its own development, China is undertaking more and more international responsibilities commensurate with its strength and status."[16] Here, China sounds comfortable with the role of supporter and happy to contribute to global governance, which serves its own interests as well as those of the international community. In the same speech, however, Yang assertively declared—in terms more consistent with a spoiler than a supporter—that China is getting stronger on the international stage; that the U.S. was violating international law by a proposed $6.4 billion arms sale to Taiwan, calling it a "violation of the code of conduct among nations" and threatening for the first time retaliatory sanctions on U.S. firms that supply arms; that China is not ready to address sanctions on Iran's nuclear program; and that China's television and radio news service contains "more solid" and reliable news than Western media.[17]

Regarding the latter, every night at 1:00 am in Beijing, China Central Television (CCTV) hands over its broadcast to its Nairobi team for *Africa Live*, an hour-long flagship program put together by a team of fifty Kenyans and ten Chinese and billed as a "new voice" for African news and Sino-African relations—one televised worldwide and that, according to CCTV Africa chief Song Jianing, tells "the real Africa story, the real story of China and the real story of Sino-African relations."[18] While CCTV Africa is clearly part of a wider Chinese strategy to remedy its negative image among many Africans, it provides a global "platform for Africans to speak their point of view," offering a uniquely non-Western view of the continent and China's relationship with it.[19] Thus, the Kenyan vice-president, Kalonzo Musyoka, echoing remarks by China's ambassador to Kenya, portrayed the channel as a means to "present a new image of the continent" that breaks with the traditional international media view of Africa as "the continent of endless calamities."[20]

The truth is that China, like the other emerging powers, does not yet have a fixed role or identity, which may explain why there is no official Chinese Communist Party (CCP) document that lays out a grand strategy for the nation's future. China, like most of the emerging powers, is a conflicted state with a political discourse grounded in several ideological strands: (1) *conservative pragmatism*—the dominant ideology among China's ruling elites but one that lacks programmatic ideas to guide policy and political action; (2) *nationalism*—fueled by the media and growing tensions between China and the West over human rights and China's rising power, nationalism has become the dominant ideology among the Chinese masses; (3) *the new left*—a minor ideological force championed by neo-Marxist and neo-Maoist academics; and (4) *liberalism*—a marginalized ideology but one that remains, over the long run, the most serious threat to the CCP regime because it is the most coherent and programmatic of all the competing ideologies in China.

China also deliberately speaks with different voices, depending on the targeted audience. Its rhetoric takes on a more nationalist tone at home than abroad. It desires to project a reassuring voice to its global and regional audiences. And in its South-South dialogue, China, as the largest and most powerful of the BRICS, would like to exude the spirit of accommodation and sensitivity. Indeed, at a time when China wants above all to impress the world with its "peaceful rise," the BRICS club offers it the perfect platform. The various institutional mechanisms of BRICS—periodic meetings among the member states, in which they share knowledge and best practices—hold enormous potential for South-South cooperation. They also further China's strategy of "multilateral diplomacy" and "partnership with the developing countries" to solve emerging global issues.[21] At the global level, the BRICS emphasis on engaging multilateral bodies like the United Nations, the Security Council, G-20, the World Bank, and the IMF furthers China's goal of being perceived by others as embedding (binding) itself within the world community as a responsible stakeholder. Of course, membership in multilateral organizations is not an especially reliable indicator of a rising power's true intentions, much less a guarantee that those intentions won't change down the road. As Jagannath Panda, a research fellow at the Institute for Defense Studies and Analyses, writes, "multilateral dialogue processes . . . allow Beijing to deflect doubt at multiple levels while continuing to raise its global power and ambitions. . . . BRIC permits China to work with mainstream developing countries to expand its clout and formulate new global rules without having to fulfill the requisites of developed countries."[22]

Whatever images it desires to project to various audiences, China must eventually define its global role—one that furthers its goals but also wins acceptance from other powers, most importantly from the United States. Indeed, the chief foreign-policy challenge going forward for Beijing, and for Washington as well, is how best to manage the Sino-American relationship. At the moment, neither side has an accurate picture of how the other views it. This is arguably most true for the United States. As Andrew Nathan and Andrew Scobell allege, "Most Americans would be surprised to learn the degree to which the Chinese believe the United States is a revisionist power that seeks to curtail China's political influence and harm China's interests."[23] Americans may be forgiven for their surprise. After all, the United States has contributed more to China's modernization than any other major power: "It has drawn China into the global economy; given the Chinese access to markets, capital, and technology; trained Chinese experts in science, technology, and international law; prevented the full remilitarization of Japan; maintained peace on the Korean Peninsula; and helped avoid a war over Taiwan. Yet Chinese policymakers are more impressed by policies and behaviors that they perceive as less benevolent."[24] Here, the Chinese rightly view the United States as being two-faced in its intentions. On the one hand, Washington wants to work cooperatively with Beijing, grasping the need for China's help to manage economic and security issues at both the global and regional levels. On the other hand, the United States is alarmed by China's rise and would like to preserve American primacy. Accordingly, the United States employs various policies to delay China's growth and to socialize and bind China within the established American Order; that is, "to remake China with U.S. values," in the words of Ni Feng, the deputy director of the Chinese Academy of Social Sciences' Institute of American Studies.[25]

Finally, with respect to China's ambitions and growing clout, it should be pointed out that any prediction regarding a country's future prospects based on its current performance is always a risky bet. There is no guarantee that an emerging power will continue to rise; no country's ascendance is inevitable or irreversible. Just ask the Japanese. Without fundamental political reforms, China may succumb to the limits of developmental autocracy—what the Chinese scholar Minxin Pei calls a "trapped transition," wherein the neo-authoritarian regime exhausts its political and economic vitality. If the Chinese economic and political situation is more precarious than it looks, the future may be one of regime exhaustion, which would undermine state capacity, heighten social tension, and threaten regime collapse. Unless it breaks with its authoritarian past, according to Pei, it is quite possible that "China may not only fail to fully realize its potential, but also descend into a long-term stagnation."[26]

Gordon Chang similarly predicts China's demise, contending that it has "just about reached high tide, and will soon begin a long painful process of falling back."[27] Other China experts are less pessimistic about emerging instability in China. Steven Jackson, for instance, recognizes that "China is facing enormous problems," but "this characterization has been true for the past 150 years." Likewise, David Shambaugh notes that China "is in a curiously ambivalent state of 'stable unrest.' "[28] Taking the middle ground, Roger Irvine writes, "If there is any consensus among observers it is possibly that on balance, China will probably manage internal challenges and maintain growth, even if at a lower rate, for perhaps another decade or more."[29]

Assuming that China manages to escape significant political and economic turmoil, then it will most likely seek and achieve (by midcentury) hegemony "over what it defiantly calls the 'First Island Chain,' which encompasses Japan, the Ryukyu Islands, parts of the Korean Peninsula, Taiwan, the Philippines, Indonesia and Australia."[30] Initially, the United States will counter China's aspirations for primacy in the Pacific by retaining a strong offshore balancing presence—one that attempts to neutralize Chinese military power within a bipolar regional structure. Ultimately, however, the United States will have to adjust to the inevitable emergence of a greater China in Central and East Asia and the western Pacific, with a substantial naval presence stretching from the East and South China Seas to the Indian Ocean.

India: An Uneasy Supporter

Like China, India has several competing visions of its role in the international system: (1) *moralists*—a Nehruvian vision that sees India serving as a moral exemplar of principled action in world politics, striving to make the international order more egalitarian in both distributive and political terms; (2) *Hindu nationalists*—who want to resurrect the glory of India by cultivating national strength, which, they believe, is rooted not only in military and economic development but ultimately in the noble and heroic virtues of Hindu society; (3) *realists*—who want India to develop its military and economic capabilities, especially a credible second-strike nuclear capability and conventional forces with the capacity to project force beyond the subcontinent; and (4) *liberals*—who, desiring India to become a great commercial power once again, emphasize interdependence fostered by globalization as the key to a prosperous India, which should model itself more on postwar Europe than contemporary China or the United States.[31]

These four visions have strikingly different views of the existing international order. Only the liberal vision, which seeks reform but not wholesale revision of the inherited Western order, is entirely consistent with a supporter or stakeholder role. The moralist vision represents the most revisionist critique of the existing order, which it views as fundamentally unjust in terms of its principles and means—its reliance on military power rather than peaceful moral suasion. That said, there is a growing consensus in India that the moralist vision has failed. Realists and Hindu nationalists want India to do whatever it takes to become a great power. And when it comes to both India's regional status and prospects as a future great power, China matters most.

Along these lines, India is poised to become the fourth largest military power in the world by the end of the decade. From 2007 to 2011, India was the world's largest importer of weapons, buying a total of $21.8 billion worth of arms, and, as of Spring 2013, its deal to buy 126 Rafale fighters from France at a cost of roughly $12 billion appears to be slowly drawing toward completion.[32] These arms purchases, however, do not signal that India is a disgruntled rising power bent on overturning the status quo. In terms of the existing international order, even India's realists and Hindu nationalists are no more than contingently revisionist, finding themselves at odds with only those aspects of the current order that complicate India's rise (for example, the nuclear nonproliferation regime).[33] Moreover, New Delhi's military thinking is still dominated not by China or the global order but by its vexatious relationship with Pakistan.

Recognizing that these visions will wax and wane with circumstances, India figures to be the United States' most likely junior partner and strongest candidate to play a supporter role within the emerging post-American international order. China is the common threat that has brought these two countries together. Unable to match China's land power, India's alternative is to respond at sea. Both China and India are rapidly building up their navies, transforming them from coastal defense forces into power-projection forces; both countries expect to have three operational carrier groups within this decade. For its part, New Delhi is most concerned about China's forays into the Indian Ocean. Maritime experts in India now worry about the increasing frequency and size of Chinese maritime contingents deployed in anti-piracy patrols off Somalia and the increasingly assertive stance taken by China's maritime policy community regarding naval bases in the Indian Ocean.

These anxieties over Chinese activities in the Indian Ocean have not kept New Delhi from also worrying about developments in the South China Sea, which is vital for India not only as a gateway for shipping in East Asia but also as a strategic maritime link between the Pacific and Indian Oceans. It profoundly affects India's strategic vision as a growing power in terms of its expanding economic and security role in the broader "Indo-Pacific," where the Indian navy is best positioned to play a crucial role. Moreover, India has an enormous economic stake in the South China Sea, with the state-owned Oil and Natural Gas Corporation's foreign arm, ONGC Videsh, involved in major oil-exploration activity off the coast of Vietnam. Accordingly, New Delhi has not hesitated lately to send the Indian navy into the waters of the western Pacific to protect its economic interests.

Geopolitically, India's "Look East" policy—initially devised two decades ago to boost trade and foster economic cooperation with Southeast Asia—has recently acquired a decidedly maritime and "anti-China" edge. The Indian navy has ramped up efforts at forging closer ties with other navies in Southeast and East Asia, each with its own interest in seeing the South China Sea remain an international waterway and concerned about Chinese assertiveness in the region. Many of India's growing maritime engagements—among them, the Indian navy's recent exercises with the Japanese navy—have been with traditional U.S. allies, giving the "Look East" strategy the appearance of a tacit alliance against China. Not surprisingly, Chinese security experts interpret India's "Look East" policy to mean "Look to Encircle China." As an article in the *People's Daily* put it: "Japan and India have both placed high expectations upon each other in combining strengths to counterbalance China."[34]

Aside from its cooperation with Japan, New Delhi has been wooing another long-term American ally in the region, South Korea. In the wake of China's rising ambitions, India and South Korea—long estranged and strategically disconnected—now share a common threat that has spawned a dynamic and growing cooperative relationship between them. Attracted by India's investment climate, South Korean companies have made India a primary base for their overseas manufacturing operations. Moreover, the two countries have deepened cooperation in the peaceful uses of outer space, the pharmaceutical and IT sectors, naval and coast guard operations, co-production of defense equipment, transfers of technology, and joint research and development.

The developing relationship between India and South Korea is based on three pillars. First, the Comprehensive Economic Partnership Agreement signed in 2009 and in effect as of January 1, 2010, jump-started the dormant economic ties between the two countries. India and South Korea recently set a bilateral trade target of $30 billion by 2014. Second, security ties, including the supply of defense equipment and joint research and development programs, have been augmented. For example, India is currently finalizing a $500 million contract with South Korean arms manufacturer Kangnam for eight minesweeper vessels. Finally, cooperation on energy security has deepened, culminating in the signing of a civil nuclear pact during Indian president Pratibha Patil's visit to South Korea in July 2011.[35] The bottom line is that, as New Delhi keeps a close eye on China's growth and strategic courtships around the world, bilateral ties between India and the United States and between India and America's allies will remain on the upswing.

Geopolitical imperatives make it a good bet that this warming trend will continue. It must be pointed out, however, that India remains somewhat uneasy with U.S. hegemony—an uneasiness it shares with other regional players, most notably Russia (India's Cold War ally). Since 2007, 80 percent of India's defense imports have come from Russia, making New Delhi the leading purchaser of Russian arms. Among the many reasons why defense cooperation between the two countries has remained strong decades after the Cold War: (1) India has an enormous legacy inventory of Soviet-based weapons that must be modernized, upgraded, and replaced; (2) Russian arms supplies continue to offer a competitive price-to-performance tradeoff; (3) both countries fear the rise of China and radical Islamic terrorism; (4) both countries are apprehensive about American military hegemony; and (5) both countries share concerns about regional instability in Central Asia. In light of the two countries' already signed arms deals worth some $11 billion and other significant joint ventures, Russia will remain India's largest defense partner for at least several years. Geopolitical ties will also remain strong, as the bilateral relationship was elevated to that of a "Special and Privileged Strategic Partnership" in 2011.[36] Hedging its strategic bets, India, like the other emerging powers, is an internally conflicted state that prefers to keep its geopolitical options open.

Brazil: Supporter-Spoiler

French president General Charles de Gaulle famously joked, "Brazil is the country of the future, and will always remain so." His point was that Brazil had great potential and it always would. Given its poor politics, inequality, dismal infrastructure, and poor economic management, Brazil seemed incapable of capitalizing on its natural resources and becoming a rich and powerful country. Though clever and memorable, de Gaulle's quip has been proven wrong. After decades of on-and-off growth and political turmoil, Brazil is finally poised to fulfill its long-unrealized potential as a global player. The South American giant is finally awake and it is holding not one but two "coming out on the world stage" parties: the World Cup in 2014 and the Olympics in 2016.

Dubbed "the breadbasket of the world," Brazil is far more than an agricultural superpower, boasting a diverse economy with strong sectors in agriculture, mining, oil, and biofuels.[37] Since the discovery of the massive pre-salt oil reservoir in the Atlantic and its enormous hydroelectricity generation capacity—including the new Belo Monte dam on the Xingu River (a tributary of the Amazon) that will be the world's third-largest in 2019—Brazil is a future energy superpower as well. The government's plan for energy expansion calls for a whopping forty-eight large dams by 2020.[38]

Brazil accounts for over 50 percent of South America's wealth, population, territory, and military budgets, making it more relatively powerful in its region than China, India, and Germany are in theirs. Over the past fifteen years, Brazil has moved from fourteenth to sixth position in the world economy; and its economic growth has averaged 4.1 percent annually since the inauguration of President Luiz Inácio "Lula" da Silva in 2002.[39] According to a study by Goldman Sachs, Brazil will likely move into fourth place among the world's largest economies by 2050, leapfrogging Germany, Japan, and the United Kingdom, to lag behind only the United States, China, and India.[40] So what does Brazil plan to do with its newfound power?

The essential goal of Brazil's grand strategy is to resist and insulate itself from American dominance. The means are twofold: soft balancing—"the conscious coordination of diplomatic action in order to obtain outcomes contrary to U.S. preferences,"[41] and (2) steering collective decisions within multilateral institutions by gaining greater influence over those institutions and strengthening their role in the management of world affairs. Brazil is not a revisionist emerging power seeking the wholesale overthrow of the American order. To the contrary, Brazilian policymakers are extremely satisfied with the current liberal order, attributing the country's recent economic and social gains to the global economy and its open trade and financial rules. There are some aspects to Brazil's foreign policy, however, that are consistent with a spoiler, at least with respect to U.S. unipolarity.

Consider Brazil's foreign policies over the past decade. In 2001, it turned down George W. Bush's offer of a position in an extended Group of Seven, claiming that the price for a seat at the top table was too high. Since 2000, Brazil's foreign minister has visited the Middle East twenty-four times, arguing that the United States is no longer the "indispensable nation" in the region. With respect to nuclear proliferation, Brazil sees the nonproliferation treaty (NPT) as a "politically driven tool in the hands of the United States to selectively 'lay down the law' on weaker states."[42] Brasilia asks, why should Iran be punished for its civilian enrichment technology, whereas Israel, which has bombs in the basement, and India, which has chosen to critique and remain outside the NPT regime, get big rewards from Washington? Indeed, Brazilian elites do not describe the Western global order in terms of multilateralism and inclusion but rather as an imposed order ruled by powerful Anglo-Saxon states, which use international institutions and arbitrarily enforced rules to control weaker, non-Western states. Global hierarchy, in their eyes, is less a function of material power than of race. Little wonder, at the height of the 2008 financial crisis, President Lula declared, "This crisis was created by white men with blue eyes." He went on to say that he had never met any "black bankers."[43]

Concerned over the budding relationship between Brazil and Iran, Hillary Clinton visited Brasilia in March 2010, seeking support for stronger sanctions on Iran's nuclear program. The trip was billed as an effort to forge ties with a country that is increasingly recognized as a global power and fellow democracy. Unfortunately, the rhetoric of partnership came easier than the reality. Clinton returned empty-handed, as Brazil's foreign minister, Celso Amorim, and President Lula refused to condemn activities that they believe any rising power has the right to engage in.

Few were surprised by the outcome. Brazil has consistently preferred a diplomatic approach to sanctions (which it sees as a step toward military force) and has demanded proof that Iran is constructing a weapon and not simply working on mastering peaceful nuclear technologies. More generally, relations between Washington and Brasilia have been strained in recent years and have not improved, as Washington had hoped, with Lula's successor, President Dilma

Rousseff. In addition to tensions over Iran, especially after Iranian president Mahmoud Ahmadinejad was warmly welcomed in Brasilia in November 2009, the U.S.–Brazil relationship has fallen victim to disagreements over Honduras, military bases in Colombia, and the World Trade Organization cotton dispute, coloring Washington's perceptions of Brazil as more of an emerging rival than a true partner. And even though trade between the countries has been expanding almost 10 percent a year over much of the past decade, America and Brazil have not signed a single economic pact for two decades—a period when Washington reached trade accords with eleven other Latin American countries; nor has there been a meeting of the minds within global or regional economic forums. The two countries hold widely divergent views "on several highly contentious issues: U.S. tariffs and subsidies that block Brazilian agricultural sales, Brazil's import barriers to services and manufactured goods, and deep discord over intellectual property." Aside from these economic issues, "U.S.-Brazil relations are strained by geopolitical tensions. Particularly galling for Brazil has been Washington's reluctance to support its bid for a permanent seat on the U.N. Security Council, even though President Obama gave U.S. backing to India two years ago."[44]

Returning to the Iranian nuclear issue, the larger and more ominous message is that Brazil and the other leading democracies of the south and east—Mexico, South Africa, India, and Indonesia among them—are ready to flex their muscles and show the world that they will no longer routinely comply with American or European desires. "We will not simply bow down to the evolving consensus if we do not agree," declared Brazil's foreign minister.[45]

The repercussions go well beyond support for sanctions against Iran in the Security Council. Two years ago, Washington was abuzz with the prospects for a "League of Democracies" that would support U.S. global leadership. In the aftermath of Cyclone Nargis, which devastated Myanmar, however, a rift opened between the democracies of the advanced north and west, which supported intervention on humanitarian grounds, and the democracies of the south and east, which lined up behind China's call for defending state sovereignty. Indeed, political autonomy from the United States and Europe has become a common theme among the BRICS countries—all of whom dream of becoming autonomous global players. Brazil's grand strategy consists of South-South alliances and agreements with nontraditional partners (China, Asia-Pacific, Africa, Eastern Europe, Middle East, etc.) to avoid asymmetric external relations with powerful countries—especially the United States, for which Brazil harbors the same resentments many Latin Americans have for the exercise of U.S. power in their region.

This rebellious spirit was evident in the Doha round of trade talks and in the ongoing climate change negotiations, where Brazil and the other emerging democracies of the south and east have been more receptive to Beijing's position than to Washington's. We see it in the way Brazil is assertively raising its profile around the world, particularly in Africa, where it is building on its historical ties from the time of the Portuguese empire. Indeed, Africa now accounts for about 55 percent of the disbursements by the Brazilian Cooperation Agency, which oversees aid projects abroad, and the charm offensive is paying off: trade flows between Brazil and Africa have surged from $4.3 billion in 2002 to $27.6 billion in 2011.[46]

Brazil's government and companies have been scouring Africa for opportunities, putting down stakes in Mozambique, Kenya, Angola, Guinea, and Nigeria, among other places. In Mozambique, for instance, a Brazilian plant makes antiretroviral drugs to fight the AIDS epidemic, and a Brazilian mining company, Vale, has started work on a $6 billion coal expansion project. Brazil is lending $150 million to Kenya to build roads and ease congestion in the capital, Nairobi. In Angola, West Africa's rising oil power, the Brazilian multinational construction company Odebrecht has become one of the largest employers.[47] Odebrecht África, Emirados Árabes e Portugal (AEP)—the operational company that provides Odebrecht's engineering and construction services to Africa, the Middle East, and Portugal—will also undertake projects in Guinea-Conakry and is currently restoring the railroad for the transport of iron ore for the company ArcellorMittal in Liberia.[48]

Meanwhile, the Brazilian government signed a new security agreement with Angola in July 2012, which will expand the training of Angolan military personnel in Brazil. The so-called Agreement on Cooperation in Defense Field between Angola and Brazil—covering defense, polity, teaching and instruction, military intelligence, military equipment and systems, peacekeeping missions, and humanitarian and "search and rescue" operations—commits Brazil to train military and technical personnel, implement and develop programs and projects for the application of defense technologies, and conduct joint scientific research and military training activities with Angola.

The foundation for today's diplomatic, economic, and military buildup in Africa was laid in the 1970s, when Brazil began its quest for autonomy from the United States. Its current forays into Africa are rooted in the same ambitions that have been driving the outward expansion of other rising powers, like Turkey's attempts to hold sway over the Arab world and India's promotion of its culture across Asia. Brazil's array of aid projects, loans, and security agreements extended to African countries points both to its goal of projecting greater influence in the developing world and to the expanding business allure of Africa, where some economies are booming. Thus, in May 2012, a leading Brazilian investment bank, BTG Pactual, started a $1 billion fund focused on investing in Africa. Indeed, new links with the continent are popping up everywhere, including a flight from Addis Ababa, Ethiopia's capital, to São Paulo; a fiber optic cable connecting northeast Brazil to West Africa; and Brazilian farming ventures in Sudan.[49]

A Divided World

As China, Brazil, India, Turkey and other emerging powers continue to gain influence around the world, the United States will suffer a corresponding loss of global influence. Power is a relative concept, after all. As such, we may all want more power, but everyone cannot simultaneously become more powerful. Just like when the entire audience stands on their seats at a rock concert, no one sees any better—if everyone has power, then no one has power. And contrary to liberal expectations, as U.S. hegemony wanes, there is little reason to expect international cooperation to fill the gap of American power. There is even less reason to expect that whatever international cooperation is achieved will reflect American interests.

Consider, for instance, the surprise agreement announced on May 16, 2010, whereby Iran agreed to ship its low-enriched uranium to Turkey, complicating the Obama administration's efforts to ratify international sanctions against Iran. Negotiated at a three-way meeting that included Brazilian president Lula and Turkish prime minister Recep Tayyip Erdoğan, Iran under the new agreement will ship 2,640 pounds of low-enriched uranium to Turkey for storage. In exchange, after one year Iran will be eligible to receive 265 pounds of material enriched in France and Russia. An Iranian foreign ministry spokesman said the country would continue to enrich uranium on its own. Iran's apparent cooperation with the new agreement makes it less likely that Russia and China will support tougher sanctions against Iran in the UN Security Council and puts President Obama in the awkward position of potentially rejecting a deal that is nearly identical to one he negotiated months earlier.

Instead of showcasing the determination of the "international community," the Obama administration's drive for sanctions against Iran ran into a BRIC wall precisely because it looks like a "Euro-Atlantic" initiative. Efforts for a new, stronger sanctions resolution against Iran are hitting not only the expected resistance from China and Russia but also reluctance on the part of Turkey and India, whose private sector shows little enthusiasm for severing commercial relations with Tehran.[50]

International politics is filled with similar stories of international cooperation at the expense of the United States. For instance, Egypt's first democratically elected president, Mohamed Morsi, chose to travel to Beijing, not Washington, on his inaugural state visit outside the Middle East, illustrating the central place China occupies in Egypt's recalibrated foreign policy strategy of balance and leverage vis-à-vis the United States. Morsi's trip yielded an estimated $4.9 billion in investment deals and joint ventures between Egyptian and Chinese firms. The opening of Egypt's political space after decades of autocracy under the Mubarak regime has unleashed political and social forces, empowering large segments of public opinion to make their voices heard on issues related to Egyptian foreign policy.[51] Given the legacy of U.S.–Egypt relations and the expressed objectives of the Morsi government to reinvent Egypt's foreign policy, China is positioned to reap significant gains.

Cairo's interest in a vibrant Sino-Egyptian relationship is partly driven by the economic imperatives of attracting Chinese investment. "We want the Silk Road to return as a direct link between Egypt and China," Morsi said.[52] The larger goal, however—one consistent with the electoral platform of the Freedom and Justice Party (FJP)—is to diversify Egypt's foreign relations portfolio away from its strong orientation toward the United States. As Nikolas K. Gvosdev, the former editor of the *National Interest*, observes: "Clearly, Egypt is looking for room to maneuver by increasing ties with China to provide balance in its relationship with the U.S."[53]

The Obama administration confronts the reality of a divided world—one that can be expected to grow more fragmented over time. It also confronts the reality that, while the United States is strong enough to do most anything it chooses without suffering dire consequences, it is arguably less capable of exerting influence over others (to get them to do things they otherwise would not do) than it was prior to becoming the undisputed top dog of international politics. Power does not map onto material capabilities as neatly as it did in the past. And as the age of entropy unfolds, power will become more and more diffuse and difficult for anyone to exercise. The upshot is that, unlike in the past, polarity will tell us little about world politics in the twenty-first century.[54]

How Power Diffusion Works
to a State's Advantage

This Is Not Your Great-Grandfather's Multipolar World

In the coming years, world politics will be characterized by several global (or macro) level features that clearly distinguish the age of entropy from past epochs. First, we will see the emergence of an international system in which states do not have the capacities to shape and direct the system, much less to create and manage a durable and legitimate international order. Unlike in the Great Power Concert model, wherein the great powers (old and new) find ways to build an architecture for joint management of the new multipolar system, no state or group of states will be in control.

Second, and contrary to the core prediction of the Great Power Conflict model, this is not a power transition process but a power diffusion process, one that will occur spontaneously as an unintended result of differential growth rates among countries. This unintended deconcentration of global power is very important and historically unique. What it means is that a global balance of power can and will be restored without traditional balancing behavior (competitive arms buildups and alliance formations) in the system's core. Thus, there is no overwhelming reason to assume, as does the Great Power Conflict model, that the new multipolar system will be permeated by the traditional problems of anarchy—insecurity, rivalry, arms races, nationalism, and competition for resources—that plagued past multipolar systems. To the contrary, the process of power diffusion will most likely unfold peacefully because, as discussed in the prior chapter, rising states are not expected to be spoilers; at worst, they will advance limited, rather than unlimited, revisionist aims. Rising powers will most likely be conflicted states, variously motivated to support, shirk, and spoil at the global level.

Third, world politics will be largely defined by three elements: (1) an abundance of security among the great powers, (2) the devaluation of territory, and (3) a fairly robust liberal consensus. The combination of these three macro features exerts a powerful effect on the orientation of state interests: great powers will be driven more by the prospect of maximizing their own *absolute gains* than by the fear of *relative losses* or the temptation to make gains at each other's expense. Actors seeking to maximize absolute gains are, by definition, inward looking—largely unconcerned by how others are doing or by the larger system in which they are embedded.

This is not to suggest that relative gains and losses are no longer of any concern to states. They most certainly do matter and will continue to matter in the future, but less for reasons of self-preservation and survival and more because states want to maximize their wealth, influence, status, and access to scarce resources, such as food, water, nonrenewable minerals, and energy. These will be the issues over which great powers struggle and compete. Multipolarity will surely heighten this competition, as new and old great powers jockey for position in the international pecking order. A relative-gains orientation will be especially evident in disputes over distributional issues that will increasingly crop up over questions about which type of international order should prevail and who should get what and for how much (a subject discussed at length in chapter 8).

The emerging multipolar world will be further defined by its global and super-sized nature, by the expectations of great powers regarding war as a legitimate tool of statecraft, and by the horizontality of international politics. It is to these unique features that I now turn.

The First Truly Global, Super-Sized Multipolar System

When India, China, Brazil, the European Union, and possibly Russia and Japan join the United States as members of the great power club, we will have entered the first truly global epoch of world politics. Past international systems that contained several great powers were merely regional European systems, not global ones. Europe was the core, everything else was considered the periphery. True, Japan and the United States eventually became poles, but they were minor players that arrived late in the game. Europe was where the top players competed.

The global nature of the coming world will afford the great powers more space to maneuver without stepping on each other's toes. It will be easier for them to carve out separate spheres of influence. As a result, the problem of colliding interests should be far less frequent and intense than under old-style multipolarity.

Future great powers also will be much larger. In terms of territory and population, India and China dwarf France, Prussia/Germany, Britain, Italy, and Austria-Hungary. Only Russia and the United States—the two continental-sized flank states—were comparable in size to India and China today, and they quickly outstripped their European counterparts to become superpowers after World War II.

The super-sized nature of the coming great powers will produce a qualitative change in their expected behaviors. Unlike past great powers, they will not need more territory or population to compete; there will be no imperial temptations for them to resist. Rather, the key to realizing their potential power will be internal growth and consolidation—processes best facilitated by a quiescent international setting.

A Restored Global Balance of Power without Traditional Balancing Behavior

As entropy increases, available energy within the system dissipates and becomes distributed in the most probable pattern: a state of equal energy among particles. This spontaneous deconcentration process describes the current pathway from global unipolarity to multipolarity. It is noteworthy not because of what states are doing to restore a global balance of power but rather what they are not doing: balancing by means of arms buildups and the formation of alliances to gain advantages in relative military power. The entropic path to equilibrium is brought about by enervation, that is, an absence of dynamism and power politics within the system's core. Major-power war becomes barely conceivable, let alone the likely consequence of a return to deconcentrated global power.

The big and important point here—one rarely, if ever, discussed in the vast balance-of-power literature—is that a global balance of power can occur in two precisely opposite ways. It may be achieved as an unintended consequence of fiercely competitive nation-states jockeying for position. This dynamic view of how equilibrium is achieved is rooted in the familiar logic of classic balance-of-power theory. A global balance may also result, however, from a world drained of useable energy, a world of diffused power, resting in a state of ultra-stable equilibrium characteristic of maximum entropy.[1] This decidedly undynamic route to equilibrium suggests that a global balance can arise without competitive balancing or power-seeking behavior.

That several great powers could coexist within a relatively peaceful system is not terribly surprising of itself. The so-called Concert system, for example, existed during a multipolar phase, roughly from 1815 to 1853. That system, however, arose from the ashes of a hegemonic war lasting more than two decades, the purpose of which was to defeat an aspiring hegemon (Napoleonic France) before it rolled up the system. The current system, however, has already been "rolled up" for all intents and purposes. So how could a balance of power be restored, not simply maintained, without deliberate balancing against an established hegemon—currently the United States? The answer is that uneven rates of growth among states seeking merely to get rich can produce a rough equivalence in capabilities among several states, none of which feels particularly threatened by the others or aggressively seeks relative gains at the expense of the others. In other words, the major actors in the system are primarily egoistic: they remain quite competitive due to social and material scarcity but not in a traditionally military sense.

This view of how balance (or equilibrium) emerges from rising entropy is similar to how it occurs in the "automatic" version of balance-of-power theory. Both are spontaneously generated balances. The difference is that in traditional balance-of-power theory, a global balance arises as an unintended consequence of the co-action of states pursuing power-maximizing strategies; that is, their intended goal is not power equality but superiority and domination over others.[2] The current pathway to multipolarity is the mirror image of an "automatic" balance of power emerging from the uncoordinated actions of power-hungry states. Major powers in the age of entropy are inward-looking states attempting to maximize consumption: they act in ways they believe will enrich their citizens. In other words, economic welfare and security have become more important to states than security defined in traditional military and territorial terms. None other than Robert Gilpin, arguably the most important and influential modern-day realist, claims that "economic issues certainly have become much more important since the end of the cold war and have displaced, for the United States and its allies, the prior overwhelming concern with military security."[3]

Domestic strategies designed to promote economic growth along with structural factors such as the diffusion of technology and the "advantages of backwardness" result in uneven growth among states, such that a balance of power will be restored—even if no actor intends this outcome. But contrary to balance-of-power theory and practice, global balance is achieved *not* by thwarting the aims of the major actors but rather as a by-product of the pursuit of the actor's main goal: domestic economic growth. Global equilibrium is neither desired nor unwanted by the actors; it isn't the essential driver of their behavior. And their behavior does not accord with the traditional balancing strategies of forming alliances and building arms. Balance or equilibrium emerges without balancing. Consistent with this nonbalancing formula for global equilibrium, a recent *China Daily* (*Zhongguo Ribao*) editorial avers, "The emerging trend in the world today is the gradual evolution of world power towards relative equilibrium. It is an inevitable outcome of the growing move toward multipolarity and of deepening economic globalization and rapid revolution of science and technology."[4] There is no mention of alliances or arms buildups; rather, emerging multipolarity is attributed to the diffusion of economic, scientific, and technological power.

Why does the logic of balance of power no longer capture the core dynamics of contemporary international politics? What has changed? Two big things. First, territory is not valued as highly as it was during the golden era of power politics. Second, the time-honored expectation among great powers that violence is a legitimate means to settle their disputes or to expand their influence no longer exists.

Great Powers No Longer Expect to Settle Their Differences by Means of War

The age of entropy is transforming the nature of power, the ability to exercise power, the way power is exercised, and the goals of power itself. Knowledge, not territory, is the key to success. To be sure, people will continue to define their identities largely by means of territory: nationalism, more so than cosmopolitan universalism, will continue to hold sway over international politics. Control over resources and access to routes (e.g., sea lanes vital for the transport of oil and projecting military power) will continue to be strategic objectives, especially among the great powers.[5] And disputes over territory and regional influence will continue to fuel rivalries among established and emerging powers and among the emerging powers themselves.

Territorial concerns rooted in balance-of-power politics are most evident between China and India, which share a disputed border that extends roughly 2,000 miles and which remain keenly sensitive to changes in their relative military capabilities. Consistent with a balance-of-power worldview, both countries perceive the other as forming balancing alliances against it. China sees India teaming up with the United States, Japan, Australia, and Vietnam; whereas India views China as working closely with Pakistan, Nepal, Burma, Bangladesh, and Sri Lanka. Yet, there has been a good deal of cooperation in their relationship as well, including ongoing border negotiations, confidence-building measures to maintain stability along the Line of Actual Control, regular summit meetings, and a growing trade relationship that could reach $100 billion in the next several years. Both countries are also members of the BRICS club.[6] And after talks in New Delhi in September 2012, Chinese defense minister Liang Guanglie and Indian defense minister A. K. Antony announced an agreement to resume joint military exercises, which had been suspended two years earlier. All of which is to say that the Sino-Indian relationship, though marred by serious disputes over borders, resources, and power politics, does not fit the standard portrait of balance-of-power politics. It is something a bit more complex. While both sides keep a vigilant watch on what the other is doing in Central Asia, Southeast Asia, the Indian Ocean, the Persian Gulf, Africa, and Latin America, they continue to look for and find ways to cooperate. If this is balance of power, it is state-of-the-art, twenty-first-century balance of power.

The bottom line is that territory still matters, such that the emerging world will not be altogether different from the old one. But geography and policies rooted in geopolitics have become less relevant to the formation of strategy and politics than they were when raw materials and land were the major prerequisites for state power. This sea change largely explains why there has been no major-power war since 1945, and there is every reason to believe that this record-setting long peace among the great powers, which shattered the old record of great-power peace from 1871 to 1914, will continue.[7]

We no longer live in a world governed by the logic of the mercantilist age, when military conquest to control territory and achieve autarky (or a monopoly on goods) was the surest route to riches and power. Today, the traditional link between territory and wealth has been largely broken. The current era of high technology, instant communication, and nuclear weapons has significantly raised the benefits of peace and the costs of war. What matters most today is not a state's ability to exert direct control over resources but its capacity to purchase them in a free global market.

Accordingly, the foundation of modern state power has shifted away from traditional military power toward an emphasis on economic production and a sustained capacity to generate ideas and commercial innovations that create wealth.

To be perfectly clear on this point, innovation and economic growth remain key building blocks of military power; I am not suggesting otherwise. Rather, I am saying that military power is no longer an essential building block of economic growth and wealth creation; this has deeply changed the nature of international politics and how the game is played.

Given the new realities of the nuclear revolution and the rise of globalization and "knowledge economies," territory is no longer the coin of the realm in terms of power assets. Taking more of it no longer makes states safer or more powerful. Indeed, land grabs, naked or clothed, will certainly make a state less safe and secure in the end. How can this be? How can territorial expansion ever become obsolete among powerful states? At a glance, this type of thinking seems like the naïve nonsense one would expect from a wooly-headed idealist. As any realist would certainly point out, so long as states operate in an anarchic world and continue to have disputes, war among them will remain a very real possibility and the struggle for power will endure. Under anarchy, the search for security in a dangerous and unpredictable world is compelling enough reason for states to seek territorial conquest. In the words of John Mearsheimer, "anarchy and uncertainty about other states' intentions create an irreducible level of fear among states that leads to power-maximizing behavior. . . . [T]he structure of the international system, not the particular characteristics of individual states, causes them to think and act offensively and to seek hegemony."[8] The motivation to attack for reasons of security is especially high when taking territory is much easier than defending it against an attack. When offensive military operations have a huge advantage over defensive ones, "the only route to security lies through expansion. Status-quo powers must then act like aggressors; the fact that they would gladly agree to forego the opportunity for expansion in return for guarantees for their security has no implications for their behavior."[9]

This is the famous logic of the security dilemma—a celebrated theory grounded in the observation that "the means by which a state tries to increase its security decrease the security of others."[10] The problem is that states can never do just one thing; they are hopelessly interconnected. So when a state tries to make itself more secure (and not threaten others in the process), it cannot help but make others less secure, even though it does not intend to do so. Moreover, because most weapons can be used for both offensive and defensive purposes, it is difficult for pure security-seeking states to differentiate themselves from aggressors. Here the problem is one of transparency and recognition of type—whether the state is a security seeker or a greedy aggressor. When offensive weapons are indistinguishable from defensive ones, security seekers cannot make their intentions known by means of the weapons they employ. Unable to distinguish between benign security seekers and dangerous aggressors, insecure states must assume that everyone is an aggressor. And when offense has a huge advantage over defense, such that preemptive incentives dominate, the consequences of a surprise attack are so dire that security seekers must act like aggressors and wage their own preemptive attacks. The logic is simple: kill or be killed.

When the security dilemma is at work, international politics can be seen as tragic in the sense that states may desire—or at least be willing to settle for—mutual security, but their own behavior puts this very goal further from their reach. As mutual suspicions grow, war becomes more likely, even among states that seek only security and nothing more.[11]

In theory, the principles behind the security dilemma are true enough. In practice, however, they beg the question: when was the last time a purely defensively minded state actually gained security by attacking its neighbors or eliminating its adversary as a sovereign state? When was the last time a security dilemma caused war? I cannot think of a single case since 1945. I suspect that the quality of information among powerful states is simply too good today for them to misperceive each other's intentions and thereby stumble into war with one another. In addition, the spread of democracy has made offensive military doctrines increasingly difficult to sell; mass publics rarely give their stamp of approval to reckless foreign policies, knowing full well that they will be the ones paying the price in blood and treasure.

Leaving aside security as a motive for grabbing territory, opportunistic expansion is a core principle of power politics. Just as nature abhors a vacuum, great powers—motivated by an irresistible temptation to cash in on an opportunity to make gains relative to their competitors—move quickly to fill power vacuums with their own power and influence. Until recently, the world has always had its share of greedy states that expanded for reasons other than security. If the future bears any resemblance to the past, therefore, we will surely see interstate wars of aggression; surely territorial expansion will remain, as it has always been, a rational policy for accumulating state power.

Does the world still operate along these lines? Here again, I cannot think of a single case in the post–World War II era when a state gained power and prestige by conquering its neighbors. If territorial expansion is still a genuine goal among powerful actors today, why has interstate war, especially major war, become such a remarkably rare phenomenon since the end of the Cold War?[12] Why have there been so few cases—and virtually no successful ones—of greedy expansion since 1945? Indeed, if a greedy state is one defined by its "nonsecurity motives for expansion, which can include the desire to increase its wealth, territory, or prestige, and to spread its political ideology or religion, when these are not required to preserve the state's security,"[13] then one would be hard-pressed to identify such a state—much less a "purely greedy state" (one entirely without security motives)—in the world today. Political scientist Peter Liberman may be correct that sufficiently ruthless occupiers can extract gain from territory, especially in industrialized countries, even in the modern world.[14] But if conquest still pays, leaders of contemporary states do not seem to know or believe it.[15]

The absence of greedy states is especially puzzling in what was formerly known as the Third Word, which consists of regions defined by significant power inequalities among neighboring states. According to balance-of-power realism, capability imbalances are dangerous precisely because they encourage opportunistic expansion. As Jeffrey Herbst observes, however, very few Third World states have fought interstate wars or even confronted major external threats: "Even in Africa, the continent seemingly destined for war given the colonially-imposed boundaries and weak political authorities, there has not been one involuntary boundary change since the dawn of the independence era in the late 1950s, and very few countries face even the prospect of a conflict with their neighbors. Most of the conflicts in Africa that have occurred were not, as in Europe, wars of conquest that threatened the existence of other states, but conflicts over lesser issues that were resolved without threatening the existence of another state."[16] Likewise, K. J. Holsti comments, "The search for continental hegemony is rare in the Third World, but was a common feature of European diplomacy under the Habsburg, Louis XIV, Napoleon, Wilhelmine Germany, Hitler, and Soviet Union and, arguably, the United States."[17]

To be sure, headlines that dominate the news today—from Indo-Pakistani clashes over Kashmir to Sino-Japanese-Vietnamese tensions over disputed islands in the East and South China Sea—suggest that plenty of states still care about territory. These issues, however, are a far cry from past bids to take over the world or a large portion of it. Indeed, the United States' most likely peer competitor, China, more resembles Wal-Mart than the former Soviet Union.

Modern leaders seem to understand that in the twenty-first century, states move up the ladder of international power and prestige by means of knowledge economies that generate dynamic growth; that the present and future competition among states will be decided by technological innovation, connectedness within global networks, the ability to steer complex technological innovation processes, and who best creates environments that facilitate flexible and timely innovation choices.

These are the kinds of issues Americans focus on—or should focus on—when they consider how to prevent their country's declining global position from accelerating. At present, their fears have little to do with security defined in the traditional terms of whether other states will attack the United States or its allies.[18] They understand that America's position in the world will be largely determined by the health of its economy—an economy saddled by enormous public debt set to double in the coming decade from $5.8 trillion in 2008 to $14.3 trillion in 2019. They have seen America's share of world product fall 32 percent since 2000.[19] As of June 2013, unemployment remained at nearly 8 percent. Foreclosures have forced millions of Americans out of their homes, and real incomes have fallen faster and further than at any time since the Great Depression.

Americans worry about having less influence in the world, about putting the country's fate in the hands of others. They worry about China and other emerging countries taking market share from U.S. companies; about dangerously high current account deficits; about the effects of globalization and outsourcing on the average American's standard of living; about the welfare and education of their children and grandchildren; about terrorism, cyberspace crime and attacks, the spread of infectious diseases and the potential emergence of a new pandemic, nuclear proliferation, climate change, energy, healthcare, savings, pensions, and biosecurity. Add to this list of potential troubles the decline of the U.S. dollar, which arguably poses the most serious threat to the future of American power. If the U.S. dollar relinquishes its status as the world's sole reserve currency to the renminbi, gold, SDR, bancor, or something else, not only will its value plunge but U.S. credit markets will collapse, commodity prices and interest rates will soar, and the Federal Reserve's balance sheet will explode.[20]

These are the issues and security threats that will determine the fate of America and the world in the twenty-first century, whether the United States remains far and away the most dominant country in the world, falls back to the pack, or, worse still, simply collapses. Only madmen still believe that the path to security and greatness lies in imperialism and territorial conquest.

Am I proclaiming the triumph of Davos-style liberal cosmopolitanism and the death of realism?[21] Certainly not. As a political realist, I firmly believe that international politics is still fundamentally a competition for power and influence over others and the environment. As in the past, states want to maximize their wealth, influence, security, prestige, political autonomy, and freedom of choice. But the world has changed in important ways. To better fit the realities of the twenty-first century, therefore, realism must be uprooted from its foundation in the industrial age, geopolitics, and concerns about military power and territory to the exclusion of everything else that matters in the world. Realism must become more a theory of consumption- and influence-maximizing—shaping others' preferences to get the outcomes you desire—than one about military capabilities and security defined narrowly as safety from territorial attack.

The devaluation of territory and the disutility of military attack as a means to power and security have profound implications for the coming multipolar system. It means that we should not expect deep and intense security dilemmas—ones that would lead to wars—among the great powers; consequently, we should not expect new-style multipolarity to behave anything like old-style multipolarity. Under traditional multipolar settings, great powers built up arms in the belief that it was not only possible but highly likely that their weapons would be used against each other. Likewise, when they formed alliances, they targeted them at one another. Balance of power—the oldest and most accepted theory of international relations—is built on the assumption that war is a legitimate instrument of statecraft, that states will settle their differences by fighting and, when the odds are right, will wage wars of aggression to expand at each others' expense. Throughout history, these expectations have profoundly influenced the behavior of states and the operation of the international system as a whole.

The long peace has fundamentally changed these great power behaviors and expectations. Great powers no longer build up arms and form alliances in the expectation that they will settle their differences by fighting. It is no longer an acceptable practice for powerful states to waltz in and take over a country for profit. Those that ignore these global norms encounter the wrath of the entire international community, as Saddam Hussein found out when he invaded Kuwait.

With interstate war no longer in play, balance-of-power theory tells us far less about what makes the clock tick in international relations than it did in the past. Contrary to the predictions of balance-of-power theory, today's great powers seem determined to do two things more than anything else: get rich and avoid catastrophic military contests. For these reasons, the coming world of many powerful states and nonstate actors will be very different from your great-grandfather's and great-great-grandfather's multipolar systems.

The Coexistence of Regional Hegemonies

As discussed, the Great Power Conflict model views the world in terms of hierarchies, namely, concerns over prestige and power. States constantly ask, "Where am I in the international pecking order and how can I move up?" The centrality of these vertical concerns eventually triggers a system-wide war between a rising challenger and a declining leader. The rising power insists on more prestige and the declining hegemon responds by resisting its demands. After all, more prestige for the challenger means less prestige for itself.

The logic seems straightforward enough until one recognizes that the theory defines prestige as nothing less than global supremacy. To be sure, the concept of hegemony implies a state so powerful that it dominates all others. No other state has the military wherewithal to put up a serious fight against it. Hegemons rule the system, which, in the Great Power Conflict model, is interpreted to mean the entire world.

The concept of a system, however, can be applied more narrowly to describe a particular region, such as Europe, Northeast Asia, the Near East, or the Western Hemisphere. In other words, one can distinguish between *global* hegemons that dominate the world and *regional* hegemons that dominate distinct geographical areas. This definition of hegemony makes sense because it is virtually impossible for any state to achieve true global hegemony. The principal impediment to world domination is the difficulty of projecting power across the world's oceans onto the territory of a rival great power. In practice, the best outcome that a great power can hope for is regional hegemony, and possibly to exert control over another region that is nearby and accessible over land. The United States, which dominates the Western Hemisphere, is the only regional hegemon in modern history; it does not control the rest of the world, though it has achieved far greater world dominance than any state in history. Other states have fought major wars in pursuit of regional hegemony—Imperial Japan in Northeast Asia; Napoleonic France, Wilhelmine Germany, and Nazi Germany in Europe—but none succeeded.

A regional conception of hegemony is important because it allows each of the various poles in what will be the first "global multipolar" system to control its own backyard. Everyone can have prestige. China's sphere of influence will be Northeast Asia; Brazil will dominate Latin America; Germany or the European Union will determine the fate of Europe; and the United States will continue to hold sway over North America and, in addition, project its power over the unclaimed regions of the globe.

It is now possible to imagine a world in which one great power's prestige does not come at the expense of other great powers. This was not possible in prior multipolar systems. When all the great powers were European states, the primary focus of power and prestige was Europe itself; it comprised the so-called core of the international system. The rest of the world was considered "the periphery," and, as such, control over parts of it could augment but not entirely satisfy the prestige demands of the central players, aside from Britain—whose maritime supremacy and insular geographic position allowed it to play the offshore balancer and kingmaker roles with respect to the Continental core. With all of the great powers vying for control over the same region, an increase in the prestige of one could only mean a corresponding loss for the others. Little wonder that we have come to associate prestige with ferocious zero-sum competition and hegemonic wars. But that was the past. The particular characteristics and dynamics of that system were as much, if not more, a function of geography as they were of the multipolar distribution of military and economic capabilities. There is no compelling reason to believe that future multipolarity will behave similarly.

Rising Entropy at the Macro Level

The World Is Not Flat in Purgatory

If the preceding description of the age of entropy were complete, there would be little reason for anxiety about the future. A world of perpetual peace—in which billions of citizens join the Great Power club and prestige can be enjoyed by all—sounds like a good place to live. The discussion to this point, however, focused only on the upbeat attributes of our entropic future. There is much about increasing entropy that will make the world a less than desirable place to live. The age of entropy promises not the hellish world of hegemonic war predicted by the Great Power Conflict scenario or the heavenly one promised by the Great Power Concert alternative but a bleak outlook akin to a permanent state of purgatory. It will be a world of banality and confusion, of anomie and alienation, of instability without a stabilizer, of devolving order without an orderer. Let us now consider these aspects of global entropy.

Chaotic Alliance Patterns and Geographic Disorder

In the age of entropy, international politics will become increasingly volatile and unpredictable. This turbulence will be strikingly evident in the realm of geopolitics, that is, in the relationship between politics and territory.[1] Let me say at the outset that I am not suggesting that territory no longer matters in the modern world, nor am I advancing a "borderless world" argument or arguing that globalization means de-territorialization. Europe's Schengen Area, which comprises twenty-six countries that agreed to eliminate border controls with each other, does not represent the future of political organization across the globe.

Geography remains an important driver of national interests and world events. To be sure, Russia's obsession with security—its fixation on the control of territory—stems from the inherently exposed nature of its borders, the unremitting grassy steppes that extend from Europe to the Far East with scarcely a mountain range or major forest to hinder an enemy attack.[2] Likewise, the successive rises to global hegemony of Britain and then the United States were in no small part due to their fortuitous geographic positions as insular states surrounded by large bodies of water, offering them both a degree of protection that afforded the luxury of idealism and direct access to the commerce of the rest of the world. China, in contrast, is hemmed in on all sides by powerful states (Russia, Japan, India, and the United States), making it doubtful that it will ever rise to the level of world hegemon. In a geographic sense, therefore, the world is certainly not "flat." Resource scarcity, historical memory, cultural and ethnic divisions, and geopolitical rivalry will continue to shape international and domestic politics, causing conflict and limiting cooperation. Only the most optimistic of observers would suggest otherwise.

Contrary to popular globaloney, the world is also far from "flat" and "borderless" in terms of the depth and breadth of global connectedness. In late 2011, DHL released its first Global Connectedness Index, which measures connectedness according to countries' participation in ten types of generally beneficial international flows: merchandise trade, services trade, foreign direct investment, portfolio equity investment, international telephone calls, international Internet traffic (as indicated by the proxy of bandwidth statistics), international trade in printed publications, international tourism, international education, and international migration. With respect to the depth of global connectedness—that is, the size of a country's international flows as compared to a relevant measure of the size of its domestic economy—the measures above range from 2 percent to 30 percent, with most of them falling significantly below 20 percent. In terms of the breadth of connectedness at the global level, 60 percent of trade takes place within continents—56 percent within regions defined more narrowly (based on the World Bank's classification system); foreign direct investment (FDI) is roughly as regionalized as trade; and nearly half of phone calls and immigration flows occur within continental regions. This underscores the point that even those countries that have achieved the world's highest levels of global connectedness in relative terms have room to significantly increase their absolute levels of connectedness. The report concludes that the data on global levels of connectedness "clearly demonstrate that we live in a semiglobalized world where levels of connectedness are only a fraction of what 'flat world' intuitions would lead one to expect, but are still sufficiently large that a fully local or national worldview also fails to accord with reality."[3]

With these caveats firmly stated, what I am suggesting is that geography matters less today than in the past. Like Russia, Germany, too, faces both east and west with no geographical features to protect it. While, in the past, this exposure led to German militarism and expansionist pathologies, there is little fear among Germans today that they will be attacked or invaded. How have German fears faded while its geography has remained constant? Even Russia, while more concerned than Germany about its territorial situation, willingly gave away two layers of empire at the end of the Cold War and allowed a united Germany to become a member of NATO. Would Russia have even considered these concessions if geography were still an extremely powerful cause of national interests and global events? Does anyone believe that this would have happened if the Red Army had not possessed nuclear weapons or if Russian leaders valued territory the way they always had prior to World War II? Surely, geography, though still important, no longer determines the fate of nations or their fears and desires the way it did in centuries past. There is nothing inevitable about geography.

I also mean to suggest that stable geographic groupings have lost salience; they were the stuff of traditional balance-of-power politics, when a few great powers managed relations among each other and the world through spheres-of-influence arrangements. Today, there is no East versus West; no North-South divide—not with the rise of China and India. These outmoded Cold War groupings have been replaced by more amorphous global divisions: the established G-7 powers versus the emerging BRICS; democratic capitalism versus authoritarian capitalism; northwest versus southeast democracies; and, most worrisome, a stable zone of peace versus an arc of instability running from the Caribbean basin through most of Africa, the Middle East, and Central and Southeast Asia, where the threats of radical Islam, terrorism, and failed states loom.

At its core, politics is about choosing one's friends and enemies. International politics is essentially the business of alliances and alignments. If entropy is rising and the international system is becoming more disordered and messy, therefore, we should expect to see it manifested in increasingly fluid and unpredictable alliance patterns. Actors, whether states or otherwise, that are aligned on certain issues and within specific regions will be on opposite sides on other issues and in other regions. These groupings will also change from one conflict to the next. The increase in cross-national and subnational loyalties associated with entropy will also result in the breakdown of clear geographical patterns demarcating friends and enemies.

And indeed we do see fluid and irregular alliances patterns. Thus, the U.S. National Intelligence Council concluded, "at no time since the formation of the Western alliance system in 1949 have the shape and nature of international alignments been in such a state of flux as they have during the past decade."[4]

Entropy will also spark a rise in cross-national and subnational loyalties at the expense of "plain old" nationalism—blurring the neat geographical lines that formerly distinguished friends from enemies. One consequence of this geographic disorder from a military standpoint is that selective targeting of individuals will become more important than firepower. An example of this kind of change is, of course, President Obama's drone program—the worst-kept official secret in the United States—and his expanded "targeted killing" policy, which, implemented by the Central Intelligence Agency, has deployed unmanned drones to kill hundreds of suspected terrorists without charge or trial. To date, the administration has yet to disclose the legal criteria and procedures it uses for targeted killing or, for that matter, the number of innocent civilians killed or harmed in drone strikes.[5] Of course, Allied soldiers landing in Normandy did not read the Germans their Miranda rights before shooting them. Why do we expect the war on terror to be fought differently? The reason has everything to do with the geography and primary targets of the two types of warfare.

Conventional warfare takes place on "known" battlefields; irregular or "asymmetric" warfare (that is, guerrilla, terrorist, insurgency, or cyber warfare) does not. In asymmetric warfare, the long-established idea of a spatial battlefield, where state-run militaries clash using heavy weapons that primarily target the opposing army away from populated centers, is replaced by dispersed combatants of a communal, religious, or ethnic nature in an urban or heavily populated environment. The nonspatial nature of the battlefield and the fact that the combatants, typically lightly armed guerrillas, enjoy widespread popular support or, at least, the passive acquiescence of the local population greatly complicates the task of identifying combatants and distinguishing them from noncombatants.

Moreover, conventional warfare targets national armies, whereas irregular war targets groups and individuals. Drone warfare is emblematic of this shift in the security practices of the most advanced industrialized countries from a focus on nation-states to individuals as the source of greatest threat. As Peter Andreas and Richard Price put it, "the role of the advanced externally oriented coercive apparatus has been shifting in emphasis from warfighting to crimefighting functions."[6] Thus, from 2002 to 2013, U.S. drones or unmanned aerial vehicles (UAV) killed upwards of 4,000 people in an estimated 425 attacks in Yemen and Pakistan. What makes possible the use of drones for targeted killing and, more generally, the deployment of the external military apparatus for operations other than state-to-state war (including a variety of international policing operations) is a large surveillance apparatus that collects and analyses information on individuals globally. Small wonder that remote-control killing by the CIA and U.S. military has come to define the war on terror. According to the *New York Times*, "Though no official will publicly acknowledge it, the bottom line is clear: killing is more convenient than capture for both the United States and the foreign countries where the strikes occur."[7]

Nevertheless, when ideas rather than territory define the enemy, it becomes extremely difficult to avoid excessive collateral damage and still fight to win (as suggested by the 10:1 ratio of the roughly 4,000 people killed in 425 U.S. drone attacks). The term *collateral damage* originated as a euphemism for the killing of noncombatants during the Vietnam War. Its moral justification relies on the doctrine of double effect (DDE), which was introduced by Thomas Aquinas and has been used to show that agents may permissibly bring about harmful effects provided that they are merely foreseen side effects of promoting a good end (hence, the double effect). With the civilian death toll in Iraq estimated at over 600,000, the DDE has become an important justificatory tool of U.S. war fighting.

Much of the world, however, views collateral damage as nothing more than a rhetorical contrivance for murder and, in this respect, no different than terrorism. Lest one think that this view is solely motivated by anti-Americanism, it is worth pointing out that the Oklahoma City bomber, Timothy McVeigh, outraged the American public when in an interview he described the 19 dead children among his 168 victims as "collateral damage." It was considered an appalling comment that made him an even more despised figure in American society. Collateral damage creates a political problem for any state combating terrorism—whether Israeli reprisals against Hezbollah in Gaza, Russian military strikes against Chechens in Georgia, or American operations in Iraq and Afghanistan. Greater selectivity in targeting provides, at best, only a partial solution to the problem.

While traditional military powers find themselves swimming against the tide of entropy, terrorists are surfing its waves. On September 11, 2001, a small group of men killed three thousand people, destroyed four expensive aircraft, a huge portion of prime real estate in New York City, and part of the Pentagon's nerve center. The ripple effects, however, multiplied the costs into the trillions of dollars. Similarly, in October of that year, a handful of 34-cent letters containing anthrax—mailed, most likely, by a single individual—killed several people, "contaminated a large portion of the postal system, paralyzed some mail delivery for long periods, provoked plans for huge expenditures on prophylactic irradiation equipment, shut down much of Capitol Hill for weeks, put thousands of people on a sixty-day regimen of strong antibiotics (potentially eroding the medical effectiveness of such antibiotics in future emergencies), and overloaded the police and public health inspectors with false alarms."[8]

In 2008, the U.S. Department of Defense suffered a massive compromise of its classified military computer networks when an infected flash drive was inserted by a foreign intelligence agency into a U.S. military laptop at a base in the Middle East. The rogue program established what amounted to a digital beachhead, silently delivering operational plans, weapons blueprints, and surveillance data into the hands of an unknown enemy (unlike missiles, cyber attacks do not come with return addresses). Since 2008, America's adversaries have acquired thousands of files from U.S. networks and those of its allies and industry partners. Every year the amount of intellectual property stolen from networks maintained by U.S. businesses, universities, and government agencies far exceeds all the intellectual property contained in the Library of Congress.[9]

Of course, the United States is no mere victim of cyber attacks and cyber espionage. Two of the three most dangerous Internet weapons ever created are widely believed to be the products of a joint American-Israeli project. The first, Stuxnet, designed to attack software in specialized industrial equipment, was used to destroy centrifuges in an Iranian nuclear facility in 2010. The second, Duqu, performed reconnaissance missions by infecting machines through a known security hole in the Windows operating software. The third and by far the biggest and most sophisticated Internet weapon ever created is known as Flame, which is not thought to be made by the same authors as Stuxnet and Duqu. Discovered in 2012 by Kaspersky Labs, a Moscow-based security research firm, Flame has been infecting computers in Iran, Israel, Lebanon, Sudan, Syria, Saudi Arabia, and Egypt for over two years, grabbing images of users' computer screens, recording their instant messaging chats, remotely turning on their microphones to record their audio conversations and monitoring their keystrokes and network traffic.[10]

As these examples demonstrate, today's global espionage scarcely resembles the Cold War capers parodied by MAD magazine's *Spy vs. Spy* comic strip. Lapel cameras and microfilm stashed in shoe heels have been replaced by computers and satellites operating within the world's most sophisticated information-collection systems—those owned by China, the United States, Russia, Israel, and India. The new battlegrounds are cyberspace and outer space, where technologies are pirated, fortunes are stolen, and attacks are launched against state and corporate rivals. Mere bugging operations have been supplanted by satellite listening stations that capture computer keystrokes, and the environment is measured in the space and corporations that a state controls. With everyone spying on and stealing from everyone else, whether technology, software, or the capacity to conduct warfare, the distinction between "friend" and "enemy" has blurred, if not vanished entirely.[11]

Espionage and theft are not the only aims driving cyber operations, however. Beginning in 2012 Iran and North Korea launched a wave of cyber attacks on banks (most recently American Express and JPMorgan Chase), oil producers, and governments designed not to steal or disable data but to destroy it. The appeal of digital weapons for "outgunned and outfinanced" rogue countries is similar to that of nuclear weapons: they level the playing field by providing relatively weak nations with the horsepower to inflict huge attacks on their far stronger enemies. "These countries are pursuing cyber-weapons the same way they are pursuing nuclear weapons," explained James A. Lewis, a computer security expert at the Center for Strategic and International Studies in Washington. "It's primitive; it's not top of the line, but it's good enough and they are committed to getting it."[12]

The obscure geographic space of an entropic world has diminished usable firepower while strongly favoring guerrilla tactics, hacker attacks, sabotage, cyber warfare, cyber espionage, and terrorism. We are left with a more level military playing field—one that approximates maximum entropy's final state of "random motion" and "equal energy among particles."

Hybrid Responses to a Hybrid World

In a constantly shifting world steered by networked arrangements for specific tasks, where states share the international arena with a wide range of multilateral organizations, nongovernmental actors, illicit enterprises, influential private sector entities, civil society groups, and individuals with significant and increasing influence in global politics, effective action to get things done will require hybrid responses, that is, integrated partnerships among states, corporations, civil society, and individuals. This has always been true for soft power—the resources for which largely lie outside of government in the private sector and civil society, in a nation's bilateral alliances, or through its participation in multilateral institutions. What is different is that these kinds of hybrid public-private partnerships will be increasingly necessary for the effective use of hard power as well. Consider, for instance, the problem of transnational criminal organizations.

Few would refute the proposition that globalization has made people all over the world, on average, healthier, better-informed, and more peaceful than at any other time in history. Moreover, nation-states have benefited from the information revolution, tighter and denser political and economic linkages, and the shrinking of geographic distance. But the global systems that carry people, goods, and data around the globe also facilitate the movement of dangerous people, goods, and data. And, unfortunately, transnational criminal networks engaged in illegal international trade in drugs, arms, intellectual property, people, and money have benefited most of all. As the internationally renowned columnist, Moisés Naím, observes:

> Never fettered by the niceties of sovereignty, [criminal networks] are now increasingly free of geographic constraints. Moreover, globalization has not only expanded illegal markets and boosted the size and the resources of criminal networks, it has also imposed more burdens on governments: Tighter public budgets, decentralization, privatization, deregulation, and a more open environment for international trade and investment all make the task of fighting global criminals more difficult. Governments are made up of cumbersome bureaucracies that generally cooperate with difficulty, but drug traffickers, arms dealers, alien smugglers, counterfeiters, and money launderers have refined networking to a high science, entering into complex and improbable strategic alliances that span cultures and continents. . . . The resources—financial, human, institutional, technological—deployed by the combatants have reached unfathomable orders of magnitude. So have the numbers of victims.[13]

Similarly, John Arquilla and David Ronfeldt argue that the "information revolution is altering the nature of conflict across the spectrum . . . favoring and strengthening network forms of organization, often giving them an advantage over hierarchical forms. The rise of networks means that power is migrating to nonstate actors, because they are able to organize into sprawling multiorganizational networks (especially 'all-channel' networks, in which every node is connected to every other node) more readily than can traditional, hierarchical, state actors. This means that conflicts may increasingly be waged by 'networks,' perhaps more than by 'hierarchies.' It also means that whoever masters the network form stands to gain the advantage."[14]

Highly networked with the ability to wage swarming attacks, "netwarriors"— be they terrorists, criminals, fanatics associated with militias and extremist single-issue movements, or anarchistic and nihilistic leagues of computer-hacking "cyboteurs"—present a challenge that can only be met successfully by means of interagency communication and coordination among governments as well as international organizations, private firms, and individuals for everything from intelligence sharing to tactical operations. What is required is a degree of cross-jurisdictional and international networking that is difficult for the hierarchies of national governments to accomplish.[15]

Nevertheless, the need for effective public-private partnerships has been quite visible in the past decade with respect to both homeland security and the problem of failing states abroad. To secure the homeland, states must be able to combat threats and hazards that include terrorism, natural disasters, large-scale cyber attacks, and pandemics. Intelligence is key, but so too is the ability to protect and reduce vulnerabilities in critical infrastructure at borders, ports, and airports, as well as to enhance overall air, maritime, transportation, and space and cyber security. Solutions to infrastructure vulnerabilities—from critical government and industry systems and networks to power and electric grids to data protection and so on—require public-private partnerships. Thus, the Obama administration acknowledged in its 2010 U.S. National Security Strategy the need for the private sector to play a major role in addressing these challenges:

> The private sector, which owns and operates most of the nation's critical infrastructure, plays a vital role in preparing for and recovering from disasters. We must, therefore, strengthen public-private partnerships by developing incentives for government and the private sector to design structures and systems that can withstand disruptions and mitigate associated consequences, ensure redundant systems where necessary to maintain the ability to operate, decentralize critical operations to reduce our vulnerability to single points of disruption, develop and test continuity plans to ensure the ability to restore critical capabilities, and invest in improvements and maintenance of existing infrastructure.[16]

With respect to the world at large, failing states breed conflict, endanger regional and global security, and provide secure home bases for terrorists and global criminal networks. Thus, the 2010 U.S. National Security Strategy elevates development and diplomacy to a position equally important as military strength in the U.S. foreign policy toolkit. U.S. Africa Command (Africom), the U.S. military's newest combatant command, for instance, operates within a modern hybrid framework that includes working relationships with nonmilitary and nongovernmental actors to achieve its mission. Johan Bergenas, deputy director of the Managing across Boundaries program at the Stimson Center, writes:

> Since 2007, Africom has been working with the private sector and regional African armed forces to not only increase countries' security potential through border and port security capacity-building, but also to train medics in African militaries, implement HIV/AIDS prevention programs, combat drug trafficking, build classrooms and participate in cattle-vaccination programs. Furthermore, USAID engages with Africom to support host nation efforts to counter radicalization, recruitment and support to violent extremist organizations. Africom represents a working model of leveraging hybrid responses to complex environments: the U.S. military working together with USAID, the private sector and civil society on issues that transcend each institution's traditional focus.[17]

In May 2010, Denmark launched a new hybrid framework, similar to the U.S. Africom model, for the implementation of an integrated government approach to stabilization and reconstruction in fragile states. The new framework deepens integration among the areas of diplomacy, defense, and development to enhance the impact and sustainability of Danish efforts in fragile states. More specifically, the Danish Defense agreement (2010–2014) established a Danish Stabilization Fund (DSF), the purpose of which is to facilitate activities in fragile states at the interface of security and development, which take place at the regional, national, or subnational levels and include, for example, capacity building of armed forces, justice and security sector reform, and activities to prevent drug trafficking and terrorism.[18]

To more effectively respond to the interconnected challenges of a globalized world, Japan, too, has also been a leader in moving beyond traditional government policies (of the hierarchical-bureaucratic variety) to more hybrid responses—ones that combine efforts to build defense and security capacity with projects to further the development needs of weak and failing states. Under the doctrine of "strategic use of aid," Japan is donating high-tech equipment and training to weak states in an effort to build robust societies that can withstand the challenges posed by transnational criminal and terrorist groups.[19]

Finally, there is the problem of the abuse of the global financial system by terrorists, proliferators, narcotics traffickers, and others for the purpose of raising, moving, and safeguarding funds that support their illicit activities. Because their support networks have global reach and are not contained by national borders, an effective strategy to attack these networks must take the form of a hybrid response that relies on financial measures, administration and enforcement of regulatory authorities, outreach to the private sector, multilateral cooperation, and collaboration on international standards and information sharing.

Not all the news about hybrid, public-private partnerships is good news. Consider, for instance, the strange case of the pirate hunters for hire in Somalia. The creation of the Puntland Maritime Police Force to defeat the pirates terrorizing the shipping lanes off the Somali coast is a sordid story that involves dozens of South African mercenaries employed and trained by a shadowy security firm, the Dubai-based company called Sterling Corporate Service, hired by the United Arab Emirates, which made millions of dollars in secret payments to Sterling, as well as a former clandestine officer with the CIA, and Erik Prince, the billionaire former head of Blackwater Worldwide. With the anti-piracy army having been abandoned by its sponsors, "the hundreds of half-trained and well-armed members of the Puntland Maritime Police Force have been left to fend for themselves at a desert camp carved out of sand, perhaps to join up with the pirates or Qaeda-linked militants or to sell themselves to the highest bidder in Somalia's clan wars—yet another dangerous element in the Somali mix."[20]

The key to getting things done in a "hybrid world" of many types of actors wielding various kinds of power will be, first, for states to recognize the limitations of traditional power bases and, second, to identify and cooperate with private actors that possess issue-specific resources, expertise, and influence with respect to the task at hand. What this means in terms of the big picture is that the twenty-first century will see the emergence of a more horizontal world. Virtually all aspects of social and political activity will be linked through dense global webs of networks. Connectedness will, therefore, become a vital base of power; only the connected will survive and thrive.

On this point, Ann-Marie Slaughter contends that network power is not the kind that imposes outcomes. Networks are not directed and controlled by powerful actors as much as they are managed and orchestrated. The ability to "steer" these networks, she suggests, will become the coin of the realm of power capabili-ties.[21] The problem with this argument is that it stretches the meaning of power and influence to the breaking point. What does managing and orchestrating mean in this view? How does one "steer" a network without controlling it? Indeed, the orchestration metaphor itself seems to contradict her core claim that networks are not directed and controlled by powerful actors. An orchestra is, after all, led by a conductor who, like a powerful dictator, imposes outcomes on others—whose every instruction must be followed faithfully (often without question) by the players within the group. This is the very embodiment of an actor that wields power in a traditional or conventional sense.

At any rate, life in this hybrid-horizontal world of networks will be far more complex, random, and resistant to order and centralized authority than in the past. As networks become exponentially denser and more complex, the world will become increasingly unknowable and interdependent. And the more dependent we are on each other and the less we understand the way the world works, the more vulnerable and less autonomous we become. In short, chaos and insecurity flourish in the absence of hierarchy.

The Governance Gap

The world of 2030 will be radically transformed from our world today: global population will rise from 7.1 billion to about 8.3 billion; the percentage of the world's population in the middle class will expand from the current 1 billion to over 2 billion; urbanization will grow from 50 percent of the world's population to about 60 percent; demand for resources—food, water, and energy—will rise dramatically; and power will shift toward multifaceted networks. These changes will put a premium on effective governance.

As power within the international system diffuses, a growing number of di-verse state, subnational, and nonstate actors will claim that they want to play important governance roles. Many will not be up to the task. Others will be seeking only the prestige associated with a seat at the table, while shirking the responsibilities and obligations that come with the role of global stakeholder. The world faces potentially serious governance deficits. As the number of players needed to solve major transnational challenges increases, decision-making will become that much more complicated, solutions even harder to achieve. The lack of consensus between and among established and emerging powers suggests that multilateral governance will be, at best, limited. A chronic deficit of interna-tional governance will reinforce the trend toward global fragmentation.

Driven by rapid political and social change, the governance gap will be just as pronounced at the state level. Advances in health, education, and income will continue and may even accelerate, requiring and, in some cases, generating new domestic institutions and governance structures. When youth bulges decline and incomes rise, transitions to democracy are much more stable and long-lasting. Both social science theory and recent history—the Color Revolutions and the Arab Spring—support the idea that political liberalization and democracy thrive with maturing age structures and rising incomes. Countries moving from autocracy to democracy, however, also have a proven track record of instability.

The problem is not just new governance structures but old ones and the incompetence, waste, and corruption they breed. Here, Hegel's thoughts on the subject of war and its relationship to state and societal development are especially relevant: "War is not to be regarded as an absolute evil. . . . Just as the blowing of the winds preserves the sea from foulness which would be the result of a long calm, so also corruption in nations would be the result of prolonged, let alone 'perpetual,' peace."[22] Notice that the "still seas" metaphor is entirely consistent with the concept of maximum entropy and the process of rising entropy, that is, our basic intuition rooted in the law of entropy that things left on their own (that are not stirred up with purpose) go to pot (become foul).

Hegel's "domestic peace results in corrupt government" hypothesis has since been empirically tested and supported by economist Mancur Olson. In his study of the rise and fall of nations, Olson found that stable societies with unchanged boundaries promote the formation of oligopolistic market structures composed of a few special-interest organizations, whose collusion effectively lessens the degree of competition among them.[23] Coordinating their efforts by means of narrow, self-interested collective action, these rent-seeking groups reduce the country's economic efficiency and aggregate income, retarding its ability to adopt new technologies and to reallocate resources in response to changing conditions. The antidote is foreign invasion and military occupation, which break apart special-interest groups (rent-seeking distributional coalitions and cartels) and disrupt social rigidities. Thus, countries that have endured wars on their own soil (through invasion or civil conflict) experienced dramatically higher rates of economic growth afterward, and their growth rates far exceeded those of countries that have remained at peace. More recently, Tanisha Fazal has similarly argued that the international norm against conquest, annexation, and occupation has not only permitted state failure but encouraged it.[24] Both studies support

Hegel's logic that maximum entropy in the form of domestic stasis leads to internal corruption, waste, underdevelopment, stagnation, state failure, and a general deterioration of society. Conversely, when domestic inertia is interrupted and uprooted, good things happen.

Modern day examples of this entropic phenomenon abound. India's outsourcing industry—its back-office information technology (IT) work for far-off Western firms—has been a capitalist marvel, bringing in annual export earnings of roughly $100 billion. But as the *Economist* points out, "at home e-commerce is in its infancy, with sales only 6% of China's. Thanks to lousy infrastructure, useless regulation and a famously corrupt telecoms sector, the web is available to only 10% of Indians, many of them squinting at screens in cafés."[25] Likewise, in the north Indian village of Ranwan, stacks of rice sat for years along the side of a highway, rotting and burning, while flies swarmed nearby over spoiled wheat. Workers were finally called in to cart off the sacks of rice to a distillery to be turned into liquor. Stimulated by agricultural innovation and generous farm subsidies, India's grain stockpile is bigger than that of any country except China. While the grain piles up, however, India's poor go hungry. Twenty percent of India's population is malnourished—a deplorable percentage that doubles the rate of China and Vietnam; and 250 million Indians do not get enough to eat. The main culprit is India's failed food policies, which, because of pervasive corruption, mismanagement, and waste, serve more to enrich government officials, who routinely steal food from various links in the distribution chain, than to distribute food to the poor. Meanwhile, India grows so much food that it has become a grain exporter to countries such as Saudi Arabia and Australia. Such is the paradox of plenty in India's food system.[26]

Just like at the level of international politics, where change and historical progress have most often been achieved through bloody global wars, the governance gap at the level of domestic politics highlights the problem of how to manage peaceful evolutionary change in a way that promotes progress and social justice—values that, hitherto, have been advanced by means of brutal wars of revolutionary change. After all, peace is not the same thing as justice: the two values are not always complementary; they do not necessarily go together. "Peace and justice," as Richard Betts notes, "are not natural allies, unless right just happens to coincide with might."[27]

The distasteful truth of history is that violent conflict not only cures the ill effects of political inertia and economic stagnation but is often the key that unlocks all the doors to radical and progressive historical change. It is a truth rooted in the principle of rising entropy and its remedy within human affairs. Insofar as it stirs things up, war performs useful social and political functions.

The Tradeoff between International Legitimacy and Institutional Effectiveness

The trend of global power diffusion means that traditionally poor states are experiencing upward mobility the likes of which they never dreamed. Quite naturally, they seek superior representation and voice at international bargaining tables commensurate with their rise in power; they talk about making the international system more democratic, about the evils of one state dominating global affairs, and about the benefits of multipolarity. And well they should talk of these things.

On the downside, however, shifts in global power and wealth spawn crises of international legitimacy. Emerging second-tier states, many of whom hold markedly different threat perceptions, political values, and economic visions than those of the established countries (particularly, the United States), are underrepresented in the international architecture that America created in the 1940s. There is no good solution to the problem of global governance reform. Reform has focused on making international institutions more efficient and more representative—two objectives that are hopelessly in tension.[28] Global reform, therefore, fails when it fails and fails when it succeeds. Let me explain.

Power is a zero-sum game. Any attempt to boost the institutional power of emerging states such as China, India, Brazil, and South Africa means a corresponding reduction in the power of established institutional players. This would not cause a problem if—and this is a very big if—there were an all-powerful sovereign arbiter above states who continually assessed the relative power of states and then adjusted their institutional power according to their overall power ranking. There is no such beast, however. For the rules of existing institutions to be rewritten, therefore, those currently enjoying the benefits of power would have to *voluntarily* surrender their perks, and this they are loathe to do. But if mismatches are allowed to persist between institutional power within global governance structures and the actual distribution of international power, then dissatisfied rising powers will use their voice option to delegitimize existing regimes and their exit option to find or create alternative institutions—ones consistent with their preferences and that best facilitate their goals.

The success of reform in terms of representativeness, however, will prove a failure in terms of effective governance. The crux of the problem lies with the incentives of the established but waning countries. They well understand that global institutions will not serve anyone's interests if powerful emerging states view them as illegitimate. But their preferred solution to the problem is not to vacate their seat at the table, handing over the institutions to the upstart nations, but rather to enlarge the table. In other words, when it comes to global governance reform, they will choose inflation over redistribution. The recent switch from the G-7 to the G-20 is an example of this kind of reform, as is the expansion of the key World Trade Organization (WTO) negotiation meetings to include India, Brazil, and China.

The problem with inflating the so-called green room is that as the number of veto players (those that can block a proposal by voting against it) expands, the likelihood of reaching consensus on negotiating issues necessarily declines. Further, the new crop of emerging powers comprises a more heterogeneous array of countries (in terms of their regime types, per capita incomes, cultures, ideologies, race, etc.) compared with their more like-minded and homogenous predecessors from the developed world; this heterogeneity will likely contribute to more diverse preferences within the great power club than has typically existed in the past. Taking into account all these factors, we can assume that global governance either will remain unreformed and grow increasingly illegitimate and irrelevant or will be reformed through expansion and become, as a result, even more dysfunctional than normal.[29] Thus, privileged nations gave up their first-class seat on the sinking ship that was the G-7, in exchange for a secure spot on a bigger boat, the G-20, with no one at the helm. The G-7 is history and the G-20 is unworkable.[30]

Consider, for example, the fate of the United Nations Security Council (UNSC). Champions of UNSC expansion suggest that enlargement will bring greater legitimacy to the body, inspiring rising powers to contribute to global public goods. In the long run, a failure to update existing institutions like the UNSC will cause powerful but underrepresented states to turn to other forums. Legitimacy, however, is also a matter of performance. Composed of a diverse group of new stakeholders, an expanded UNSC is more likely to produce gridlock than consensus on global flashpoints such as Darfur, Iran, or North Korea. It would also hopelessly undermine the workings of the already dysfunctional International Criminal Court (ICC).

Created by the Rome Statute and signed by 120 member states in 2002, the ICC embodies a fragile international consensus that leaders should be held accountable for crimes against their own people. To date, only three heads of state are in international custody, one (President Omar Hassan al-Bashir of Sudan) has been indicted but not apprehended, and only one, Charles Taylor, has been convicted of war crimes. There has been no indictment of President Bashir Assad of Syria for the contemptible carnage in Homs and elsewhere; no ICC investigation into the deaths of tens of thousands of Sri Lankan civilians trapped on a beach between government forces and the Tamil Tigers at the bloody end of the country's civil war in 2009; no indictment of Yemen's former president, Ali Abdullah Saleh, for the autocratic leader's decision to turn the guns of his security forces on unarmed protesters, leaving hundreds dead and many more maimed; and no investigation of criminal charges in Gaza and Bahrain. The explanation lies in power politics.

International justice has become the prisoner of international politics. Why should anyone expect otherwise? Law, after all, is intended to constrain power, and what all countries, especially great powers, jealously protect and always want more of—what they are most addicted to—is power. This is why realists hold such low expectations for the ICC and international law in general. Great powers are likely to support a law-based international order only so long as it binds others' power but leaves their power relatively unconstrained. For justice to be legitimate, however, it must be applied equally to all. Clearly this is not happening at the international level. All five veto-holding members of the Security Council—the United States, Russia, Britain, France, and China—refuse to subject themselves to ICC jurisdiction; none is willing to send one of its nationals to the ICC should he or she be accused of crimes against humanity.

More important, the ICC does not have universal jurisdiction. It can only investigate crimes in nations that signed the Rome Statute or when cases are referred by the Security Council. All five permanent members, however, can veto any referral to the court from the UNSC. Thus, in the Middle East, where few nations signed the Rome Statute and many have powerful patrons on the Security Council, authoritarian leaders can commit despicable atrocities with impunity. In the cases cited above, Sri Lanka is a close ally of China; Bahrain and Yemen are supported by the West's veto-holding members (the United States, Britain, and France); and Syria's president Assad is protected by China and Russia. As citizens of the Middle East persistently demand that the court prosecute autocrats ousted in the Arab Spring, the ICC's failure to do so continues to erode their faith in international justice. Indeed, the general perception, especially among Africans, is that the ICC focuses exclusively on Africa, where many countries ratified the Rome Statute. In their eyes, justice appears reserved for outcast African leaders from weak states with no powerful patrons.[31]

Now if this is the ICC's record and the perception of international justice when the UNSC has only five veto-holding members, imagine how hamstrung the ICC would be if the UNSC went from five to twenty or more permanent members. If politics prevents justice today, how much more so will it prevent justice if and when international institutions in the future more accurately represent actual power in the international system? So the world confronts a dilemma: providing rising states with greater voice and representation would help solve the legitimacy crisis but would further impair the efficiency and competence of international institutions—inefficiency that would come at a time of serious transnational challenges, including climate change, the threat of global pandemics, nuclear proliferation, terrorism, and the need for international financial reform.

The proliferation of institutions and nonstate actors as power brokers, the decoupling of power from influence, and the further erosion of the American Century will combine to make it far more difficult to forge consensus, especially around U.S. preferences. Global governance—already in an all-too-familiar messy and anemic condition—will become increasingly more enfeebled and dysfunctional over time. And with no solution to the emerging institutional crisis, international politics will become more confrontational. The world needs urban renewal. What it will get is unplanned suburban sprawl.

Economic Statecraft and Neo-Neocolonialism

As the age of entropy unfolds, the nature of power itself is changing. Military power still matters, but not as much as it once did. We no longer live in a world defined by close allies and conflicts against sworn enemies. Rather, relationships are ambiguous, anxieties are driven more by internal than external problems, and leaders assess other countries based on whether they can make their domestic problems better or worse. As David Brooks puts it, "Today, the world is like a cocktail party at which everybody is suffering from indigestion or some other internal ailment. People are interacting with each other, but they're mostly focused on the godawful stuff going on inside. Europe has the euro mess. The Middle East has the Arab Spring. The U.S. has the economic stagnation and the debt. The Chinese have their perpetual growth and stability issues."[32] In this inwardly focused "everyone for themselves" environment, states can scarcely rely on military hardware to solve their most pressing problems. They must turn, instead, to less traditional, more subtle forms of statecraft to survive and thrive.

We see this in the anxieties of the BRICS and the kinds of power most useful for their particular needs. Like growing kids, rising economic powers are insatiably hungry for resources. To secure their required daily calories, emerging economies use trade, finance, foreign direct investment (FDI), and foreign aid as their preferred bases of power—preferred because they deliver the most bang for the buck. These tools of economic statecraft foster relationships of asymmetric dependence with poorer, resource-exporting economies—relationships in which the more powerful state gains influence within, and reliable access to the resources of, the weaker, more dependent country. Critics further claim that the terms of trade tend to favor the advanced economies and prevent the growth of functioning domestic markets within the poorer regions of the world. Not surprisingly, such strategies often inflame the inhabitants of developing countries, setting off charges of neocolonialism. Witness the backlash to Beijing's economic policies in Africa.

Pouring billions of dollars into building roads and developing the energy sector across the African continent, China has emerged as Africa's main trading partner and chief source of investment for infrastructure development. According to Chinese statistics, trade between China and Africa reached $166.3 billion in 2011, while over the past decade, African exports to China have risen from $5.6 billion to $93.2 billion. And the good times just keep rolling.[33] Recently, Lu Shaye, director-general of African affairs for the Chinese Foreign Ministry, announced that China will further open its borders to African goods by expanding the scope of African products that enjoy zero tariffs to 95 percent from the current 60 percent. In terms of FDI, China has invested billions of dollars in Africa. Writing in *China Daily*, commerce minister Chen Deming claimed that direct Chinese investment in Africa reached $14.7 billion by the end of 2011, a 60 percent increase from two years earlier. The Industrial and Commercial Bank of China alone has invested more than $7 billion in various projects across the continent.[34]

In return, China gets a steady stream of commodities and energy resources, with the continent becoming a major source of oil from Sudan and Angola, and copper from Zambia and the Democratic Republic of Congo. But that's not all it gets. China's ties with Africa have also fueled a backlash of angry feeling among Africans. Critics say that China's projects—its roads, pipelines, and ports—are mainly intended to benefit China's extractive industries, not African people.

They grumble about labor abuses, corruption, and the other downsides of being locked in a tight embrace with the resource-hungry Asian economic power. And there is substance to their complaints. In November 2011, Human Rights Watch reported that safety and labor conditions at Chinese-owned copper mines in Africa were worse than at other foreign-owned mines. The report also noted that Chinese mine managers persistently violate government regulations. One of the low points came in 2010, when a Chinese mining boss in Zambia shot nearly a dozen local miners during a riot. Finally, Chinese state-owned firms in Africa were criticized for using imported labor to build government-financed projects, such as roads and hospitals, while pumping out resources and leaving little for local economies.[35]

More generally, African leaders have accused China of taking a neocolonialist approach to the continent and exploiting Africa's natural resources. Addressing the July 2012 Forum on China-Africa Cooperation in Beijing, South African president Jacob Zuma warned that the unbalanced nature of Africa's burgeoning trade ties with China is "unsustainable" over the long term. "Africa's commitment to China's development has been demonstrated by supply of raw materials, other products, and technology transfer. This trade pattern is unsustainable in the long term. Africa's past economic experience with Europe dictates a need to be cautious when entering into partnerships with other economies."[36] These comments come from the leader of a fellow BRICS country (South Africa joined the group in 2011). Echoing Zuma's sentiments, most African nations want China to import more than just resources.

In response, President Hu Jintao attempted to repair China's neocolonial image by introducing several Africa-friendly measures at the forum. In addition to pushing for expanded African roles at the United Nations, Mr. Hu pledged $20 billion in loans to Africa—double the amount China gave the continent three years ago at the same forum; vowed to focus on cooperation in agriculture, infrastructure, cultural exchanges, and more scholarships for African students to study in China (specifically, Mr. Hu said that China will train 30,000 Africans, offer 18,000 scholarships, and send 1,500 medical personnel to Africa); and will encourage Chinese infrastructure and resources companies to expand private investment in Africa, with the goal of shifting low-end manufacturing to the continent.[37] This won't be easy, however. Chinese firms planning to move to Africa face stiff competition from other low-cost producers such as India, Bangladesh, Vietnam, Mexico, and Turkey. Moreover, as Jeremy Stevens, a Beijing-based China economist at Standard Bank, observes, "It is more costly to make something in Africa because of bottlenecks in infrastructure, human capital and access to finance, which have been exacerbated by poor governance and mismanagement."[38]

For Africans, the specifics of China's commitment to grassroots projects in Africa—how the aid will be dispersed and where it will go—will be difficult to determine, since Beijing does not clearly document its aid programs to Africa. Thus, the U.S. Congressional Research Service concluded in its assessment of China's aid programs that "China appears to administer foreign aid in an ad hoc fashion, without a centralized system, foreign aid agency and mission or a regularized funding schedule."[39] China also defines foreign aid differently than the West, claiming that roads and other infrastructure benefit the people when the real aim is to strengthen the legitimacy of the government and China's extractive capacities within the region. The bottom line is that no one can come up with an accurate number of what China actually gives, not even the Chinese themselves. Africans will simply have to take Beijing's word for it—or not.

Broadly speaking, the enhanced importance of economic power relative to military power—of internal growth and development relative to external security and territorial concerns—has both good and bad consequences for the age of entropy. On the positive side, it instills a healthy amount of caution among leaders of rival nations, even those with the type of disputes that would have sparked full-out war in the past. Examples abound. In September 2012, for instance, the long-running Sino-Japanese dispute over the islands in the East China Sea, called the Diaoyu by the Chinese and the Senkaku by the Japanese, erupted into protests in more than eighty Chinese cities. Precipitated by the Japanese government's decision to buy three of the islands from their private Japanese owners, the protest spread to urban centers where Japanese car dealerships and electronics plants were damaged, reaching a peak on the anniversary of the September 18, 1931, Mukden Incident that led to the Japanese invasion of Manchuria. While it appears that permission for the protests was granted at the highest levels, including senior members of the Politburo's Standing Committee, Beijing's handling of the dispute highlighted the interdependence of the Chinese and Japanese economies and the limitations on what the leadership could allow. At a time when overall foreign investment in China is shrinking, Japan's investment in China rose by 16 percent in 2011, reaching $12.6 billion, according to the Japan External Trade Organization, compared with $14.7 billion in the United States. Despite the outpouring of nationalism, the Chinese leadership never entertained the notion of punishing Tokyo economically for buying the islands, recognizing that such punitive actions would not only be foolish but self-defeating for China. Indeed, all of Asia would face a serious economic downturn if Japanese investments in China were threatened.[40]

China's recent restraint in this case is in sharp contrast with its behavior in 2010, when it imposed an unofficial embargo on rare earth shipments to Japan in reaction to the Senkaku/Diaoyutai Island dispute. China mines 95 percent of the world's rare earth elements, which have broad commercial and military applications and are vital to the manufacture of products as diverse as cellphones, large wind turbines, and guided missiles. The danger for China is that by using mineral embargoes to "punish" countries with which it has disputes, it runs the risk of alerting Japan and other potential rivals (including the United States) of the risks inherent in China's virtual monopoly over rare earth production, provoking efforts to open up alternative sources of supplies.[41]

Thus, economic statecraft and the benefits of trade and investment provide strong incentives for leaders to avoid not just full-blown war over disputes with their rivals but even the slightest possibility of uncontrolled escalation that could lead to such wars. That's the upside. There is a downside, however. Unable to settle their disputes on the battlefield (especially nuclear-capable rivals) and unwilling to settle them at the negotiating table, rival states will find themselves stuck in tense relations over conflicts that simmer but never quite reach the boiling point. Political scientists call this state of affairs an *enduring rivalry.* The age of entropy will be defined by these enduring rivalries: pairs of states locked in frigid relations of cold peace and cold war—relations that, incidentally, conjure up images consistent with the universe's impending heat death.

Conflict in Cyberspace

Cyberspace is the quintessential example of how the age of entropy is undermining geography and changing the nature of power, with potentially huge geopolitical implications. Indeed, the revolution in cyber capabilities over the coming decades will arguably reshuffle the geopolitical deck much like the Industrial Revolution reshaped power in the nineteenth and twentieth centuries—when mechanization not only created new industries and weapons but altered many of the basic relationships among nations and elements of power. The key questions today are:

- How will novel applications of these capabilities alter power relationships over the next several decades? Who is most likely to benefit: states, opposition movements, companies, organized crime, or individuals?
- What is the trajectory of future technologies, and how will the wide-scale application of those capabilities change power relationships among states, nonstate groups, social movements, and individuals?
- What must the United States do to ensure it prospers and maintains its national influence and power in this new environment? How must the United States adapt?

What we do know for certain about conflict in cyberspace is that it is very different from conflict in physical space—what is called traditional kinetic conflict (TKC).[42] Specifically, TKC differs from cyber conflict in five significant ways. First, military activities in TKC occur in space that is largely separate from the space in which dense civilian populations are found. In contrast, civilians are ubiquitous in the space where cyber conflict takes place. Second, offense and defense in TKC are typically in rough balance with each other; neither is inherently superior to the other. In cyber conflict, offense enjoys a huge advantage over defense because the former needs to be successful only once, whereas the latter needs to succeed every time. "Cyberwarfare is like maneuver warfare, in that speed and agility matter most"; to stay ahead of attackers, a defender "must constantly adjust and improve its defenses."[43] Third, TKC is conducted by military forces presumed to be under the control of national governments. No such presumption exists with respect to actors in cyberspace; computer viruses generally do not come with return addresses, making definitive identification of attackers extremely difficult, if not impossible. Fourth, nonstate actors produce relatively small effects (little damage) in TKC situations compared to those that can be produced by nation-states. In cyber conflict, nonstate actors are able to generate large-scale effects associated with big and powerful actors such as states; nonstate actors can compete with states because the playing field is more level than the TKC field. Finally, in TKC, power (projection) is degraded by distance, and penetrations of national boundaries are significant feats. In cyber conflict, distance is irrelevant, and penetrations of national boundaries for purposes of attack and espionage occur routinely and without notice.

Cyber conflict is stealth welfare par excellence, conducted by phantom soldiers who are effectively invisible to their enemies. One never truly knows when the cyber enemy is sharing one's space within a computer system or network, obtaining information resident on or transiting through it. Finally, the goals of cyber attacks, what they can actually achieve, are decidedly negative, namely, "to alter, disrupt, deceive, degrade, or destroy computer systems or networks," in the words of Herbert Lin.[44] Here again, we see the changed nature of power in the age of entropy. Power is increasingly about the ability to disrupt, block, disable, and destroy rather than to adopt, enable, repair, and build.

The New Global Res Publica

There is yet another way in which geography is becoming less meaningful: the blurring of the traditional boundary that separates domestic politics (what lies inside a government and its administration) and international politics (politics among states that happens outside national boundaries). In the words of political scientist James Davis, "The classical distinction between the domestic and global public spheres is being eroded by the emergence of new technologies and economies of transportation and communication as well as new actors and forms of organization and political mobilization which those technological innovations make possible."[45] A new global public domain is emerging, within which a heterogeneous collection of actors—states, NGOs, civil society organizations (CSOs), transnational corporations (TNCs)—are taking responsibility for providing public goods at the global and regional levels. "The effect of the new global public domain is not to replace states, but to embed systems of governance in broader global frameworks of social capacity and agency that did not previously exist."[46] This so-called global governance—governance beyond the nation-state— is a wide-ranging, fragmented, and partial, not global, set of policymaking processes rooted in and pursued through transnational networks.

Some tout the global governance project's political virtues, claiming that it promises to enhance political participation, individual autonomy, and the efficient and effective provision of essential goods and services. Others, correctly in my view, see it as both illegitimate and incoherent. Regarding the former, the shift in the provision of public goods from the state toward an array of international and transnational public, semipublic, and private actors undercuts fundamental aspects of constitutional rule and, therefore, democratic accountability. As Jeremy Rabkin points out,

> In democratic countries, a legislature literally 'embodies' the diversity of the nation, so that representatives of many different localities, different interests, and different opinions, can claim, in the end, to speak as one body with authority

to decide for the whole. A legislature is an institutional monument to differences among voters as well as to their willingness to be bound, in the end, by a common rule. Global governance not only thwarts or distorts the policy impulses of legislatures, but denigrates the principle that stands behind legislative authority—that a diverse electorate will accept the results of an ultimate legislative decision so that "we" can be governed in common.[47]

To alleviate the "democratic deficit" problem, proponents of cosmopolitan government call for new global institutions that would allow the participation of every eligible voter on the planet, regardless of their particular national circumstances. But, as James Davis avers, global political deliberation of this kind "is impractical, inefficient, and presumes a degree of shared values or a common 'life world' that today is lacking."[48] Clearly it would not serve the essential goal of "liberal" democracy, which is to protect the individual and minority from undue coercion by the state, majority, or other groups that would violate their basic rights. In reality, the global governance project would not empower individuals but rather unaccountable technocrats—technical experts from public-private partnerships, who the project's proponents believe would be free from the pernicious effects of politics and special interests. Alas, the search for a depoliticized global government is a chimera, and not a very pleasant one at that.

In terms of its incoherence, global governance amounts to little more than a chaotic, horizontally arranged world on automatic pilot. Just as individuals are freer than ever before to pick and choose "facts" to fit their personal beliefs, states are now able to engage in what is known as *forum shopping*, selecting from among countless international institutions the specific venues that are most likely to elicit decisions that favor their particular interests. Like the choice-enabling infosphere with its unlimited facts, the number and density of international organizations has grown exponentially over the past few decades, creating a sea of nested, partially overlapping, parallel bodies and agreements.

What some call global governance is little more than a spaghetti bowl of clashing agreements brokered within and among thirty thousand or so international organizations of varying significance, from the Inter-American Tropical Tuna Commission to the United Nations. One wonders how states make decisions and forge long-run strategies these days when it is virtually impossible for them to figure out where international authority over any issue resides and which agreements, interpretations, and implementations of rules and laws have salience and should come to dominate.

The downside is that nobody wins and nothing gets done. The upside is that no one loses. Once a state or group of states has been outmaneuvered in one venue, the "loser" merely shifts the negotiations to other parallel regimes with contradictory rules and alternative priorities. Thus, when developing countries lost at the WTO and World Intellectual Property Organization on the Trade-related Aspects of Intellectual Property Rights (TRIPS) agreement, they "regime-shifted" to the friendlier World Health Organization (WHO), Food and Agricultural Organization, and Convention on Biological Diversity, where they won. They then went back to the WTO invoking these victories and renegotiated the TRIPS agreement to have the revisions—drafted in parallel regimes—written into the global rules.

The messiness of this state of affairs contradicts a rare consensus in the field of international relations that concentrated power in the hands of one dominant state is essential to the establishment and maintenance of international order. According to the theory, the demand for international regimes is high but their supply is low because only the leadership of a hegemonic state can overcome the collective-action problems—mainly the huge start-up costs—associated with the creation of order-producing global institutions. The current world has turned this logic on its head, however. Real demand for regimes—particularly effective ones that can coerce powerful states to change their behavior and solve global problems—is low, whereas, the supply of regimes has soared.

The problem is the virtual absence of barriers to entry. Most new treaty-making and global governance institutions are being spearheaded not by an elite club of great powers (as they always have been in the past) but rather by civil-society actors and nongovernmental organizations working with middle-level states. Far from creating more order and predictability, this explosion of forums and players has increased the chaos, randomness, fragmentation, ambiguity, and impenetrable complexity of international politics. There is no locus of authority, no accountability, no measures of success. Witness the recent remarks of the WHO general-secretary, Margaret Chan: "In this overcrowded, competitive, messy, sometimes perilous and unhealthy landscape of public health, who is the boss? Who is accountable for successes and failures? Who shows the way forward and, equally important, sets the pace? Is it the country, the donors, the global health initiatives, the foundations that provide the greatest slice of funds, or the member states of WHO?"[49] Indeed, the labyrinthine structure of global governance is more complex than most of the problems it is supposed to be solving.

In addition, what little international order exists promises to become less orderly, for there is little incentive for the United States to continue to provide order
on its own. Quite the opposite. Status-quo powers pursue extroverted foreign
policies when they confront dangerous threats to their survival; otherwise, they
become introverted. None of the future great powers (poles) are especially revisionist, and there is no reason to expect any to become unlimited-aims revision-
ists in the future. Global security, therefore, is and will likely remain relatively
plentiful. This is a recipe for American retrenchment and universal shirking behavior with respect to global obligations for order management. Relatively un-
threatened but in decline, U.S. liberal internationalism will suffer a domestic
backlash against the costs of maintaining Pax Americana, as the public's mood
swings back to its tradition of foreign policy isolationism in the form of "Come
Home, America" populism. As the process of power diffusion continues and the
world flattens, a more balanced multipolarity will emerge with no single dominant power capable of providing global order. The system will then be on automatic pilot.

Discontinuous Change and Intense Corporate Warfare

Global communication networks combined with rapid and unpredictable
technological innovation have ignited fierce corporate competition, compelling
firms to abandon the traditional end-to-end vertical business model in favor of
dynamic specialization, connectivity through outsourcing and process networks,
and leveraged capability building across institutional boundaries. They have also
caused public policies to converge in the areas of deregulation, trade liberalization
and market liberalization. Never before has instability ruled the marketplace like
it does today. Frequent discontinuous change in industry structure, technological
innovation, macroeconomic trends and crises, regulatory and legal requirements,
and market and competitive forces mean that successful companies must now be
"change-capable"; they must recognize change as a constant feature of the landscape, with stability as the exception to this rule. In an environment of rising
entropy, one that is disordered and unpredictable, "strength lies not in order and
structure but in responsiveness and flexibility."[50]

All of these trends have combined to create relentless and intense competition on a global scale. So while we may indeed be looking more alike, what
precisely are the traits that we share? Sameness in the "horizontal" world of entropy, where the main challenge is not profitability but mere survival, breeds
cutthroat competitors no more likely to live in harmony with each other than the

unfortunate inhabitants of Hobbes's state of nature. Instead of shooting wars and arms buildups, we see intense corporate warfare, with firms engaging in espionage, information warfare (such as the hiring of "big gun" hackers), and guerilla marketing strategies.

The picture that emerges from these global trends at the macro level is one of historically unprecedented change consistent with increasing entropy: unprecedented hegemonic decline; an unprecedented transfer of wealth, knowledge, and economic power from West to East; unprecedented information flows; and an unprecedented rise in the number and kinds of important actors. Nonmilitary means of warfare, such as cyber-, economic-, resource-, psychological-, and information-based forms of conflict, will become more and more prevalent among state and nonstate actors. Advances in information technologies and spaced-based information systems will continue to breed innovative war-fighting synergies through combinations of advanced command and control, enhanced precision weaponry, and much improved target and surveillance capabilities. Related to these developments, the traditional battlefield will continue to see an expanding use of artificial intelligence and robotics. And because information is supreme in the twenty-first century, entities from nation-states to terrorist groups to individuals will seek to gain advantages over their adversaries by developing and mastering new tools and techniques to conduct cyber warfare.

None of this signals a future that resembles the past. To the contrary, like automatons buffeted about by forces beyond their control, we are being steered by the rise of entropy toward an ultimate state of inert uniformity and unavailable energy. Time does have a direction in international politics, and there is no going back—the initial conditions of the system have been lost forever. But entropy is not only on the rise at the level of the international system. Individuals, too, are suffering from it, primarily because the human brain was not designed to handle many of the properties characteristic of the digital revolution. This is the subject of the next chapter.

Rising Entropy at the Micro Level

Information Overload and the Advent of Truthiness

In the midst of information's increased quantity and speed of transmission, modern people may feel, as psychologist and philosopher William James did in 1899, that an "irremediable flatness is coming over the world." This is not to suggest that the world is becoming flat in Thomas Friedman's sense of greater connectivity and a more level global playing field, though this is partly occurring. Flatness here refers, instead, to a general sense of banality and loss of meaning in life. Information rains down faster and thicker by the day. Rather than a heightened sense of stimulation and awareness, information overload produces boredom and alienation.[1] Why? The answer lies in the field of economics—the study of how to allocate scarce resources.

What is scarce in the information economy? Certainly not information; we're drowning in that. What is in short supply is human attention. As the economist Herbert A. Simon explains, a "wealth of information creates a poverty of attention." This is because in "an information-rich world, the wealth of information means a dearth of something else: a scarcity of whatever it is that information consumes. What information consumes is rather obvious: it consumes the attention of its recipients."[2] Thus, modern society suffers from collective attention deficit disorder, and this problem has migrated to the front of our cultural awareness. No matter how much we pump up our brains to superhuman levels with drugs originally intended to treat Alzheimer's and narcolepsy or by means of "brain-training" games like Cogmed or Lumosity, we remain terminally distracted by Google, tweets, e-mail, power browsing, iPhones, Blackberrys, Kindles, iPads, RSS readers, Netflix, cable television, Firefox tabs, and Flickr photostreams. Finding our way in today's world requires effective strategies to allocate our limited attention efficiently among the overabundance of information sources that might consume it.

Just as human beings must learn how to drink from the fire hose, organizations, too, must figure out how to usefully and efficiently process the enormous quantity of information that either flows their way or that they themselves collect. The U.S. National Security Agency alone intercepts and stores nearly two billion separate e-mails, phone calls, and other communications every day. "The complexity of this system defies description," lamented John R. Vines, a retired army general who reviewed the Defense Department's portion of the intelligence last year. "We consequently can't effectively assess whether it is making us more safe."[3] The larger point is that wisdom does not come from greater quantities of information at our fingertips.

Personal Worlds Grounded in Truthiness

The more information is repeated and duplicated, the larger the scale of diffusion, the greater the speed of processing, the more filtering of messages, the more kinds of media through which information is passed, the more decoding and encoding and so on, the more information becomes noise. This is what is known as information entropy: the degradation of information through monotonous repetition and meaningless variety. Just as matter and energy degrade to more probable, less informative states, the more information processed or diffused, the more likely it will degrade toward meaningless variety akin to noise, information overload, or sterile uniformity. Information entropy is, in this sense, a measure of the degradation of information as a result of its transmission. The high noise levels and distortions of signals associated with information entropy are emblematic of the hugely encoded digital age, where information is lost, distorted, buried in noise, irrelevant, ambiguous, complicated, cluttered and overloaded.

Consider the effects of the infosphere: the "million-channel media universe" of talk radio, cable television, and the Internet (YouTube and the blogosphere). With so many contradictory "facts," "truths," and "informed opinions" being hurled at the public like free food on a cruise ship, people everywhere can essentially select and interpret facts in ways that accord with their own personal, idiosyncratic, and often flat-wrong versions of reality. Knowledge no longer rests on objective information but rather on seductive "true enough" facts. A truth pocked with holes but one that is "true enough" will nonetheless hold sway over those who choose to believe it because it *feels* right.

This is what the comedian Stephen Colbert calls "truthiness," the belief that feeling right is more important than being right. The U.S. invasion of Iraq was an archetype of truthiness logic. "If you *think* about it, maybe there are a few missing pieces to the rationale for war," Colbert remarked. "But doesn't taking Saddam out feel like the right thing, right here in the gut?" Truthiness drives all kinds of far-fetched but widely held political beliefs—claims that the U.S. government carried out the 9/11 attacks, that Republicans rigged the 2004 election, that HIV does not cause AIDS—as well as nonpolitical beliefs, e.g., 51 percent of Americans, including 58 percent of women, believe in ghosts; 75 percent of Americans believe in paranormal activities; 42 percent of Americans believe that "people on this earth are sometimes possessed by the devil," and so on.[4]

The point is that we have entered a new social landscape composed of personal worlds, where individuals can construct and live in their own unique, fact-resistant spaces. Our arrival at this particular destination rather than somewhere else is no accident: "personal world-dom" is precisely where the vehicles being built by today's cutting-edge technology companies are designed to take us. The purpose of Amazon, Facebook, Microsoft, Google, Apple, LinkedIn, Zynga, Instagram, and Twitter is, after all, to empower the individual by eliminating gatekeepers— the Blue Meanies who would prevent us from chasing our dreams, publishing our own books, starting our own companies, and running our own absurdly complex algorithms. Now, thanks to the powerful computing and storage facilities available to the masses via "cloud" computing, "I see the elimination of gatekeepers everywhere," proclaims Jeff Bezos, the founder of Amazon.com, who further points out, "Sixteen of the top 100 best sellers on Kindle today were self-published."[5] This explosion of new voices and startup firms may prove, on balance, to be a very good thing. But it will surely result in increasingly fractured and incoherent national and international narratives, obstructing the kind of decisive government action and international cooperation that provides needed public goods and solutions to our collective troubles.

Of course, most of us will not have a voice in this new "let a million flowers bloom" hyped future. Instead, we will supply the ears and eyeballs that observe and validate the moving and shaking activities of the nouveau billionaires.

Warmly outfitted in our Snuggies and Slankets, we will be asked merely to live comfortable and secure lives in a state of perpetual torpor, drifting in and out of consciousness on our well-worn couches. Yes, the individual is indeed taking center stage, just as the Internet and social network sages predicted. But the role is more about addiction (to the Web and games within virtual worlds), alienation, cognitive overloading, and sluggishness than heroism.

The infosphere demands our attention and distracts us from engaging in social and political activities. Americans watch an average of six hours of television a day—a habit that drains both their time and energy to respond to what they see. Plugged into the digital universe, they have become an atomized mass of self-conscious watchers who, statistics show, mostly watch alone. As voyeurism becomes an addiction, the infosphere's power to disconnect and deactivate grows. When everything and its opposite are claimed to be true, people stop trusting what they hear and the messengers from whom they hear it. Thus, Gallup reported in September 2012, that Americans' distrust of traditional media had hit a historic high, with 60 percent saying they have little or no trust in the mass media to report the news fully, accurately, and fairly; the poll also found fewer Americans closely following political news than in previous election years.[6] They either tune it all out or heavily discount the information. This produces disinterested, cynical, and solipsistic citizens—people who scarcely fit the mold of potential warriors for various political causes. Inasmuch as increasing information entropy generates ambivalent paralysis, the main political effect of the infosphere will be a joyless peace rooted in apathy.

Occasionally, the numbing silence will be interrupted by the erratic power of social media, often in the form of a pitch-perfect YouTube video that transforms a distant conflict into an online cause célèbre. Such was the case with Invisible Children's viral sensation *Kony 2012*, a thirty-minute film about the murderous activities of Uganda's Joseph Kony and the Lord's Resistance Army that began popping up on viewers' Facebook feeds when Oprah Winfrey, with her nearly 10 million Twitter followers, decided to post messages about it. Part of *Kony 2012*'s appeal to slacktivism, the pejorative term for armchair activism done mostly online by a younger generation, was the filmmaker's decision to caricature the issues and distort the facts. As Jason Russell, the co-founder of Invisible Children, explained, "No one wants a boring documentary on Africa," so "we have to make it pop, and we have to make it cool"—a process that typically entails concocting core "facts" to suit a Pixar version of a human rights story. Thus, *Kony 2012* implies that there are thirty thousand child soldiers in Mr. Kony's army, even though the entire Lord's Resistance Army, after years on the run, is believed to be down to hundreds of fighters.[7]

Do the facts matter? Not really. As most people seem to intuitively understand, *Kony 2012* was little more than a very bright and noisy explosion in the continuous fireworks display that is today's news culture, just another burst of light from nowhere that burns brightly for a moment only to be extinguished just as quickly.[8] It happens all the time. There's pink slime in our hamburgers. Click. There's an Iranian plot to assassinate a Saudi diplomat on U.S. soil. Click. Seventy-eight people, half of them women and children, burned alive by Syrian government troops in the tiny hamlet of Qubeir. Click. Apple exploits Chinese workers! Click. How about a stranger than fiction story that combines China and Syria? Appearing in a YouTube video shot in northern Syria, wearing camouflage fatigues, firing a Kalashnikov rifle, calling himself "Yusef," and denouncing the government of Bashar al-Assad in Mandarin, Bo Wang becomes the first known example of a Han citizen of China joining a jihadist group in the Arab world.[9] Click. Star Wars Kids, Obama Girl, Maru the cat. Click. Click. Click.

Far greater dangers lurk in the sea of ennui, however. For heavy information flows create not only boredom, distortions, and "flash in the pan" news stories but also psychosis and political extremism. To see this, let us return to the saga of Jason Russell. Unfortunately for him, his story didn't end with the fading away of *Kony 2012*. Far from it. Russell went temporarily iCrazy, becoming a victim of the very social media he himself had mastered and exploited. Tony Dokupil's *Newsweek* feature, "Tweets. Texts. Email. Posts. Is the Onslaught Making Us Crazy?" documents his descent into madness:

> The same digital tools that supported his [Russell's] mission seemed to tear at his psyche, exposing him to nonstop kudos and criticisms, and ending his arm-length relationship with new media.
>
> He slept two hours in the first four days, producing a swirl of bizarre Twitter updates. He sent a link to "I Met the Walrus," a short animated interview with John Lennon, urging followers to "start training your mind." He sent a picture of his tattoo, TIMSHEL, a biblical word about man's choice between good and evil. At one point he uploaded and commented on a digital photo of a text message from his mother. At another he compared his life to the mind-bending movie *Inception*, "a dream inside a dream."
>
> On the eighth day of his strange, 21st-century vortex, he sent a final tweet—a quote from Martin Luther King Jr.: "If you can't fly, then run, if you

can't run, then walk, if you can't walk, then crawl, but whatever you do, you have to keep moving forward"—and walked back into the real world. He took off his clothes and went to the corner of a busy intersection near his home in San Diego, where he repeatedly slapped at the concrete with both palms and ranted about the devil. This too became a viral video.[10]

Russell was subsequently diagnosed with "reactive psychosis," an Internet-induced form of temporary insanity. Others have what is termed Internet Addiction Disorder, which will be included for the first time in the upcoming Diagnostic and Statistical Manual of Mental Disorders. According to the director of the Semel Institute for Neuroscience and Human Behavior at UCLA, Peter Whybrow, "the computer is like electronic cocaine," stimulating cycles of mania followed by depressive spells.[11] The average teen sends or receives about 3,700 texts a month! That's double the 2007 figure. The Internet "fosters our obsessions, dependence, and stress reactions," argues Larry Rosen, a psychologist and expert on the Net's effects; it "encourages—and even promotes—insanity."[12] Little wonder that America runs on Xanax and other antidepression drugs.

Individual psychosis is just one aspect of the Internet's contribution to the great American crack-up.[13] Political extremism is yet another deleterious societal effect, as old as hyperlinks themselves, that is poisoning our collective mind. More and more people are turning to conservative and liberal blogs for news and commentary, with little cross-traffic between them. Composed of countless moneymaking operations competing for eyeballs, the infosphere predictably treats politics as entertainment, as mere titillation to escape the boredom. Its audience demands heat, not light; thoughtful analysis, after all, is often tedious. The more extreme the views, the louder the opinions expressed, the more outlandish the caricatures, the more mindless the debate, the better. Whether it tunes in or drops out, the public has allowed, even encouraged, the political conversation to be hijacked by extremists—whose dogmatic views, demagoguery, and often utterly delusional thinking further polarize our politics and decrease our ability to reconcile differing views.

A likely consequence of this polarization within national societies is that individuals will now be more disposed than in the past to hold cross-national, supranational and subnational loyalties, identities, and attachments. Consider the growth of hacktivist organizations such as Anonymous, a leaderless global movement opposed to state institutions and companies that work with them. Consider, too, the new strategic geography of the worldwide grid of global cities that connects major international business and financial centers, including New York, London, Tokyo, Paris, Frankfurt, Zurich, Amsterdam, Los Angeles, Sydney, Hong Kong, Sao Paulo, Shanghai, Bangkok, Taipei, and Mexico City. The intensity of market, financial, and investment transactions among these cities makes this new strategic space an ideal breeding ground for the formation of transnational identities and communities. While the proliferation of these types of interaction opportunities could facilitate bridge building across groups, there is little reason to expect conflict-dampening links to emerge among highly polarized, fact-resistant individuals and groups.

Structural Entropy at the Micro Level

To this point, the discussion has focused on rising information entropy—systemic processes and emerging properties associated with the digital-information revolution—and its effects on individuals and groups at the system's micro level. The rise of structural entropy, too, has implications for micro-level phenomena. These effects, however, are mostly social and psychological rather than political. Given the concerns of the present work, therefore, the following analysis of structural entropy at the micro level will be rather brief and deliberately more sketchy than the prior discussions regarding the other three cells presented in Table 2.1.

There are two broad aspects of the emerging system's structure that are of particular interest with respect to the micro level. First is the virtual nature of reality and the anonymity of cyberspace, which have opened up new political, social, and normative spaces—virtual worlds within which individuals and groups can now behave for all intents and purposes unconstrained by established social norms and moral codes. The other structural-systemic property that exerts considerable causal weight at the micro level is what might be called "the inherent unknowability of the emerging world." As global entropy rises, the exponentially increasing speed, complexity, and unpredictability of the world make it that much more difficult to comprehend. One behavior consequence of this unintelligibly complex state of affairs is that leaders can be expected to impose, with bad results, unjustifiable certainty on inherently uncertain situations.

Social Aspects of Cyberspace

Just like the communication breakthroughs that preceded it (print, radio, telephone, television), the Internet has been said to promote both pro-social and antisocial behaviors. On the bright side, Internet tools such as social media allow individuals to share information and develop relationships with people on a massive scale at the click of mouse. Little wonder that online networking has become an indispensable tool for political groups to reach and organize targeted members (e.g., union leaders seeking to connect with workers). Indeed, many liberal observers believe that the democratization of communications and connection technologies will bring about the democratization of the world.[14] According to this favorite view of the Internet, large numbers of citizens, armed with nothing but cell phones, take part in rebellions that challenge the authority of their nondemocratic political leaders and regimes. The Internet facilitates the formation of transnational virtual communities that empower citizens to confront their governments; it has given birth to what some have called a new "interconnected estate," "a place where any person with access to the Internet, regardless of living standard or nationality, is given a voice and the power to effect change."[15]

On the darker side, a recent psychological study found that too much time spent on social networking sites, such as Facebook, Twitter, MySpace, and Google+, can cause teens to develop narcissistic tendencies, antisocial behaviors, mania, and aggressive tendencies. "While nobody can deny that Facebook has altered the landscape of social interaction, particularly among young people, we are just now starting to see solid psychological research demonstrating both the positives and the negatives," said Larry Rosen, professor of psychology at California State University, where the study was conducted.[16]

What is beyond debate is that social identity, social interaction, and relationship formation are very different on the Internet than in real life. Studies have shown that virtual environments allow individuals to dramatically alter their self-representation, creating online personas that are wildly different from their real-world ones.[17] Antisocial, norms-transgressing behaviors abound within the myriad virtual worlds from which we may choose to operate anonymously. These behaviors include carrying out illegal activities, such as gambling and selling fake products; propagating offensive pornographic materials; cyberbullying; distributing libelous, unfounded, and misleading statements about people; and cheating others through clever scams. Much of this antisocial behavior is related to Internet addiction disorders (IAD) or what some call pathological Internet use (PIU), such as *cybersexual addiction*, spending excessive amounts of time on adult cyberporn websites; *cyber-relationship addiction*, becoming heavily involved in online relationships; *Net compulsions*, obsessively gambling, shopping online, instant messaging; *information overload*, displaying compulsive web surfing and database searches; and *computer game addiction*, obsessively playing online games.[18]

In short, the virtual nature of reality in cyberspace offers an environment for seemingly normal people to engage in all sorts of antisocial behaviors. While these antisocial aspects are surely worth pointing out, their effects are more psychological, social, and cultural than they are in any sense political, much less political in an "international relations" sense. For this reason and because it is still far too early to reach any firm conclusions regarding the effects of the Internet on human nature and behavior (especially with respect to future generations), it makes little sense for the purposes of this book to dwell on this topic, so I won't.

Misplaced Certainty in an Increasingly Unknowable World

Everyone agrees that international politics takes place in a mostly uncertain environment. Within the anarchic realm of international politics, structural uncertainty always operates as a permissive cause of conflict, and security dilemmas and conflict spirals are purportedly rooted in that uncertainty. However, leaders that must make decisions in the moment face more proximate uncertainties, and the pressure to decide often leads them prematurely and unjustifiably to impose certainty on their environment.[19]

Excessive and unwarranted certainty arises for many reasons, both political and psychological. Leaders, especially those operating in domestic systems in which power is decentralized, oversell their policies, particularly when they call for widespread and deep sacrifices from the citizenry.[20] Sometimes elites come to believe their own exaggerated rhetoric, invented myths, and self-serving propaganda for subconscious psychological reasons. Motivated cognitive biases, for instance, may cause them to blur the line between sincere belief and tactical argument, valid strategic arguments and opportunistic strategic rhetoric, fact and fiction.[21] Moreover, psychological experiments have shown that people tend to treat extremely probable outcomes as if they were certain (the so-called certainty effect).[22]

Excessive certainty also results from the desire of intelligence analysts to please policymakers either by telling them what they want to hear or, more normally, "by being able to reach a firm conclusion rather than writing in the typical and disliked style of 'on the one hand, on the other hand.'"[23] Under many circumstances, however, honest intelligence warns its consumers to be sensitive about the lack of good evidence—the kind of evidence that would be required to reach certainty about a situation; that is, good intelligence often asks decision makers to be less certain about their conclusions. Policymakers, however, rarely welcome uncertainty, which is why they often call for better intelligence but usually don't want it.[24]

Thus, before the U.S. invasion of Iraq in 2003, key members of the Bush administration claimed to be absolutely certain that Saddam Hussein was hiding weapons of mass destruction (WMD) and had ties to al-Qaeda. Despite the usual gaps and discrepancies in the available intelligence information, the Bush administration made its case in terms that were "clearer than truth," as Dean Acheson would have put it.[25] Thus, at the national convention of the Veterans of Foreign Wars on August 26, 2002, Vice President Dick Cheney framed the matter in no uncertain terms: "Simply stated, there is no doubt that Saddam Hussein now has weapons of mass destruction. . . . There is no doubt that he is amassing them to use against our friends, against our allies, and against us."[26] Even if we grant that Cheney made his point "clearer than truth" to gin up public and legislative support for the war, few would disagree that he and other top officials were extremely confident that Iraq had weapons of mass destruction. We now know that this was false and that the Bush administration's "certain knowledge" to justify preventive war was misplaced.[27]

If one has complete and correct knowledge of all the relevant information, then certainty is warranted. In most situations, however, certainty is unwarranted. Let us call this type of cognitive error *misplaced certainty* and define it as a situation in which uncertainty has been prematurely eliminated. Thus understood, misplaced certainty is comprised of two equally important dimensions. First, the decision-maker's subjective probability estimates do not line up with objective probabilities. Mistakes of this kind are, in some sense, inevitable: decision-makers rarely, if ever, know all the relevant information and so are always placing bets to some extent. Seen in this light, international politics is like the stock market: longs bet that a stock will go up, while shorts bet that it will go down; both sides cannot be correct.[28] Both have some degree of confidence in their assessment, but one of the traders must be misestimating the future price of the stock. Most everyday decisions are low-risk, low-cost bets under uncertainty, and mistakes are common.

Misplaced certainty, however, is not merely a mistake or bad bet. It is a bet placed without recognition that it is only a bet. Instead, the bettor rigidly and persistently imposes a singular reading of the situation, confident that the bet will be confirmed even though the evidence is indeterminate. The mind "seizes and freezes," as Arie Kruglanski and Donna Webster put it.[29] It is this unwarranted cognitive closure, which follows the initial imposition of certainty, that distinguishes misplaced certainty from a mere mistake. Mistakes are cases in which one chooses, sometimes with exaggerated and arrogant confidence, a course of action but then realizes that the initial judgment was mistaken and changes course. Trumped by reality, this preliminary hubris is eventually replaced by a measure of humility. With misplaced certainty, in contrast, new information that objectively undermines one's beliefs and assumptions does not result in less certainty about the initial judgment. Rather, certainty about the situation hardens over time, even in the face of incoming information that clearly contradicts the assessments at the core of the decision. Discrepant information is either manipulated to support the initial judgment or ignored.

Misplaced certainty is an information processing error, the result of a bias. It might have cognitive roots—the limits of human cognitive capacities in complex environments induce decision-makers to rely on shortcuts such as heuristics or analogical thinking rather than looking to update existing "prior" beliefs in the light of new evidence.[30] Or it might have affective roots—a subconscious psychological need to see objects we value (people, policies, or states) in a certain way that causes blind spots in information processing, so-called motivated bias.[31] Whatever its cause, its effect is to render decision-makers unable to process information or update correctly, which can cause bad decisions that result in unnecessary conflict.

Consider, for example, Cheney's apparent certainty about Iraq's WMD and links to al-Qaeda. At several points he acknowledged that the physical evidence did not yet support his certainty. But he confidently asserted that what the United States needed was one more informant, one more hiding place, and so on. What makes this a case of misplaced certainty is not that it led to a bad outcome but that Cheney's judgment reflected a disconnect between what the world was telling him and his cognitive-affective response. It's not just that his assumptions were wrong but his certain belief in those assumptions, given countervailing evidence, that makes it a case of misplaced certainty. Even if Cheney had been proven right eventually, his certainty was misplaced.[32]

Of course, misplaced certainty in world politics is not an altogether new phenomenon. Consider, for example, British certainty in the 1930s that the Germans possessed an aerial "knockout blow," which Hitler would not hesitate to unleash if provoked by the West; Israel's certainty that Egypt and Syria would not attack in October 1973; Russia's certainty that Japan posed no real military threat in 1904; or British certainty in 1915 that Gallipoli would be an easy victory.[33] In all of these cases, unwarranted confidence about an adversary's capabilities or intentions, or both, formed and persisted in the face of disconfirming evidence.

Obviously misplaced certainty is not altogether new, but as global entropy rises over the coming decades, it will become increasingly widespread with damaging results. The post-fact world of the age of entropy provides richly fertile ground for this type of information-processing error: it is easier than ever to impose certainty on uncertain situations and then, despite evidence to the contrary, steadfastly cling to one's mistaken judgment. With so many facts to choose from, people can avoid confronting their lack of understanding about complex cause-and-effect relationships. Psychologists call this the "illusion of explanatory depth," whereby we typically feel that we understand how complex systems work even when our true understanding is superficial. It is not until we are asked to explain how such a system works that we realize how little we actually know.[34] Dangerous consequences often follow such illusions. As the popular nineteenth-century American humorist Artemus Ward famously quipped, "It ain't so much the things we don't know that get us in trouble. It's the things we know that just ain't so."[35]

Moreover, as the world becomes increasingly unknowable and events more random, it is not just the ease of reaching cognitive closure by imposing certainty on a messy reality that increases. The incentives and temptations for doing so grow stronger as well. It is entirely understandable, after all, that decision-makers finding themselves in crisis situations that require bold and timely decisions should, under the pressure to act decisively, seek and succumb to the comforts of certainty, real or imagined. But like the sweet and alluring song of the Sirens, it is an appeal that is hard to resist but, if heeded, may lead to dire consequences.

I conclude with a brief but nonetheless illustrative anecdote that epitomizes much of what has been discussed in this chapter. The first debate between President Obama and the Republican challenger, Mitt Romney, drew media criticism from several sides of the spectrum, most loudly from the left, focused on the moderator, Jim Lehrer. The left accused Mr. Lehrer of having lost control of the debate to Mitt Romney, who, they claim, "ran all over him like a truck crushing a bug."[36] Richard Kim of the *Nation* concluded that Lehrer's style of moderation "is fundamentally unequipped to deal with the era of post-truth, asymmetric polarization politics—and it should be retired."[37] Only in an age of entropy would a statement like this one be quoted without explanation in the *New York Times*, whose editors must have assumed its readership could easily decipher the meaning of the phrase "post-truth, asymmetric polarization politics." Such a phrase would have made little sense to most anyone twenty-five years ago. It makes plenty of sense today, and this is one of the big ways that the world we live in is vitally different from everything that has come before it. Information entropy is rising, politics are polarizing, and truths—the things we know that just ain't so—are more idiosyncratic, malleable, and dangerous than ever.

Maxwell's Demon and Angry Birds

Big Data to the Rescue?

If and when we reach a state of maximum entropy, much of international poli-tics as we know it will have ended. It will be a world full of fierce international competition and corporate warfare but little traditional military balancing; information overload, boredom, apathy, low levels of attention and trust, and continued extremism; powerful nonstate identities that frustrate purposeful na-tional action and impede international cooperation; and new non-geographic political spaces that bypass the state, favor low-intensity warfare strategies, and undermine the formation of stable alliances. Is there anything we can do to fore-stall or even escape this future? Or are we doomed by it, with no choice but to adapt? Perhaps, like scientists, we should search for the answer in an allegory.

Modern science regularly employs allegory as thought experiments that bridge the gap between visible reality and the invisible realm of theory, between the concrete and the abstract. Allegory often combines human and divine char-acteristics within the form of a demon: an agent of communication that typically performs the function of messenger, guardian, or sage, depending on what the larger allegorical scheme demands.

Arguably the most famous of all scientific demons is the "very observant and neat-fingered being" invented in 1867 by the British physicist James Clerk Maxwell to counteract increasing entropy and the relentless drift to thermal equilibrium as mandated by the Second Law. How does the demon defeat entropy? By sorting molecules. Maxwell's demon is a sorter extraordinaire, who performs the impossible operation of sorting slower and faster molecules into separate vessels without expenditure of work.[1]

Recognizing the probabilistic nature of rising entropy and seeking to outwit chance, James Clerk Maxwell imagined "a creature whose talents are so extraordinary, that it can trace the orbit of each molecule. The demon guards a door between two volumes of a gas with different temperatures. It allows only the fast molecules from the cold side to pass and only the slow molecules from the hot side."[2] Thus, the cold side becomes colder, the warm side warmer, and entropy thereby decreases.

More specifically, Maxwell's thought experiment supposes two vessels, A and B, divided by a wall (CD), within which there is a frictionless sliding door. Both vessels contain an equal number of molecules in a state of agitation, striking each other and the sides of the vessels and the wall that separates them. The demon, strategically positioned by the frictionless sliding door, possesses the superhuman capacity to (1) observe individual molecules, (2) know their paths and velocities, and (3) by opening and closing the sliding door, sort the molecules, allowing certain ones heading for the hole to pass from one vessel through to the other. By selecting molecules with more than the mean square velocity of A and allowing them to pass from B into A, and by selecting molecules with less than the mean square velocity of B and allowing them to pass from A into B, the demon reverses the natural tendency of heat to pass from hotter to colder regions. The number of molecules in each vessel remains the same but the energy in A increases (A gets hotter) and that in B diminishes (B gets colder). And no work is done, no energy expended. The Second Law is thereby circumvented by nimble sorting.

Now let us return to the earlier example of the thoroughly shuffled deck of cards. It was not entirely correct of me to say that the disorder from shuffling can never be undone. The statement holds true only if your activity is limited to absent-minded shuffling. If you were not so limited, you could easily sort the cards back into their original order or any order you so choose. The point is that, unlike Nature, human beings can undo the disorder caused by the introduction of a random element; we can not only shuffle absent-mindedly but also sort, order, and arrange. In the words of Henry Adams, "Chaos [is] the law of nature, Order . . . the dream of man."[3]

Maxwell's Demon Is a Big Data Cyberazzi

There is an emerging Maxwell's demon in today's world. It is a super-intelligent sorter, the likes of which the world has never seen before. It can scarcely be called a savior, however, certainly not for international politics. In the age of entropy, Maxwell's demon is Big Data.[4] IBM estimates that 2.5 quintillion (that's seventeen zeros!) new bytes of data are generated every day (90 percent of which was created in the past two years)—information that Big Data fashions into personal profiles for the purpose of targeting advertisements more accurately.[5]

It would be wrong, however, to understand this revolution solely in terms of the massive amount of information collected. Big Data is also distinguished by its quest to take all aspects of life and turn them into data, a process that has been called *datafication*.[6] Location, words, friendships and "likes," even people's posteriors are being "datafied," transformed into numerically quantified formats. The core idea driving the rise of Big Data is that "we can learn from a large body of information things that we could not comprehend when we used only smaller amounts."[7] In the age of entropy, Maxwell's demon is a particular data giant, whose 23,000 computer servers process 50 trillion "data transactions" a year, mapping, sorting, and sharing our "consumer genome." Its name is the Acxiom Corporation, a "data broker" headquartered in Little Rock, Arkansas, and analysts say that it has amassed the world's largest commercial database on consumers. Few people have ever heard of this quiet leader of the multibillion-dollar database marketing industry. But Acxiom certainly knows who you are, what you do, where you live, your race, sex, weight, height, marital status, education level, political preferences, buying habits, household health concerns, vacation dreams, and much, much more. After all, knowing everything about you is the business Acxiom is in, and it is a lucrative one. With customers ranging from Toyota and Ford, to Macy's, E*Trade, Wells Fargo, and HSBC, Acxiom posted profit of $77.26 million dollars in 2011–2012, on sales of $1.13 billion.[8]

In the hyperkinetic world of digital advertising these days, powerful algorithms use myriad data points to size us up based on what we Google, what sites we visit, what ads we click. The chance to show us an advertisement is then auctioned to the highest bidder (among marketers seeking to identify their best prospects and pitch them before they move on to the next Web page). All of this happens in milliseconds, and the entire process is invisible. This worries some regulators and consumer advocates, who see the emergence of a "computer-generated class system," of an "ad-driven Internet powered by surveillance."[9]

Like helpless molecules in Maxwell's original thought experiment, we are being observed, understood, and super-sorted—captured before we know it. Sophisticated biometric data-gathering systems can identify us through voice-, facial-, and vein-pattern recognition software. Have you had your palm scanned yet? If not, you will.[10] In the age of entropy, Maxwell's demon is a Big Data cyberazzi. In a broader sense, however, we are all becoming Maxwell's demons of sorts. To explain this, a brief digression on the social significance of games is needed.

Scholars who study games (yes, they exist) have shown that they reflect the societies and times in which they were born and popularized. Thus, Monopoly, a game that allowed anyone to pretend to be a tycoon, arrived during the Great Depression; Risk, a literal expression of Cold War realpolitik, appeared in the 1950s; and Twister, the first popular American game to use human bodies as playing pieces, captured the sexual revolution of the 1960s; one critic branded it "sex in a box."[11] The next blockbuster was Trivial Pursuit. Called "the biggest phenomenon in game history" by Time magazine,[12] Trivial Pursuit is a board game in which progress is determined by a player's ability to answer general knowledge and popular culture questions; that is, the game rewards the player who has stored the largest amount of meaningless information. Not coincidentally, the popularity of Trivial Pursuit peaked with over 20 million games sold in 1984—a time of transition to the information age, spanning from the advent of the personal computer in the late 1970s to the Internet's reaching a critical mass in the early 1990s. Then entropy began its steady rise in world politics.

As the Berlin Wall fell in 1989, signaling the collapse of the Soviet satellite system and the onset of the Cold War's endgame, Tetris became a global addiction. Invented in 1984 in a Soviet computer lab, the game did not become popular until Nintendo's Game Boy was bundled with a Tetris cartridge. Sam Anderson writes, "The enemy in Tetris is not some identifiable villain (Donkey Kong, Mike Tyson, Carmen Sandiego) but a faceless, ceaseless, reasonless force that threatens constantly to overwhelm you, a churning production of blocks against which your only defense is a repetitive, meaningless sorting."[13] Voila! The enemy is disorder, randomness, chaos, and our task is to sort—repetitively, meaninglessly. You may be thinking, "No one plays Tetris anymore." Not true. Tetris has sold more than 100 million copies for cell phones alone since 2005 and has spawned dozens of "touchscreen puzzle-block" spinoffs.[14] The game Unify, for instance, is simply a bidirectional form of Tetris, in which colored blocks drift in from opposite edges of the screen and meet in the middle. Anderson continues, "In the nearly 30 years since Tetris's invention—and especially over the last five, with the rise of smartphones—Tetris and its off-spring (Angry Birds, Bejeweled, Fruit Ninja, etc.) have colonized our pockets and our brains and shifted the entire economic model of the video-game industry. Today we are living, for better and worse, in a world of stupid games."[15]

In the age of entropy, we are all Maxwell's demons. Some of us will never be more than mere clumsy, naïve demons; while others, particularly those of the new and yet-to-come generations, will become super-intelligent, nimbly fingered demons. Thus, as the amount of information grows seemingly beyond our reckoning—to the point that we shout back, "TMI! Enough already!"—we become ever more adroit information processors. Storing, manipulating, and sharing knowledge, we have become expert users of information technology; we stream information, filter it, save it, text it, sort it, and Google it.[16] While we cannot reverse the process of information overload, we can figure out how best to adapt and maybe even learn how to turn floods of information into useful and reliable knowledge. Creating order from disorder is, after all, humankind's most essential and ubiquitous task. We are constantly pushing back against the natural forces of dissipation, chaos, and randomness, fighting against the rising tide of entropy that threatens to engulf us. As the father of cybernetics, Norbert Wiener, poetically observed, "We are swimming upstream against a great torrent of disorganization, which tends to reduce everything to the heat death of equilibrium and sameness. . . . This heat death in physics has a counterpart in the ethics of Kierkegaard, who pointed out that we live in a chaotic moral universe. In this, our main obligation is to establish arbitrary enclaves of order and system. . . . Like the Red Queen, we cannot stay where we are without running as fast as we can."[17]

Wiener's insight—*that our main obligation is to establish arbitrary enclaves of order*—is the key to finding a remedy for increasing entropy in international politics. Unlike in Nature, the process of entropy can be arrested and undone in world politics. But there are two requirements for this reversal to happen: (1) a benevolent and powerful hegemon that is willing to provide and manage an international order—one broadly if not universally recognized as legitimate—and (2) an international landscape wiped clean of its inefficient international institutions, leaving a tabula rasa upon which the newly crowned hegemon (which may be the old hegemon in what amounts to a second term of global leadership, such as the one Britain received after its coalition defeated Napoleonic France in 1815) can create an efficient and workable global architecture. At the zenith of its power, a hegemonic leader is tantamount to Anaxagoras's Mind (Nous), the sorting action of which supplies order (Cosmos) from Chaos. But how can such a global power and institutional transformation take place without a major war or other cataclysmic event to reboot the system? Is there some other way to hit the reset button?

The only solution is an enormous shock to the system, a calamity of huge proportions that cracks through the closed system's outer crust and injects the world with new, useful energy to do work again. Aside from, perhaps, an appalling natural disaster, global pandemic, or series of coordinated worldwide terrorist attacks against major cities, such as New York, Tokyo, Berlin, London, Paris—cures surely worse than the disease—there is no force other than a hegemonic war that can fix the problem, no other engine of destruction that can set the stage for global renewal. A technological fix may arrive in time to save the day. But technology is a large part of the problem; it is difficult to imagine how it becomes the solution.

Catastrophes: Mechanisms of Change and Renewal

Great catastrophes may not necessarily give birth to genuine revolutions, but they infallibly herald them and make it necessary to think, or rather to think afresh about the universe.[18]

—FERNAND BRAUDEL (INAUGURAL LECTURE GIVEN
TO THE COLLÈGE DE FRANCE, DECEMBER 1, 1950)

The principle of creative destruction lies at the core of most processes of change. One observes a cyclical pattern: an original period of stasis and equilibrium followed by a period of chaotic destabilization (turbulence), which then establishes a second equilibrium that may differ radically from the one that preceded the initial destructive disruption. This pattern, known as *punctuated equilibrium*, describes not only change in the natural world but also socioeconomic and political change.[19] Most important to the present concerns, it is the time-honored dynamic that has triggered the most significant changes in world politics.

Deep-seated change most often comes in one of two guises: (1) low-probability events known as fatal discontinuities that "change everything" in an instant and (2) persistent, gradually unfolding trends (political, demographic, environmental, social, technological, energy, and economic shifts) that have no less far-reaching consequences over the long term.[20] Rising global entropy is a gradually unfolding trend, which can be reversed by a fatal discontinuity that wipes the slate clean and sets the course of world history on a different track. The twenty-first century offers many potential hazards that could result in a fatal discontinuity. As Martin Rees, the Cambridge don and Astronomer Royal, conjectures:

> Populations could be wiped out by lethal "engineered" airborne viruses; human character may be changed by techniques far more targeted and effective than the nostrums and drugs familiar today; we may even one day be threatened by rogue Nanomachines that replicate catastrophically, or by super intelligent computers. . . . Experiments that crash atoms together with immense force could start a chain reaction that erodes everything on Earth; the experiments could even tear the fabric of space itself, an ultimate "Doomsday" catastrophe whose fallout spreads at the speed of light to engulf the entire universe.[21]

While fascinating and imaginative, these scenarios, especially the latter ones, seem exceedingly unlikely. There are, however, many other potential "global catastrophe" candidates that could materialize and cause upward of 10 million fatalities or $10 trillion dollars worth of economic loss—any one of which might, in some ways, substitute for hegemonic war as a cataclysmic cure for rising international entropy.[22] These include an immensely diverse collection of events ranging from volcanic mega-eruptions to viral pandemics, nuclear wars to large-scale terrorist attacks, out-of-control scientific experiments to climatic changes, encounters with extraterrestrial objects to economic collapse.[23] Of these, a nuclear exchange between India and Pakistan or China or a nuclear war in the Middle East involving Iran and Israel are more probable than most of the others. But the emergence of a deadly viral pandemic caused by a disease passing from animals to humans seems the most likely candidate of all as the source of the next global catastrophe, one on a similar scale as past hegemonic wars.

Modern technology and globalization have connected viruses to humanity in dangerous ways. SARS, HIV, Ebola, and avian influenza are well known enough that their mere mention makes us anxious. So far, humanity has been very lucky, especially over the past couple of generations. As the Stanford University biologist and director of global viral forecasting Nathan Wolfe points out: "We would have to call [HIV] the biggest near-miss of our lifetime. Can you imagine how many people would already have died if HIV could be transmitted by a cough?"[24] How long before our luck runs out?

Suppose we remain lucky with respect to pandemics. There will always be embittered loners, fanatics, social misfits, and dissident groups. Advances in technology will beget far more deadly and accessible instruments of terror and destruction than we have today; instant global communications will augment their societal impact. How long can we hope to survive in a future world with hundreds of independent fingers on the button of a doomsday machine?

Of course, doomsday scenarios are not new to this century. At the turn of the last century, H. G. Wells gave his provocative lecture "The Discovery of the Future" at the Royal Institution in London in 1902, wherein he provided a list of potential catastrophes that ends with the certain heat death of the universe by the forces of entropy:

> One must admit that it is impossible to show why certain things should not utterly destroy and end the entire human race and story, why night should not presently come down and make all our dreams and efforts vain. It is conceivable, for example, that some great unexpected mass of matter should presently rush upon us out of space, whirl sun and planets aside like dead leaves before the breeze, and collide with and utterly destroy every spark of life upon this earth . . . that some pestilence may presently appear, some new disease, that will destroy, not 10 or 15 or 20 per cent of the earth's inhabitants as pestilences have done in the past, but 100 per cent; and so end our race . . . that some great disease of the atmosphere, some trailing cometary poison, some great emanation of vapour from the interior of the earth . . . [or] new animals to prey upon us by land and sea, and there may come some drug or a wrecking madness into the minds of men. And finally, there is the reasonable certainty that this sun of ours must radiate itself toward extinction; that, at least, must happen; it will grow cooler and cooler, and its planets will rotate ever more sluggishly until some day this earth of ours, tideless and slow moving, will be dead and frozen, and all that has lived upon it will be frozen out and done with. There surely man must end. That of all such nightmares is the most insistently convincing.[25]

Perhaps betraying himself as a naïve optimist of sorts, Wells concluded the lecture by saying that he does not believe "in these things because I have come to believe in certain other things—in the coherency and purpose in the world and in the greatness of human destiny. Worlds may freeze and suns may perish, but there stirs something within us now that can never die again."[26] To date, all have turned out to be failed forecasts, thankfully, with the exception of the concluding sanguine one. This is not terribly surprising, for, as Francis Bacon noted four hundred years ago, the most important advances are usually the least predictable.[27]

Alas, Doomsday Events Are No Substitutes for Hegemonic War

Cataclysmic events share two important characteristic with hegemonic wars: they shake things up and result in great losses of blood and treasure. Indeed, war is the most destructive form of human behavior, and its consequences are as deep as they are wide: profound losses in economic development, environmental devastation, the spread of disease, state expansion, militarized societies, disrupted families, and traumatized people. In its profoundly disruptive effects on society, economics, and politics, war resembles epidemics, which also "have the capacity to induce profound turmoil but often function as catalysts of change, generating transformation in the belief structures of survivors, in the micro- and macro-level social and economic structures of affected polities, in the relations between the state and society, and ultimately between countries."[28] More generally, war determines the changing shape of world politics, the institutional structures and cultures within states, and the trajectory of history itself.[29]

But war is not merely a cataclysmic event, a natural catastrophe; it is a political act. The military's mission is to kill people and break things; its skill is the management and application of violence. It is the political purpose of that violence that fundamentally distinguishes war from an act of mass murder. Under the direction and coordination of political leaders, soldiers fight on behalf of a larger collective political unit to advance the goals of the collectivity or, at least, of its leadership.[30] As Carl von Clausewitz famously stressed in *On War*, his classic unfinished work on war and military strategy, war is a "political instrument, a continuation of political activity by other means. . . . The political object is the goal, war is the means of reaching it, and means can never be considered in isolation from their purpose."[31] War in the Clausewitzian model is the rational control of violence to serve political ends. And it is precisely the political ends of hegemonic wars that distinguish them and the crucial international-political functions they perform—most important, crowning a new hegemonic king and wiping the global institutional slate clean—from mere cataclysmic global events. Indeed, without a hegemonic war, the world is less likely than if one were fought to escape the kinds of catastrophic events that appear as substitutes for hegemonic wars. Why? The answer is bound up with the larger question: what is the source of international order? The key is the relationship between hegemonic wars and the provision of global public goods.

What Is a Global Public Good?

Preventing global pandemics, averting asteroid strikes, mitigating the effects of climate change, securing "loose nukes" are all examples of global public goods; they make people everywhere better off and, as such, are universally desired.[32] Public goods are defined by two characteristics: they are nonexcludable and non-rival. Once a public good is provided, no one can be excluded from partaking of it (the concept of nonexcludability); and one's enjoyment of the good does not impinge on the consumption opportunities of others; that is, an individual's use of the good does not reduce the availability of the good to others and the benefit that one receives must neither be seriously impaired by another's enjoying the good nor come at the expense of another's enjoyment (the concept of nonrivalry).[33] Examples of public goods include a beautiful scenic view, national defense, bridges, clean air, and street lights. Seems like a win-win situation; everyone enjoys and benefits from the provision of public goods, so there should be lots of them, right? Wrong. Because no one (not even those that do not contribute) can be excluded from enjoying a public good once it has been supplied, public goods are often underprovided or not provided at all. Oddly, the problem is not one of collective irrationality but collective rationality: people tend to act rationally to the incentive structure of a public good. Let me explain.

The provision of a public good typically requires small contributions from a large number of people, such that each individual contribution makes little difference (is relatively insignificant) to the overall amount required for the good's provision. This means that one's contribution is costly to oneself but has no appreciable effect on the outcome of whether the good is supplied or not. There is no rational reason, therefore, to contribute, especially given the good's property of nonexcludability. The rational incentive is, instead, to ride free on the efforts of others. Of course, some people will contribute because it is the right thing to do whether others contribute or not. But if most people act rationally and attempt to ride free on the contributions of others, the good will not be provided; in which case, one is still better off having not paid for a benefit they will not receive. So either way—whether the public good is provided or not—one is better off free-riding than contributing to the public good.

This is where the state's coercive institutions come into the story. Institutions are designed to change and mold incentives; that is what they are meant to do. The underprovision of public goods rests on the "free-rider" or "collective action" problem. The distinct incentive structure of collective action and public goods results in a perverse system effect: individual rationality produces collectively suboptimal outcomes. The solution to this incentive problem—to overcoming the failings of volunteerism in situations when it is rational to shirk—is enforcement through fear. Just as the Mob has vicious enforcers to keep people in line, the state has coercive institutions (such as the Internal Revenue Service) that compel citizens to contribute their fair share to the provision of national public goods, ensuring that they are supplied in abundance. Taxation and regulation (for example, that limits the emissions of polluters in order to provide the public good of clean air) are the two most common institutional mechanisms by which governments solve the free-rider problem. The state extracts resources from the people via taxation to fill its coffers and war chest. These revenues are then channeled into what the state deems to be national public goods—building infrastructure (e.g., roads and bridges) or the coercive machinery of the state (the military and police), so as to provide internal and external security or to project power abroad for purpose of national growth and expansion—which are then delivered to and enjoyed by not just its citizens but anyone living within the state's borders. Employing its coercive power to impose penalties for shirking behavior, the state changes the citizenry's incentives, compelling individuals and firms to contribute their fair share to, and to behave in ways consistent with, the national public good.[34]

There is no equivalent to the coercive state in the realm of international politics. States are sovereign. This means that there is no authority above them, no world government, no supranational institution with the power to tax and regulate states, no sovereign arbiter to make and enforce agreements among them. There are instead nearly two hundred states, each recognized by international law as sovereigns over their territorial boundaries. Simply put, the ordering principle of international politics is anarchy. What this means is that, in the absence of a powerful hegemonic state that is both able and willing to provide global public goods solely by means of its own efforts, the provision of global public goods depends on the voluntary efforts of states—on international cooperation under conditions of anarchy. Given the logic of the collective action and the free-rider problem, it is no wonder that global public goods have been underprovided or not provided at all.

Nevertheless, global public goods have existed in the past and continue to exist. They are most prevalent during the zenith of a powerful hegemon's reign, particularly those of liberal hegemons like Great Britain in the nineteenth century and the United States in the twentieth and twenty-first centuries. The creation and crowning of new hegemons is one of the core functions of hegemonic wars; this is why such wars usher in unmatched periods of durable and productive peace.

Remember, hegemonic wars perform three essential political tasks that restore international order. First, they concentrate power in the hands of one dominant state: a newly crowned hegemon, which alone possesses the capabilities, willingness, and legitimacy to create a new international order that transforms and reconstructs a world in ruins. Second, hegemonic wars destroy the old order, leaving a tabula rasa upon which a new global architecture can be built. Third, hegemonic wars make it clear to everyone who has power and who does not; they clarify the bargaining situation among the great powers—confusion over which caused war to break out in the first place.

None of these core international-political functions can be expected to arise from a global pandemic or any of the other aforementioned catastrophes. Such cataclysmic events might engender the benefit of increased international cooperation, but only temporarily and under certain conditions (for example, when the best efforts of a single state acting unilaterally cannot provide the global public good, when there is a workable consensus on the cause of the problem and its remedy, and so on). Catastrophes bring destruction and revolutionary change, but seldom are they followed in their immediate aftermath by political order and stability; seldom do they crown global leaders and clarify the bargaining situation among actors. Moreover, most catastrophes do not pass the Goldilocks test. Their effects are either too weak and temporary to wipe the slate of international institutions clean, or they are too strong, such that they obliterate the global architecture and everything else along with it. They are rarely "just right." Which is to say, the effects of catastrophic events do not "matter" in the same way or to the same degree that the effects of hegemonic wars "matter" to the nature and evolution of world politics.

What Hegemons Do

The primary service that the hegemon performs is international leadership for the provision of global public goods and international regimes (global governance structures) in various issue-areas, such as trade, monetary, security, technology, and energy. Essentially, the hegemon acts like the state in a domestic setting, with one big difference: it provides public goods free of charge (or at much reduced cost) to the rest of the world. The reason why a hegemon is crucially important is because "international public goods are unlikely to exist unless the group is 'privileged' so that a single state has sufficient interest in the good to be willing to bear the full costs of its provision. This outcome will be most likely when some single state, the hegemonic power, is sufficiently large relative to all others that it will capture a share of the benefit of the public good larger than the entire cost of providing it."[35]

Like a state delivering goods and services to its citizens, the hegemon provides the world with international peace, security, and order, goods that only it can deliver. Unlike the state, however, it allows others to take advantage of it. To be sure, the hegemon benefits (it turns a net profit by supplying the goods), but smaller states benefit even more.[36] Here we have a rare case in international politics in which "the weak exploit the powerful," to turn a core realist principle on its head. Thus, the hegemon stabilizes entire regions by extending its security umbrella; it answers the phone when distressed states dial 911; it provides the international economy with a stable currency, a large and open domestic market, free-trade institutions and norms, and a counter-cyclical lender of last resort; its teeth give international law its enforcement bite.

Unlike the binding decisions and authoritative processes within states, international politics is a realm "in which choices are made continuously over a period of time by actors for whom 'exit'—refusal to purchase goods or services that are offered—is an ever-present option. This conforms more closely to the situation faced by states contemplating whether to create, join, remain members of, or leave international regimes."[37] Under these circumstances, cost-effective global leadership (the kind that pays more than it costs) requires legitimacy and voluntary followers. One of the keys for a hegemon's longevity, therefore, is that it be far-sighted, that it transcend its narrow self-interest in favor of the collective long-run interest. "Do good for others in order to do well for yourself," is the proper maxim for an unchallenged hegemon.[38]

The Declining Hegemon: From Benevolent to Coercive Leadership

As a hegemon declines, however, it becomes less enamored with the long-run benefits it receives from its world order and more concerned over the immediate costs of managing the international system. Accordingly, it becomes less other-regarding and generous and more narrowly self-interested and coercive. There are three principal reasons for this change in ruling style: (1) the hegemon can no longer deliver the goods solely by its own efforts, even if it desired to do so, or it can supply them but only at a prohibitive cost to itself; (2) with the emergence of peer competitors, the hegemon no longer desires to supply the world with free goods, even if it still possesses the capability to do so; (3) some or all rising powers no longer view what the hegemon supplies as public goods. These three reasons may be stated less succinctly as follows.

First, an aging hegemon, while still the dominant power, has diminished capabilities to provide global goods (international peace, stability, and order) solely by means of its own assets. Second, the appearance of one or several peer competitors forces a declining hegemon—if it seeks to have any chance at maintaining its "top-dog" position—to play the game more fiercely (without a hint of altruism or misplaced generosity) than it did when it was at its apex in relative power. Finally, rising powers invariably challenge the hegemon's authority and the legitimacy of its existing international order; that is, they no longer see the services delivered by the hegemon as "public goods" but, instead, as things that benefit the declining hegemon far more than everyone else. This is why dramatic shifts in power among states, especially rapid shifts, almost always cause instability.

Less able and willing than in the past to provide global public goods, the hegemon now sees "benevolent leadership" as no longer worth the candle. Instead, it will continue to provide international order only if it is able to extract contributions toward the good from subordinate states. In effect, the declining hegemonic power now constitutes a quasi-government, supplying public goods and taxing other states to pay for them. Subordinate states, having grown accustomed to free-riding, will be reluctant to be taxed; if they can be coerced by the hegemonic state's still-preponderant power, however, they will succumb. Indeed, if they receive net benefits (i.e., a surplus of public good benefits over the contribution extracted from them), they may recognize hegemonic leadership as legitimate and so reinforce its performance and position. Nevertheless, the system is becoming more fragile as it transitions out of a period of splendid stability to the next phase within the hegemonic life-cycle, one characterized by persistent crises and instability.[39] World politics has either just entered this phase or is fast approaching it.

Why Not a Co-Managed Order?

The presence of a hegemon willing and able to provide world leadership— what the famous economist Charles Kindleberger approvingly calls a "benevolent despot"—is a sufficient condition for the supply of global public goods.[40] It is not a necessary condition, however, for their provision—at least, not in theory. Put differently, the core assumption of "the impossibility of collective action" (advanced by theories of benevolent hegemonic leadership) is logically false.

Secondary powers will be willing to participate in collective action provided that they benefit from the provision of the global public goods and are sufficiently powerful to have an impact on their provision. Of crucial importance is the minimum number of states that will benefit from cooperation despite the continuing noncooperation of others. If a small number of large actors benefit from the provision of a public good, then they will have an incentive to cooperate to preserve the goods after hegemony.[41] This minimum number (let us call it k) exists at the point where the benefits of cooperation for the cooperating states begin to outweigh the costs. Once k or more states cooperate, cooperators do as well as or better than they did before cooperation, even though free-riders do even better and incentives to join them (to defect from cooperation) persist.[42]

And so, in theory, declining hegemony does not mean the end of international order and the underprovision of global public goods; in theory, there is no "impossibility of collective action." A small group of large countries that share a common interest in the supply of public goods can cooperate to provide them (think of it as a benign form of collusion). Collective action is, in theory, a viable alternative to hegemonic leadership. In practice, however, the world is messier and more intractable than it is in theory.

As power diffuses throughout the international system, questions about "which order should prevail" become relatively more important than fondness for "any order rather than chaos," so the assumption that international order is a public good becomes less tenable. The problem is one of nonrivalry. When there is widespread disagreement about the desired nature of international order—its particular social purposes, rules, conventions, and decision-making procedures—the mere presence of international regimes and institutions is not itself evidence of nonrivalry. Lacking the required property of nonrivalry, international order becomes more of a contentious distributional issue over who gets what and how much than a global public good that is universally enjoyed.

The very notion of a public "good" assumes a concert of like-minded nations that share fundamentally compatible ideas on what constitutes a legitimate, fair, and acceptable order. Widespread global agreement of this kind does not exist today and is unlikely to exist in the future. There remains a deep divide between advanced and emerging countries over core features and issues that will define domestic, regional, and global orders, including Westphalian sovereignty, nuclear proliferation, climate change, and the proper operation of global markets.

There is no reason to expect, for instance, that the West's model of modernity will be embraced and replicated by the rising non-Western world. To most leaders of emerging economies, such a linear version of history would appear as not only quaint and passé but downright paternalistic and patronizing. They would point out that in our current interdependent world of increasing speed, fluidity, porous borders, and discontinuous technological changes, centralized and autocratic governments have regularly outperformed their more laissez-faire and democratic counterparts.[43]

Whether or not, on this question, emerging countries are on the "right side of history" is not of immediate importance. Though governed in part by the Darwinian logic of survival of the fittest, the international system is not so finely calibrated that it automatically and efficiently selects winners and losers; it is not the equivalent of a well-functioning market. For long stretches of time, it can tolerate a diversity of competing practices, ideas, beliefs, cultures, and priorities, all existing at the same time. It took almost fifty years and the exogenous shock of the information revolution to select out the Soviet-style socialist system. Simply put, the world can fall into a state of dissensus, and that is the direction we're heading.[44]

A Crisis of Global Legitimacy

One sign of this dissensus (that entropy is on the rise) is the decline in U.S. legitimacy to rule and provide order. Curiously, however, this crisis of global legitimacy has not been matched by a willingness among the emerging powers to band together and counterbalance U.S. military and political power. Why not? The answer resides in an entirely overlooked feature—one unique to unipolarity as opposed to any other international structure (e.g., multipolarity, tripolarity, or bipolarity). Under unipolarity and only unipolarity, balancing is the policy of revision, not the status quo. Any state or coalition seeking to restore a balance is, by definition, revisionist in an essential way: it seeks to overthrow the established order of unbalanced power characteristic of a unipolar system and replace it with a balance-of-power system. The goal is a change *of* system, not a change *within* the system, so it will alter the very structure of international politics from unipolarity to bipolarity or multipolarity. Because balancing under unipolarity is revisionist, any state intent on restoring system equilibrium will be labeled an aggressor. This huge ideational hurdle and the enormous power disparity between U.S. military capabilities and anyone else's military capabilities have been the main obstacles to balancing behavior at the global level.

For hard military balancing to occur under unipolarity, it has to be preceded by a delegitimation phase.[45] Delegitimation is similar to what others have called "soft balancing," but it is more encompassing. It includes not just practices of re-sistance, which impose costs on the hegemon short of balancing against it, but also a discourse of resistance, that is, criticism of the existing order and a com-pelling blueprint for a new one. States must first come to see U.S. hegemony as so incompetent and dangerous that its rule must be overturned. Otherwise, the risks and high costs of attempting to restore a global balance will be prohibitive. Thus, unipolarity requires both delegitimation and deconcentration to occur si-multaneously as one phase. Delegitimation provides the prerequisite reasons (embodied in a discourse and practice of resistance) for internal and external balancing practices; whereas deconcentration, by dispersing power more evenly throughout the system, lowers the barriers to both the discourse and actual prac-tice of resistance to hegemonic rule. In other words, delegitimation affects the will to pursue costly balancing strategies, while deconcentration affects the abil-ity to do so.

What is being undermined and then challenged is the legitimacy of the hege-mon's right to rule and its established order—the system's institutions, gover-nance structures, and principles that guide, among other things, the use of force. This begs the question: why would states want to delegitimize the existing order? The standard story is that the law of unequal growth among states disrupts sys-tem equilibrium by creating a disjuncture between actual power and prestige (the reputation for power). Another reason why states might want to modify or overturn an existing hegemonic order is that it does not work to their benefit anymore. The genius of Pax Americana was that the United States understood the maxim "Do good for others in order to do well for yourself."[46] As long as America provided necessary public goods to the rest of the world, resentment about its privileged position remained dormant.

The 2008 financial crisis brought to the surface resentment of U.S. hegemony, especially its macroeconomic policies. In the eyes of many, the global crisis was rooted in American incompetence (U.S. deregulation and the lack of transpar-ency caused the spread of its "toxic assets" to the rest of the world) and an inher-ently unfair playing field that permits reckless U.S. monetary expansion (the dollar depreciated against every other major currency except the Chinese yuan). As such, the economic meltdown portended not only the beginning of the end of American unipolarity but also a potentially momentous global political change. Just as the Great Depression ushered in fascism, Stalinism, and, of course, World War II, a recurrence of the latest Great Recession may be of sufficient magnitude that we can expect deep and far-reaching political repercussions.

One of these political repercussions will be to strengthen an already existing trend, the rise of authoritarian capitalism.[47] The West's old Cold War rivals, China and Russia, are now authoritarian-capitalist great powers. Such states have been absent since the defeat of Germany and Japan in 1945 but are now poised to make a comeback—a big comeback. Russia and China are much larger in terms of population, territory, and resources than imperial and fascist Germany and Imperial Japan ever were or could have hoped to become. The return of authoritarian-capitalist great powers may foreshadow a re-creation of the Cold War global alignments: a democratic First World competing with a nondemocratic Second World for the allegiances of nonaligned states in the Third World. But there is one fundamental difference this time around. Whereas the old Second World operated outside the global capitalist system, the new Second World is now fully integrated within the global economy, with its members participating on their own terms, just as their nondemocratic-capitalist predecessors did prior to 1945.

The potential development of a new Second World raises two important questions. Will Beijing, Moscow, and their future followers be openly antagonistic toward the democratic-capitalist countries, raising the specter of a new Cold War? And if the world experiences another round of the last financial crisis, will the effects of this next global economic turndown subject newly democratized countries to increasing social and economic pressures that undermine liberal institutions, weaken the grip of liberal democracy, and increase the appeal of authoritarian-capitalism? Either of these two possibilities would delegitimize the current global order. In many respects, both trends are already playing themselves out: to reiterate the general point, the world is fast approaching a state of dissensus and confusion characteristic of the age of entropy.

The processes of delegitimation and deconcentration (power diffusion), however, are merely *preconditions* for states to engage in traditional military balancing against a declining unipolar power; their simultaneous presence is no guarantee that states will adopt traditional balancing behaviors (building arms and forming military alliances). To the contrary, and for reasons discussed in prior chapters, we should not expect to see a return of the classic multipolar, balance-of-power system characteristic of international politics prior to 1945. We will witness, instead, the emergence of a global balance without traditional balancing behavior in the core. Persistently rocked by turbulence and discontinuous change, it will be a world characterized not only by rough equilibrium in terms of its system-wide distribution of capabilities but also by its increasing complexity, both organized and disorganized, and intensified conflict over vital issues, such as international macroeconomic coordination, financial regulatory reform, trade policy, and climate change.

Adaptation and Strategies for Success

Operating within this confused and messy external environment, those actors most likely to thrive, whether individuals, groups, corporations, bureaucratic organizations, or nation-states, will be the ones that can best cope with complexity and uncertainty. Actors must learn to manage discontinuous changes shaped by external forces—technological, competitive, and regulatory innovation or the decline and rise of whole industries and regional economies—that engineer radical breaks with the past. There are many strategies for reducing complexity and productively adapting to rapidly changing environments, but none guarantee success.

Organizations have experimented with decentralized but mutually coordinated decision-making centers. This is because in today's world, the most valuable and complex technologies are increasingly innovated by self-organizing networks—linked organizations (e.g., firms, universities, government agencies) that create, acquire, and integrate diverse knowledge and skills required to innovate complex technologies. *Self-organization* here refers to the networks' capacity to constantly combine and recombine learned capabilities without centralized, detailed managerial guidance.[48]

Effective participation in these self-organizing innovation networks requires that long-established, inflexible operating principles be replaced with flexible learning procedures based on self-observation, networks of small production units, just-in-time production, demand-flow technology, outsourcing, enterprise clusters, and so on. Because innovation is characterized by rapid, highly disruptive, and unpredictable change, managers must avoid the temptation to control every decision and instead learn to steer the innovation process, shaping the organizational environment within which choices emerge.

The goal is to create boundaries for effective, improvised, and self-organized solutions. As environmental uncertainty increases, therefore, smart organizations tend to become more organic, that is, they decentralize authority and responsibility, moving it down to lower levels; they encourage employees to take care of problems through teamwork, working directly with one another; and they take an informal approach to assigning tasks and responsibilities.[49] Communication becomes more horizontal, and the location of knowledge and control of tasks becomes dispersed throughout the organization.[50] Accordingly, the organization is more fluid and able to adapt continually to changes in its external environment.[51]

For firms operating in a turbulent market, adaptation is essential not just for success but for their very survival; those that fail to adapt through innovation or by emulating the most successful practices of their competitors will fall by the wayside. Self-described realists claim that world politics obeys a similar logic. There is little leeway in the cutthroat arena of international politics for slow learners, who, realists assert, are selected out of the game in ruthless Darwinian fashion. Here, realists have taken the analogies of free market economics and natural selection too far.

States are not firms, and contemporary international politics is a much more forgiving environment than a well-functioning market. One need only consider the persistent life of "failed" states in Africa, whose artificially drawn borders have, nonetheless, proven remarkably inviolable. This is no accident. Postcolonial African leaders deliberately reinforced the salience and viability of their received colonial boundaries. As Jeffrey Herbst argues, the "fundamental problem with the boundaries in Africa is not that they are too weak but that they are too strong."[52] The international norm of state sovereignty has become so salient that territorial boundaries, no matter how poorly they mirror actual state power and consolidation, prevent any notion of territorial competition. Indeed, most African regimes control only the capital city but are nevertheless recognized as sovereign rulers over everything within the territorial borders of the state. With territorial conquest consigned to the historical dustbin, governing regimes no longer need to consolidate their rule by broadcasting power over the hinterlands to the full extent of their state's borders. In contrast with the European state-building experience, when "war made the state, and the state made war,"[53] rulers in much of the developing world are not compelled by their external environment to protect and preserve their borders by means of military strength. The existence of boundaries alone maintains their territorial integrity and externally recognized sovereignty. War, however, remains, as Samuel Huntington argued, "the great stimulus to state building."[54] One of the consequences of perpetual peace is pathological and incomplete state consolidation and, ultimately, state failure—a subject to which we now turn.

Rising Entropy, Failed States, and Global Indifference

Given the present hegemonic grip of the norm of state sovereignty, the lust for territorial conquest no longer threatens another global conflagration. Interstate war among developed countries has become an antiquated mode of settling international disputes—an institution in decline, deemed today to be more or less as uncivilized as dueling and slavery.[55] For this we should be happy. The world will not soon tumble over the edge into primal chaos as it did twice in the prior century because of the innate threat that great powers present one another. But all is not well. Certain regions of the world have fallen, and will continue to fall, into a state of primal chaos—one rooted *not* in a clear-cut, understandable struggle between the forces of good and evil, as we have grown accustomed, but rather in the impenetrable darkness of inscrutable and unsolvable messes forged by political and economic weakness, in wars rooted in symptoms associated with rising entropy.

Since 1996, for instance, 5 million people have died and hundreds of thousands of women have been raped in the Congolese war, also known as the Great War of Africa. Most of the killing and rapes have been carried out at short range with hatchets, knives, and machetes. Yet it is not an unambiguous story of good versus evil but, instead, a rather abstruse one about state weakness and failure. Specifically, the contradiction of states with little or no control over their hinterlands but full claims to sovereignty could not remain submerged forever. The hinterland has begun to strike back. Rebel armies (recall the discussion of violent nonstate actors, or VNSAs, in chapter 3) have formed to challenge African governments in Rwanda, Zaire, Ethiopia, Liberia, Sierra Leone, Somalia, Congo-Brazzaville, and Chad, and many of them are winning.

In addition, Africa has recently witnessed a spate of spectacular state failures—states collapsing from internal rot largely because leaders have stolen so recklessly from their countries that they managed to kill off most of the productive sources of the economies. Thus, the collapse of the Democratic Republic of the Congo (DROC), a country the size of Western Europe and home to 60 million people, has facilitated the ceaseless proliferation of insurgent groups, still numbered at around twenty-nine in late 2010. These militias from various countries and regions within the DROC fight brutal insurgencies and counterinsurgencies that are less about controlling territory than controlling civilians to obtain resources and in retaliation for attacks by rival groups.[56] What the Congolese war demonstrates is that nonterritorially oriented conflict in the age of entropy can be just as brutal and catastrophic as in the prior age when the great powers fought over territory, considered to be the most important currency of power. What is very different about today's conflicts, even large-scale ones, however, is that much of the world has ignored Africa's Great War, and those who are aware of it have little interest in understanding its origins or driving forces. As Jason K. Stearns writes,

> The Congolese war must be put among the other great human cataclysms of our time: the World Wars, the Great Leap Forward in China, the Rwandan and Cambodian genocides. And yet, despite its epic proportions, the war has received little attention from the rest of the world. The mortality figures are so immense that they become absurd, almost meaningless. From the outside, the war seems to possess no overarching narrative or ideology to explain it, no easy tribal conflict or socialist revolution to use as a peg in the news piece. In Cambodia, there was the despotic Khmer Rouge; in Rwanda one could cast the genocidal Hutu militias as the villains. In the Congo these roles are more difficult to fill. There is no Hitler, Mussolini, or Stalin. Instead it is a war of the ordinary person, with many combatants unknown and unnamed, who fight for complex reasons that are difficult to distill in a few sentences—much to the frustration of the international media. How do you cover a war that involves at least twenty different rebel groups and the armies of nine countries, yet does not seem to have a clear cause of objective?[57]

In late November 2012, one of Congo's biggest eastern cities, Goma, fell to a powerful rebel force, M23, marking the latest episode of a long struggle by Rwandan-backed rebels to take control of a piece of the DROC. After victory, M23 rebels began making noises about continuing all the way to Kinshasa, 1,000 miles to the East, to take over the country, and most observers expect them to be successful. M23's victorious march through the country, which, according to Anjan Sundaram, "threatens to redraw the map of Africa," has "highlighted the ineptitude of the United Nations mission, one of the world's largest and most expensive, charged with keeping Congo's peace."[58] What is most surprising is just how few soldiers are needed to overthrow some sub-Saharan political regimes, many of which are strangely deficient in military and police capabilities to defend themselves. "In the end, some 3,000 Congolese soldiers, backed by hundreds of U.N. peacekeepers with air power, were unable to contain M23 forces numbering *in the few hundreds*."[59] Unlike the inherited borders of African states, which have proven remarkably stable, African regimes opposed by a few hundred rebels often topple like chaff scattered by the wind.[60]

The Congolese War offers a fitting analogy for world politics in the age of entropy. Just as a house infested with active termites may appear quite sturdy at a glance, the apparent robust stability of state borders suggested by the dearth of interstate wars conceals the ubiquitous problem of internal rot and decay. For instance, the Peterson Institute for International Economics projects that the United States' current account deficit will rise from a prior record of 6 percent of GDP to over 15 percent (more than $5 trillion annually) by 2030, with net debt soaring to $50 trillion—the equivalent of 140 percent of GDP![61]

China's new leadership team is in for a rough ride as well. Chinese annual growth is slowing dramatically, tumbling from double digits to 7 percent or even less as the world economy marks its worst year since 2009. Against the backdrop of a decelerating economy, heightened corruption, and myriad social problems, the perennial task of combining economic growth with political stability is proving increasingly difficult. We know this because the rapid development of China's social media services has opened a window onto the public mood, and what it reveals is a shared tone "of profound mistrust of the party and its officials."[62] Soon the new Chinese leader, Xi Jinping, will be faced with a stark choice: clamp down on internal dissent or make a break with the past by starting to loosen the party's control over the country. Whatever Mr. Xi decides, China's future hangs in the balance.

Meanwhile, Russia grows more dependent on oil exports, which have kept Prime Minister Vladimir Putin in power and the corrupt system of his United Russia party running. The spectacular growth of state income generated by oil profits largely explains how Putin comfortably won the first round of the presidential election in March 2012—mere months after the wave of mass demonstrations the previous winter had broken the surface calm of Russian politics. In the coming years, however, Russia will be running out of cheap oil: what remains in the ground will become harder to find and more expensive to produce. At the same time, the country is progressively suffering from what economists call "Dutch disease," economic stagnation caused by an overreliance on commodity exports at the expense of other parts of the economy. As growth slows in China and the advanced industrial world, these countries will buy less oil and the price will drop accordingly (it is useful to remember that Russia's GDP fell by 7.8 percent, more than any major economy, as a result of the 2008 global financial crisis and recession that followed). Signs of trouble abound, but given the vice grip of Putin's system of centralized control, it is uncertain that needed reforms will be undertaken.[63] The same can be said for the other petro-dictatorships in Africa, Latin America, and the Middle East.

Brazil, too, has its share of internal rot and decay, mostly rooted in corruption and other problems associated with failed state consolidation. For instance, in

São Paulo, the largest city in the southern hemisphere and Americas, lax control of firearms, porous borders, and a lucrative drug trade—problems endemic to Brazil and other Latin American governments—have given rise to a blood feud between the police and an organized crime group, the First Command of the Capital (known by its Portuguese initials, PCC), that saw ninety-four officers killed in 2012, twice as many as in 2011. For their part, on-duty police officers killed 119 people in the metropolitan area between July and September 2012 alone.[64] We can add this mess to Brazil's other domestic troubles, including its infrastructure deficit, Rio de Janeiro's gang problems, and civil unrest in the Amazon in retaliation for the government's plans to build sixty dams there. Regarding the latter issue, the strategic priority of Brazil's army in the coming years will be the Amazon. The number of border posts where troops will be stationed will be increased, and still more soldiers will be trained in the art of jungle warfare. The strategy's raison d'être has little to do with external threats, however. Brazil has long been at peace with its seven neighbors in the Amazon (its last scrap was with Bolivia roughly 110 years ago). Rather, the military's interest in the Amazon is to use "the army for nation-building in the jungle," "as a way to break down class divides in Brazil," and to protect Amazon borders from drug exporters seeking to establish drug routes through Brazilian territory.[65] Here as elsewhere, internal security concerns trump external ones.

In the Middle East, Syria is in the throes of a bloody, two-year civil war that has claimed at least forty thousand lives and threatens to destabilize the region. Egypt is currently undergoing the worst outbreak of violence between political factions since Gamal Abdel Nasser's coup six decades ago.[66] This time the battle is between Islamist supporters of President Mohamed Morsi, a former leader of the Muslim Brotherhood, and their secular opponents. Things have gotten so bad that President Morsi announced impending martial law, marking the steepest escalation yet in the political battle between Egypt's new Islamist leaders and their secular opponents over a referendum to allow a thorough overhaul of the proposed Islamist-backed constitution. Liberal groups claim the proposed charter has inadequate protection of individual rights and provisions that could someday give Muslim religious authorities new influence, especially over the legal system. Acknowledging the danger of protests and violence that might disrupt the referendum and the parliamentary election to follow, the military has thrown its support behind President Morsi's plan to impose martial law. In a statement read over state television, a military spokesman, warning of "divisions that threaten the State of Egypt," echoed Morsi's own words: the military "realizes its national responsibility for maintaining the supreme interests of the nation and securing and protecting the vital targets, public institutions and the interests of the innocent citizens."[67] Even some members of the opposition see no other way out. "Under the present circumstance, how can you conduct a referendum or an election when chaos is reigning and you have protests everywhere?" asked Amr Moussa, a former foreign minister under Mr. Mubarak and now an opposition leader.[68] Chaos (entropy) reigns supreme.

The façade of state capacity—that is, the myth that rulers can govern effectively and control the environment within their territorial borders—is not just a problem endemic to sub-Saharan African. It is a global problem that signals the oncoming age of entropy. Indeed, President Morsi himself, in his Delphic interview with *Time* magazine, offers an explanation of how the world works that is entirely consistent with the age of entropy: "The world is now much more difficult than it was during your revolution. It's even more difficult. The world. More complicated, complex, difficult. It's a spaghetti-like structure. It's mixed up."[69]

The age of entropy will be one of disorder, to be sure, but it will be a restless disorder, for there are no clear lines of advance. We live in a time when new forms "of art as of life seem exhausted, the stages of development have been run through. Institutions function painfully. Repetition and frustration are the intolerable result. Boredom and fatigue are great historical forces," as the cultural historian Jacques Barzun so eloquently wrote in his magisterial work *From Dawn to Decadence.*[70] The upshot of all this restiveness will be an aimless but nonetheless forceful hostility to the way things are—a hostility that inspires the pervasive use of the dismissive prefixes *anti-* and *post-* (as in anti-Western, post-American, postmodern) and the promise to *reinvent* much or all of the present global order and its associated institutions. But the hope that getting rid of "what is" will by itself spawn something new and workable to take its place is just that, mere hope.

None of this is to suggest, however, that we will inhabit a miserable world of endless gloom and doom or that we and future generations are fated to endure wretched lives of perpetual unhappiness. There is much good about the way things are, and much to be thankful for and joyous about the way things will be. Disorder does not suppress all that is good in the world. We are blessed to exist in enormously peaceful and prosperous times. Disorder is not necessarily something to fear or loathe. We may, instead, embrace the unknowable, embrace our unintelligible world, our futile struggle to come to terms with its incomprehensibility.

In this embrace, we are all akin to Sisyphus, who, according to Greek mythology, was condemned by the gods to repeat forever the same meaningless task of pushing a boulder up a mountain, only to see it roll down again. "The struggle itself," as Albert Camus famously pointed out, "is enough to fill a man's heart. One must imagine Sisyphus happy."[71] Or as Michael Stipe of R.E.M. sang, "It's the end of the world as we know it, and I feel fine."[72]

Notes

INTRODUCTION: Navigating the Chaos of Contemporary World Politics

1. Over fifty years ago, a modern-day pioneer of international relations theory, John H. Herz, predicted the breakdown of the territorial state and modern states system. His prediction was rooted in different causes, however, from those typically mentioned today. See John H. Herz, "The Rise and Decline of the Territorial State," *World Politics*, vol. 9, no. 4 (July 1957), pp. 473–493, and *International Politics in the Atomic Age* (New York: Columbia University Press, 1962).

2. See the articles by Brent Scowcroft, Robert Merry, Christopher Layne, Christopher Whalen, and Gideon Rachman in the special issue "Crisis of the Old Order: The Crumbling Status Quo at Home and Abroad," *National Interest*, no. 119 (May/June 2012).

3. Robert Pape, "Empire Falls," *National Interest*, No. 99 (January/February 2009), pp. 21 and 24. Pape may be technically correct in his claim that U.S. decline is unprecedented. However, the United States, given its historically unparalleled share of global power (between 25 and 40% over the past six decades), has much farther to fall than previous so-called global hegemons, such as Britain in the nineteenth century, which were never unipolar powers but first among equals. For a powerful counter-declinist argument, claiming that the United States will maintain its global supremacy for decades to come, see Stephen G. Brooks and William C. Wohlforth, *World Out of Balance: International Relations and the Challenge of American Primacy* (Princeton, NJ: Princeton University Press, 2008).

4. Josef Joffe, "Declinism's Fifth Wave," *American Interest*, vol. 7, no. 3 (January/February 2012).

5. See, for instance, Ezra F. Vogel, "East Asia: Pax Nipponica?" *Foreign Affairs* (Spring 1986), www.foreignaffairs.com/articles/40804/ezra-f-vogel/east-asia-pax-nipponica, and *Japan as Number One: Lessons for America* (Cambridge, MA: Harvard University Press, 1979).

6. I borrowed this line from Aaron Friedberg, "Same Old Song: What the Declinists (and Triumphalists) Miss," *American Interest*, vol. 5, no. 2 (November/December 2009), pp. 28–35 at p. 28.

7. Carmen M. Reinhardt and Kenneth S. Rogoff, *This Time Is Different: Eight Centuries of Financial Folly* (Princeton, NJ: Princeton University Press, 2009).

8. Niall Ferguson, "Europe's Lehman Brothers Moment," *Newsweek* (June 18, 2012), pp. 34–37. As the Eurocrisis unfolds, we have learned what many suspected when the single European currency was created thirteen years ago: monetary union among otherwise

sovereign states is unstable and courts disaster. Unlike the United States, with its federal system that shares the burden of financial crises among the states of the Union, Europe has virtually none of the institutions that would make that possible. For example, revenues of the European Central Bank are less than 1% of the European Union's gross domestic product (GDP). Unfortunately for the rest of the world, this is not just a European problem anymore.

9. Since 2008, the ratio of total debt relative to GDP has actually grown for most major economies, except for those of the United States, Australia, and South Korea. In the ten largest developed economies (all belonging to the United States and its allies), deleveraging has only just begun. See "Debt and Deleveraging: Uneven Progress on the Path to Growth," *McKinsey Quarterly* (January 2012), www.mckinsey.com/Insights/MGI/Research/Financial_Markets.

10. The Hays/Oxford Economics Global Report, "Creating Jobs in a Global Economy 2011–2030" (April 2011), www.oxfordeconomics.com/Free/pdfs/Hays_OE_Global_Report_2011.pdf.

11. A developing economy is one listed as low-income, lower-middle-income, and upper-middle-income according to the World Bank official classification. The World Bank defines an emerging market economy (EME) as an economy with low to middle per capita income. EMEs are considered emerging because of their developments and reforms; they are transitioning from a closed economy to an open market economy while building accountability within the system. A key characteristic of the EME, therefore, is increased local and foreign investment (portfolio and direct), indicating that the country has been able to build confidence in the local economy. Such countries constitute approximately 80% of the global population and represent about 20% of the world's economies.

12. United States National Intelligence Council (NIC), *Global Trends 2030: Alternative Worlds* (Washington, DC: U.S. Government Printing Office, 2012), p. 19.

13. World Bank, *Global Development Horizons 2011: Multipolarity—The New Global Economy* (Washington, DC: International Bank for Reconstruction and Development/World Bank, 2011). The six major emerging economies are Brazil, Russia, India, China, South Korea, and Indonesia.

14. International Institute for Strategic Studies (IISS), *The Military Balance 2012* (London: IISS, 2012).

15. Goldman Sachs Economic Research, "The N-11: More Than an Acronym," *Global Economics Paper no. 153* (March 28, 2007), www.chicagobooth.edu/alumni/clubs/pakistan/docs/next11dream-march%20'07-goldmansachs.pdf; and NIC, *Global Trends 2030*, p. 20.

16. World Bank, *Global Development Horizons 2011*, p. 4. By 2010, emerging economies held over $7.4 trillion in international reserves—roughly three times the $2.1 trillion in reserves held by advanced economies.

17. Among the G-20 today, for instance, the average debt-to-GDP ratio is over three times higher for the rich countries than for the developing countries. See "Public Debt," in United States Central Intelligence Agency, *The World Factbook*, www.cia.gov/library/publications/the-world-factbook/rankorder/2186rank.html (accessed March 21, 2013).

18. Goldman Sachs Economic Research, "The N-11," p. 4.

19. World Bank, *Global Development Horizons 2011*, p. 1.

20. "Double Your Income," *Economist Online* (December 7, 2011). www.economist.com/blogs/dailychart/2011/12/gdp-person; Frederick Kempe, "Does America Still Want to Lead the World?" *Reuters Blogs: Thinking Global* (April 18, 2012), http://blogs.reuters.com/thinking-global/2012/04/18/does-america-still-want-to-lead-the-world; NIC, *Global Trends 2030*, pp. 1 and 21.

21. The article went on to say, "Never before has China received so much attention from the world, and the world until now has never been more in need of China." *People's Daily Online*, "What Make China Accomplish a 'Glorious Decade,'" edited and translated by Mimie Ouyang (July 4, 2012), http://english.peopledaily.com.cn/90883/7865436.html.

22. Pew Research Global Attitudes Project, "China Seen Overtaking the U.S. as Global Superpower" (July 13, 2011), www.pewglobal.org/2011/07/13/china-seen-overtaking-us-as-global-superpower/4/.

23. Ibid.

24. "Internal Reference on Reforms: Report for Senior Leaders," quoted in "China's New Leadership: Vaunting the Best, Fearing the Worst," *Economist*, vol. 405, no. 8808 (October 27-November 2, 2012), p. 22.

25. Michael Beckley, "China's Century? Why America's Edge Will Endure," *International Security*, vol. 36, no. 3 (Winter 2011–12), pp. 41–78 at p. 61.

26. Jonathan Anderson, "How to Think about China, Part 2: The Aging of China," *UBS Investment Research* (February 7, 2005), p. 2.

27. Ibid., pp. 26–28.

28. The costs to the hegemonic leader are exorbitant because those who consume and enjoy the global public goods it provides (e.g., economic prosperity, a stable global currency reserve, international security, etc.) do not pay their fair share of the costs for these goods. This is the familiar free-rider problem associated with collective action and the provision of public goods. See Mancur Olson, *The Logic of Collective Action: Public Goods and the Theory of Groups* (Cambridge, MA: Harvard University Press, 1965).

29. See John Lewis Gaddis, *We Now Know: Rethinking Cold War History* (Oxford: Oxford University Press, 1998), p. 49, and Geir Lundestad, *The United States and Western Europe since 1945: From "Empire" by Invitation to Transatlantic Drift* (Oxford: Oxford University Press, 2005).

30. See Barry R. Posen, "Pull Back: The Case for a Less Activist Foreign Policy," *Foreign Affairs*, vol. 92, no. 1 (January/February 2013), pp. 116–128.

31. Quoted in Tim Arango and Clifford Krauss, "China Is Reaping Biggest Benefits of Iraq Oil Boom," *New York Times* (June 3, 2013), p. A1.

32. Fareed Zakaria, "Can America Be Fixed? The New Crisis of Democracy," *Foreign Affairs*, vol. 92, no. 1 (January/February 2013), pp. 22–33 at p. 31.

33. Richard Burt and Dimitri K. Simes, "Morality Play Instead of Policy," *National Interest*, No. 121 (September/October 2012), pp. 5–9 at p. 6.

34. The federal debt-to-GDP figure is from the Congressional Budget Office; the federal debt-to-revenue ratio is from the International Monetary Fund. Both quoted in Niall Ferguson, "Why Obama Must Go," *Newsweek* (August 27, 2012), pp. 20–25 at p. 22.

35. Pew Research Center, "Views of Middle East Unchanged by Recent Events: Public Remains Wary of Global Engagement" (June 10, 2011), http://pewresearch.org/pubs/2020/poll-american-attitudes-foreign-policy.

36. Chicago Council on Global Affairs, *Foreign Policy in the New Millennium: Results of the 2012 Chicago Council Survey of American Public Opinion and U.S. Foreign Policy* (Chicago: Chicago Council on Global Affairs, 2012), pp. 24 and 41.

37. Philip Stephens, "The U.S. Is Becoming a Selective Superpower," *Financial Times* (September 13, 2012), p. 6.

38. Ibid.

39. See Kenneth E. Boulding, *The Meaning of the 20th Century: The Great Transition* (New York: Harper & Row, 1964), chap. 7.

40. Rudolf Arnheim, *Entropy and Art: An Essay on Disorder and Order* (Berkeley: University of California Press, 1971).

41. Sriram Chellappan and Raghavendra Kotikalapudi, "How Depressives Surf the Web," *New York Times* (June 17, 2012), Sunday Review, p. 12.

42. Hedley Bull, *The Anarchical Society: A Study of Order in World Politics* (New York: Columbia University Press, 1977), p. 4.

43. Quoted in ibid.

44. David Weinberger, *Everything Is Miscellaneous: The Power of the New Digital Disorder* (New York: Times Books, 2007), p. 11.

45. Garrett Hardin, "The Cybernetics of Competition: A Biologist's View of Society," *Perspectives in Biology and Medicine*, vol. 7, no. 3 (Autumn 1963), pp. 63–64, 73.

46. Ibid., p. 61.

47. The term *butterfly effect* grew out of an unpublished academic paper that Edward Lorenz presented in 1972 entitled "Predictability: Does the Flap of a Butterfly's Wings in Brazil Set Off a Tornado in Texas?" http://web.mit.edu/newsoffice/2008/obit-lorenz-0416 .html.

48. Andrew Blum, "Speed Trap: We Built the Internet. Now We're Stuck with It," *Newsweek* (September 24, 2012), p. 5. In this short *Newsweek* piece, Blum makes many insightful observations about the implications of the Internet and the unleashed power of viral media.

49. Ibid. Initially, the Obama administration blamed the video for the death of a much-beloved U.S. diplomat, J. Christopher Stevens, and three other Americans in an attack by Benghazi militiamen with possible al-Qaeda affiliations on the American consulate compound. Two weeks later, the administration had backtracked from its initial claim that the incident was a spontaneous, unplanned attack by Libyans enraged by the video. They are currently trying to determine if al-Qaeda urged a Libyan group to launch the assault.

50. In his classic work, *On the Origin of Species*, Charles Darwin drew the connection between the populations of cats, mice, humble bees (now known as bumblebees), and clover. A contemporary of his, Thomas Henry Huxley, extended the chain (in a spirit of humor) to include old maids who keep cats as pets. Huxley, *Conditions of Existence as Affecting the Perpetuation of Living Beings* (Gloucester, UK: Dodo Press, 2008), p. 48. More recently, the chain has been extended to cattle, roast beef, and British soldiers.

51. Conventional explanations of world history focus too narrowly on the strategy and tactics of national leaders and the role of political elites. Refuting this "Great Man" theory of history, Leo Tolstoy showed in the pages of *War and Peace* that history is seldom so neat or vertically driven; the fate of mankind is more often determined by unanticipated events, blind luck, and irrational folly. Explanations of history that rely on chance,

irrationality, and dumb luck are, at best, intellectually unsatisfying and, at worst, the product of lazy thinking. Theories are useful when they make the world more, not less, understandable and predictable. The study of nonlinear, complex systems is no exception; after all, chaos is defined as a degree of order embedded within apparent turbulence. The more complex is the subject, the greater the need for theory to make sense of it, to find order and predictability. The trick is to uncover reliable patterns and processes that allow the researcher to cope with the chaos and uncertainty that appear on the system's surface.

52. Douglas Coupland, "Convergences," *New York Times Book Review* (March 11, 2012), p. 1.

53. Charles A. Kupchan, "The Democratic Malaise: Globalization and the Threat to the West," *Foreign Affairs*, vol. 91, no. 1 (January/February 2012), pp. 62–67.

54. Within the Chinese Communist Party's central committee, opponents of market-oriented changes gained a louder voice during the global financial crisis, when the Chinese government's intervention in the economy increased and intensified. More recently, however, projections of slowing economic growth have spurred debate within China as to whether the "China model" is sustainable.

55. "Incoming President Xi Jinping: Changes Ahead for U.S.-China Relations," *Knowledge@Wharton*, Wharton School of the University of Pennsylvania (March 14, 2012). www.knowledgeatwharton.com.cn/index.cfm?fa=printArticle&articleID=2557&languageid=1

56. Michael Wesley, "Asia's New Age of Instability," *National Interest*, no. 122 (November/December 2012), pp. 21–29 at p. 28.

57. Ibid., p. 24.

58. Xi Jinping, as quoted in Jane Perlez, "In Powerful China, a Likely Leader's Army Ties May Mean a Shifting Path," *New York Times*, November 4, 2012, p. 6.

59. Henry Kissinger as quoted in Sandy Fitzgerald, "Kissinger: Arab Spring Begins 'Complicated' Transformation," *Newsmax* (October 28, 2011), www.newsmax.com /TheWire/kissinger-arab-spring/2011/10/28/id/416011.

60. See Francis Fukuyama, "The Future of History: Can Liberal Democracies Survive the Decline of the Middle Class?" *Foreign Affairs*, vol. 91, no. 1 (January/February 2012), pp. 53–61; Charles A. Kupchan, *No One's World: The West, the Rising Rest, and the Coming Global Turn* (New York: Oxford University Press, 2012).

61. Condoleezza Rice, "Rethinking the National Interest: American Realism for a New World, *Foreign Affairs*, vol. 87, no. 4 (July/August 2008), p. 2.

62. This definition appeared in a 1983 study of the nation's economic competitiveness problem issued by a commission established by President Ronald Reagan. See Laura D'Andrea Tyson, *Who's Bashing Whom?: Trade Conflict in High-Technology Industries* (Washington, DC: Institute for International Economics, 1992), p. 1.

63. See, for instance, Paul R. Krugman, ed., *Strategic Trade Policy and the New International Economics* (Cambridge, MA: MIT Press, 1986).

64. Bill Emmott's *The Sun Also Sets* was a runaway bestseller in Japan when the Japanese translation first appeared in 1991. Unlike most "scholarly" observers, normal Japanese citizens rightly sensed that something was amiss. See Bill Emmott, *The Sun Also Sets: The Limits to Japan's Economic Power* (New York: Touchstone, 1989).

65. Mary E. Sarotte, *1989: The Struggle to Create Post-Cold War Europe* (Princeton, NJ: Princeton University Press, 2009), p. 2.

66. Quoted in Josef Joffe, *Überpower: The Imperial Temptation of America* (New York: W. W. Norton, 2006), p. 16.

67. According to the U.S. Department of Commerce: Bureau of Economic Analysis, the nation's personal saving rate (PSAVERT) as a percentage of disposable personal income (DPI) in January 2013 was a scant 2.4, the lowest it has been since November 2007. For the PSAVERT numbers from 1961 to the present, see http://research.stlouisfed.org /fred2/data/psavert.txt.

68. The U.S. trade deficit hit a seven-month high in November 2012. And while the trade gap has narrowed a tiny bit since 2011, it remains huge. The National Association for Business Economics predicts that the trade deficit for 2013 will total $533 billion—a small improvement from the 2012 trade deficit of $540 billion deficit and the 2011 trade deficit of $546.6 billion, http://rt.com/usa/us-trade-deficit-percent-827/.

69. The boom in entitlement spending and the decline in revenues from the Bush-era tax cuts are mostly responsible for America's parlous fiscal state. That noted, the wars in Afghanistan and Iraq also cost American taxpayers trillions of dollars, which, combined with the costs of the financial bailout (in the form of TARP) and stimulus packages in response to the subprime mortgage and financial credit crises, also battered the economy.

70. See Philip Coggan, *Paper Promises: Debt, Money, and the New World Order* (New York: PublicAffairs, 2012).

71. See Josef Joffe, "Europe's American Pacifier," *Foreign Policy*, vol. 54 (Spring 1984), pp. 64–82; John J. Mearsheimer, "The Future of the American Pacifier," *Foreign Affairs*, vol. 80, no. 5 (September/October 2001), pp. 46–61; Robert J. Lieber, "Asia's American Pacifier," in *The American Era: Power and Strategy for the 21st Century* (New York: Cambridge University Press, 2005), chap. 6.

72. See Michael Mandelbaum, *The Case for Goliath: How America Acts as the World's Government in the Twenty-First Century* (New York: PublicAffairs, 2006); *The Frugal Superpower: America's Global Leadership in a Cash-Strapped Era* (New York: PublicAffairs, 2010); and "America's Coming Retrenchment: How Budget Cuts Will Limit the United States' Global Role," *ForeignAffairs.com* (August 9, 2011), www.foreignaffairs.com/articles/68024/michael-mandelbaum/americas-coming-retrenchment.

73. Robert Kagan, *The World America Made* (New York: Alfred A. Knopf, 2012), pp. 40–41.

74. See "Sequestration Update" (May 2013), report by Democrats on the House Committee on Appropriations, Rep. Nita Lowey (D-NY), Ranking Member, p. 14, http:// democrats.appropriations.house.gov/images/Sequestration%20Update%20-%20Full %20report.pdf.

75. Pessimists are, for the most part, offensive realists. See John J. Mearsheimer, "Back to the Future: Instability in Europe after the Cold War," *International Security*, vol. 15, no. 4 (Summer 1990), pp. 5–56, and *The Tragedy of Great Power Politics* (New York: W. W. Norton, 2001).

76. See Bruce Russett and John R. Oneal, *Triangulating Peace: Democracy, Interdependence, and International Organizations* (New York: W. W. Norton, 2001); G. John Iken-

berry, *Liberal Leviathan: The Origins, Crisis, and Transformation of the American World Order* (Princeton, NJ: Princeton University Press, 2011); Ikenberry, *After Victory: Institutions, Strategic Restraint, and the Rebuilding of Order after Major Wars* (Princeton, NJ: Princeton University Press, 2001); and Daniel Deudney and G. John Ikenberry, "The Myth of the Autocratic Revival: Why Liberal Democracy Will Prevail," *Foreign Affairs*, vol. 88, no. 1 (January/February 2009), pp. 77–93.

77. Secretary of State Hillary Rodham Clinton, "Foreign Policy Address at the Council on Foreign Relations," U.S. State Department, Washington, DC (July 15, 2009), www .state.gov/secretary/rm/2009a/july/126071.htm.

78. See Stephen Jay Gould, *Time's Arrow, Time's Cycle: Myth and Metaphor in the Discovery of Geological Time* (Cambridge, MA: Harvard University Press, 1987).

79. Steven Pinker, *The Better Angels of Our Nature: Why Violence Has Declined* (New York: Penguin Books, 2011), pp. 242–243.

80. Arthur Conan Doyle, *His Last Bow: A Reminiscence of Sherlock Holmes* (New York: George H. Doran Company, 1917), p. 308.

81. James Glanz, "Power, Pollution and the Internet: Industry Wastes Vast Amounts of Electricity, Belying Image," *New York Times* (September 23, 2012), pp. 1, 20–21, at p. 1.

82. Nicholas Carr, *The Shallows: What the Internet Is Doing to Our Brains* (New York: W. W. Norton, 2011), p. 10.

83. Ron Deibert, "Social Media, Inc.: The Global Politics of Big Data," *World Politics Review* (June 19, 2012), www.worldpoliticsreview.com/articles/12065/social-media-inc -the-global-politics-of-big-data.

84. Michael Wines, "Google to Alert Users to Chinese Censorship," *New York Times* (June 1, 2012), www.nytimes.com/2012/06/02/world/asia/google-to-alert-users-to-chinese -censorship.html?_r=1.

85. Rebecca MacKinnon, "Consent of the Networked: How Googledom, Facebookistan, and Other Sovereigns of Cyberspace are Handling Their Unprecedented Power," *Slate* (January 31, 2012), www.slate.com/articles/technology/future_tense/2012 /01/consent_of_the_networked_how_google_facebook_and_other_cyberspace_power-houses_handle_digital_power_.html. Also see Rebecca MacKinnon, *Consent of the Networked: The Worldwide Struggle for Internet Freedom* (New York: Basic Books, 2012), chap. 1.

86. For two exceptional works on the subject, see F. H. Hinsley, *Sovereignty*, 2nd ed. (Cambridge: Cambridge University Press, 1986), and Stephen D. Krasner, *Sovereignty: Organized Hypocrisy* (Princeton, NJ: Princeton University Press, 1999).

87. See Adam Thierer, "Book Review: *Consent of the Networked* by Rebecca MacKinnon," *Technology Liberation Front* (January 25, 2012), http://techliberation.com/2012/01 /25/book-review-consent-of-the-networked-by-rebecca-mackinnon/.

88. Robert Jackson, *Sovereignty: The Evolution of an Idea* (Malden, MA: Polity Press, 2007), p. x.

89. Thierer, "Book Review: *Consent of the Networked*."

CHAPTER ONE: **Understanding the Language of Energy**

1. Crosbie Smith, *The Science of Energy: A Cultural History of Energy Physics in Victorian Britain* (London: University of Chicago Press, 1998), chap. 1 and pp. 15–17.

2. Ibid., pp. 15–17. See also the excellent biography by Harold Issadore Sharlin in collaboration with Tiby Sharlin, *Lord Kelvin: The Dynamic Victorian* (University Park: Pennsylvania State University Press, 1979).

3. This also put the age of the earth's at over 100 million years. Today we know that the earth is roughly 4.6 billion years old.

4. James Johnstone, *The Philosophy of Biology* (Cambridge: Cambridge University Press, 1914), pp. 63–64.

5. Reverend Thomas Chalmers on the transitory nature of things, circa 1830s. Quoted in Smith, *The Science of Energy*, p. 15.

6. James Gleick, *The Information: A History, A Theory, A Flood* (New York: Pantheon, 2011), p. 269; also see James Johnstone, "Entropy and Evolution," *Philosophy*, vol. 7, no. 27 (July 1932), pp. 287–298.

7. Clifford A. Truesdell, *The Tragicomical History of Thermodynamics, 1822–1854*, Studies in the History of Mathematics and Physical Sciences, vol. 4 (New York: Springer-Verlag, 1980), p. 51.

8. Bruce Clarke, *Energy Forms: Allegory and Science in the Era of Classical Thermodynamics* (Ann Arbor: University of Michigan Press, 2001), p. 18.

9. Ibid., p. 21.

10. Smith, *The Science of Energy*, p. 126.

11. The *American Heritage Dictionary* gives as the first definition of *entropy*: "For a closed system, the quantitative measure of the amount of thermal energy not available to do work."

12. The resulting disordered motion explains why it is often said that thermodynamic entropy measure not just the energy unavailable for work but also the disorganization in a system.

13. Rudolf Julius Emanuel Clausius, "Über die bewegende Kraft der Wärme und die Gesetze, welche sich daraus für die Wärmelehre selbst ableiten lassen" (On the Motive Power of Heat and on the Laws Which Can Be Deduced From it For the Theory of Heat Itself), in J. C. Poggendorff, *Annalen der Physik und Chemie*, vol. 79, ser. 3 (Leipzig: Barth, 1850), part 1, pp. 368–397; part 2, pp. 500–524, at p. 500. Translated in part in Truesdell, *The Tragicomical History of Thermodynamics*, chap. 8.

14. Rudolf Julius Emanuel Clausius, *The Mechanical Theory of Heat, with Its Applications to the Steam-Engine and to the Physical Properties of Bodies* (London: John Van Voorst, 1867), p. 117.

15. This means that a perpetual motion machine is impossible.

16. Rudolf Julius Emanuel Clausius, "Ueber verschiedene für die Anwendung bequeme Formen der Hauptgleichungen der mechanischen Wärmetheorie" (On Several Forms of the Fundamental Equations of the Mechanical Theory of Heat That are Useful for Application), in J. C. Poggendorff's *Annalen der Physik und Chemie*, vol. 125, no. 7 (Leipzig: Barth, 1865), pp. 353–400 at p. 400; translated and excerpted in William Francis Magie, *A Source Book in Physics* (1935; reprint, Cambridge, MA: Harvard University Press, 1963).

17. Léon Brillouin, "Life, Thermodynamics, and Cybernetics" (1949), in Harvey S. Leff and Andrew F. Rex, eds., *Maxwell's Demon 2: Entropy, Classical and Quantum Information, Computing* (Bristol, UK: Institute of Physics, 2003), p. 77.

18. As Crosbie Smith put it, "The great goal of Glasgow engineers and natural philosophers alike was . . . to minimize waste and maximize useful work, that is to attempt to approach the economic goal of a perfect thermodynamic engine through an understanding of the causes of waste." *The Science of Energy*, p. 154.

19. Sir Joseph Larmor, "William Thomson, Baron Kelvin of Largs, 1824–1907 (Obituary)," *Proceedings of the Royal Society*, vol. 81 (Appendix, 1908), pp. iii–lxvii at p. xxix.

20. Quoted in Sharlin, *Lord Kelvin*, p. 171.

21. See Smith, *The Science of Energy*, pp. 172–174.

22. The concept of root metaphor first appeared in Stephen Pepper, *World Hypotheses: A Study in Evidence* (Berkeley: University of California Press, 1948).

CHAPTER TWO: **Entropy as Metaphor**

1. James Johnstone, *The Philosophy of Biology* (Cambridge: Cambridge University Press, 1914), p. 54 n.1 (emphasis in original).

2. Use of the concept of entropy is widespread within the sciences. Biologists calculate the entropy increase in the diversification of species; economists estimate the distribution of goods by use of entropy; ecologists employ the term to talk about the dissipation of resources; and sociologists have developed a theory of socio-thermodynamics that ascribes an entropy of mixing to the integration of ethnic groups and a heat of mixing to their tendency to separate. See Ingo Müller, *A History of Thermodynamics: The Doctrine of Energy and Entropy* (Berlin: Springer, 2007), p. 73 and 159–164.

3. Percy W. Bridgman, *The Nature of Thermodynamics* (Cambridge, MA: Harvard University Press, 1941), p. 116.

4. John von Neumann as quoted in Myron T. Tribus and Edward C. McIrvine, "Energy and Information," *Scientific American*, vol. 225, no. 3. (September 1971), pp. 179–188 at p. 180.

5. See Jean-Bernard Brissaud, "The Meanings of Entropy," *Entropy*, vol. 7, no. 1 (March 2005), pp. 68–96, and Jos Uffink, "Bluff Your Way in the Second Law of Thermodynamics" (July 5, 2001), http://philsci-archive.pitt.edu/313/1/engtot.pdf.

6. University of Michigan, "Entropy Can Lead to Order, Paving the Route to Nanostructures," *Science Daily* (July 26, 2012), www.sciencedaily.com/releases/2012/07/120726142200.htm.

7. According to Sir William Thomson, credited with the idea of the universe's heat death, the Second Law's principle of the universal dissipation of mechanical energy produces "gradual augmentation and diffusion of heat, cessation of motion [useful work], and exhaustion of potential energy through the material universe. The result would inevitably be a state of universal rest and death, if the universe were finite and left to obey existing laws." William Thomson (Lord Kelvin), "On the Age of the Sun's Heat," *Macmillan's Magazine*, vol. 5 (March 5, 1862), pp. 388–393. Reprinted in William Thomson, *Popular Lectures and Addresses*, vol. 1, *Constitution of Matter* (London: Macmillan, 1889), quoted material from p. 349.

8. Arieh Ben-Naim, *Entropy Demystified: The Second Law Reduced to Common Sense* (Hackensack, NJ: World Scientific, 2007), chap. 6.

9. Ludwig Edward Boltzmann as quoted in Ingo Müller and Wolf Weiss, *Entropy and Energy: A Universal Competition* (Berlin: Springer-Verlag, 2005), p. 236.

10. "For very large N, more frequently equates with always!" Ben-Naim, *Entropy Demystified*, p. 144.

11. This example comes from Arthur Stanley Eddington, *The Nature of the Physical World* (Cambridge: Cambridge University Press, 1928), pp. 63–65.

12. In much the same way, order in the universe is being relentlessly replaced by increasing disorder; at least, that is how true believers in the universal applicability of entropy and the Second Law of Thermodynamics see it.

13. Peter T. Landsberg, *Entropy and the Unity of Knowledge* (Cardiff: University of Wales Press, 1961), p. 16.

14. James Clerk Maxwell to John William Strutt, 6 December 1870, in Elizabeth Garber, Stephen G. Brush, and C. W. F. Everitt, eds., *Maxwell on Heat and Statistical Mechanics: On "Avoiding All Personal Enquiries" of Molecules* (London: Associated University Presses, 1995), p. 205.

15. A macrostate is derived from its microscopic dynamics, such that a given macrostate may be represented by many different microstates, e.g., different configurations of molecular motion; different configurations of a pair of dice that yield the number seven, etc. Moreover, various macrostates can be realized by largely differing numbers of corresponding microstates. Equilibria are those macrostates that are most likely to appear because they have the largest number of corresponding microstates. See Andreas Greven, Gerhard Keller, and Gerald Warnecke, eds., *Entropy* (Princeton, NJ: Princeton University Press, 2003), chap. 1.

16. Anaxagoras's ideas about matter paved the way for atomic theory. See C. C. W. Taylor, "Anaxagoras and the Atomists" in C. C. W. Taylor, ed., *From the Beginning to Plato: Routledge History of Philosophy, Vol. 1* (New York: Routledge, 1997), pp. 208–243.

17. David Hawkins, *The Language of Nature: An Essay in the Philosophy of Science* (San Francisco: W. H. Freeman, 1964), pp. 206, 216.

18. Sir Oliver J. Lodge, *Life and Matter: A Criticism of Professor Haeckel's "Riddle of the Universe,"* 2nd ed. (London: Williams & Norgate, 1905), chap. 9.

19. Entropy is a time-asymmetric principle: it *increases* over time. There is, however, a corresponding puzzle of thermodynamic time-asymmetry (or T-asymmetry), which may be stated as follows: "There are many common and familiar physical processes, collectively describable as cases in which entropy is increasing, whose corresponding time-reversed processes are unknown or at least very rare. Yet, the dynamical laws governing such processes show no such T-asymmetry—if they permit a process to occur with one temporal orientation, they permit it to occur with the reverse orientation." Huw Price, "Time's Arrow and Eddington's Challenge," *Séminaire Poincaré*, vol. 15, *Le Temps* (2010), p. 119.

20. The British astronomer Sir Arthur S. Eddington, who coined the term "time's arrow," concluded, "If as we follow the arrow we find more and more of the random element in the state of the world, then the arrow is pointing towards the future." Eddington, *The Nature of the Physical World.*

21. Eric Zencey, "Entropy as Root Metaphor," in Joseph W. Slade and Judith Yaross Lee, eds., *Beyond the Two Cultures: Essays on Science, Technology, and Literature* (Ames: Iowa State University Press, 1990), p. 190.

22. Quoted in James Gleick, *The Information* (New York: Pantheon, 2011), pp. 273–74.

23. See Stephen G. Brooks and William C. Wohlforth, *World Out of Balance* (Princeton, NJ: Princeton University Press, 2008), p. 4.

CHAPTER THREE: **The Multidimensions of Disorder**

1. Halford J. Mackinder, "The Geographical Pivot of History," *Geographical Journal*, vol. 23, no. 4 (December 1904), pp. 421–444, reprinted in *Geographical Journal*, vol. 170, no. 4 (December 2004), pp. 298–321 at p. 299.

2. The U.S. naval base at Guantánamo, which occupies forty-five square miles on the southeastern end of Cuba, is "one of the known world's last no man's lands, an island out of time, a place without a state"; it is, accordingly, "the legal equivalent of outer space." Jill Lepore, "The Dark Ages: Terrorism, Counterterrorism, and the Law of Torment," *New Yorker* (March 18, 2013), pp. 28–32 at p. 29.

3. Thomas Pynchon, "Entropy" in *Slow Learner* (New York: Little, Brown, 1984), pp. 88–89.

4. In 2006, U.S. defense expenditures accounted for 65.6 percent of total defense expenditures among the great powers (the United States, China, Japan, Germany, Russia, France, and Britain). For this figure and U.S. defense expenditures as a percentage of world defense expenditures, see G. John Ikenberry, Michael Mastanduno, and William C. Wohlforth, "Introduction: Unipolarity, State Behavior, and Systemic Consequences," *World Politics*, vol. 61, no. 1 (January 2009), pp. 1–27 at p. 7.

5. Barry R. Posen, "Command of the Commons: The Military Foundation of U.S. Hegemony," *International Security*, vol. 28, no. 1 (Summer 2003), pp. 5–46.

6. See Stephen G. Brooks and William C. Wohlforth, *World Out of Balance* (Princeton, NJ: Princeton University Press, 2008).

7. There is one important way by which unipolarity constrains other powers: no state can balance the unipolar power. Under bipolarity, in contrast, each pole can balance the other solely by its own internal means.

8. For the record of post–Cold War U.S. interventions, see Nuno Monterio, "Unrest Assured: Why Unipolarity Is Not Peaceful," *International Security*, vol. 36, no. 3 (Winter 2011/2012), pp. 9–40.

9. Kenneth N. Waltz characterized unipolarity as a structure prone to overextension by the unipole, implying that unchecked power results in its reckless and capricious exercise. See Waltz, "Structural Realism after the Cold War," *International Security*, vol. 25, no. 1 (Summer 2000), pp. 5–41 at p. 13.

10. Charles L. Glaser, "Structural Realism in a More Complex World," *Review of International Studies*, vol. 29, no. 3 (July 2003), pp. 403–414 at pp. 412–413.

11. Robert Jervis, "Force in Our Times," in James W. Davis, ed., *Psychology, Strategy and Conflict: Perceptions of Insecurity in International Relations* (London: Routledge, 2012), pp. 220–241 at p. 227.

12. For a comprehensive review of power transition theory, see Jonathan M. DiCicco and Jack S. Levy, "Power Shifts and Problem Shifts: The Evolution of the Power Transition Research Program," *Journal of Conflict Resolution*, vol. 43, no. 6 (December 1999), pp. 675–704. For a critique of power transition theory, see Steve Chan, *China, the U.S., and the Power-Transition Theory* (New York: Routledge, 2008).

13. Aaron L. Friedberg, "Hegemony with Chinese Characteristics," *National Interest*, no. 114 (July/August 2011), p. 18.

14. Michelle Murray, "Identity, Insecurity, and Great Power Politics: The Tragedy of German Naval Ambition before the First World War," *Security Studies*, vol. 19, no. 4 (October–December 2010), pp. 656–688.

15. See Robert Gilpin, *War and Change in World Politics* (New York: Cambridge University Press, 1981).

16. Alastair I. Johnston and Sheena Chestnut, "Is China Rising?" in Eva Paus, Penelope Prime, and Jon Western, eds., *Global Giant: Is China Changing the Rules of the Game?* (New York: Palgrave Macmillan, 2009), pp. 242–243.

17. The Doors, "Roadhouse Blues," music and lyrics by John Densmore, Robby Krieger, Ray Manzarek, and Jim Morrison, *Morrison Hotel* (Elektra/Warner Brothers, 1970).

18. Conspiracy theories are driven by this incongruity. The average person doesn't want to believe that an insignificant person like Lee Harvey Oswald could have been the lone assassin of John F. Kennedy.

19. Niall Ferguson, "Complexity and Collapse: Empires on the Edge of Chaos," *Foreign Affairs*, vol. 89, no. 2 (March/April 2010), p. 32.

20. Similarly, Barry R. Posen notes, "One reason for this [narrowing gap between the great powers' military capabilities and those of middle powers, small states, and non-state actors] was the collapse of the Soviet Union and Warsaw Pact, which permitted a vast outflow of infantry weapons. At the same time, some of the former Soviet republics and East European Warsaw Pact states inherited arms production capabilities in search of markets." Posen, "Emerging Multipolarity: Why Should We Care?" *Current History* (November 2009), reprinted in Robert J. Art and Robert Jervis, eds., *International Politics: Enduring Concepts and Contemporary Issues*, 11th ed. (Upper Saddle River, NJ: Pearson Education, 2013), pp. 552–560 at p. 557. See also Jeffrey Herbst, *States and Power in Africa: Comparative Lessons in Authority and Control* (Princeton, NJ: Princeton University Press, 2000), p. 255.

21. Posen, "Emerging Multipolarity," p. 558.

22. The Federation of American Scientists, "Liberation Movements, Terrorist Organizations, Substance Cartels, and Other Para-State Entities," www.fas.org/irp/world/para/index.html.

23. Phil Williams, *Violent Non-state Actors and National and International Security* (Zurich: International Relations and Security Network, 2008), p. 18.

24. See Jakub Grygiel, "The Primacy of Premodern History," *Security Studies*, vol. 22, no. 1 (January–March 2013), pp. 1–32, esp. pp. 27–29, and Rupert Smith, *The Utility of Force* (New York: Knopf, 2005), p. 273.

25. Richard N. Haass, "Paradigm Lost," *Foreign Affairs*, vol. 74, no. 1 (January/February 1995), pp. 43–58, and "The Age of Nonpolarity: What Will Follow U.S. Dominance," *Foreign Affairs*, vol. 87, no. 3 (May/June 2008), pp. 44–56 at p. 56; Ann-Marie Slaughter, "America's Edge: Power in the Networked World," *Foreign Affairs*, vol. 88, no. 1 (January/February 2009), pp. 94–113; Fareed Zakaria, *The Post-American World* (New York: W. W. Norton, 2008), p. 243.

26. See Stewart Patrick, "Prix Fixe *and* à la Carte: Avoiding False Multilateral Choices," *Washington Quarterly*, vol. 32, no. 4 (October 2009), pp. 77–95.

27. Richard L. Armitage and Joseph S. Nye Jr., "Introduction: How America Became a Smarter Power," in *CSIS Commission on Smart Power: A Smarter, More Secure America* (Washington, DC: Center for Strategic and International Studies [CSIS] Press, 2007), p. 7; Chester A. Crocker, Fen Osler Hampson, and Pamela R. Aall, "Leashing the Dogs of War," in Crocker, Hampson, and Aall, eds., *Leashing the Dogs of War: Conflict Management in a Divided World* (Washington, DC: U.S. Institute of Peace, 2007), p. 13; Suzanne Nossel, "Smart Power," *Foreign Affairs*, Vol. 83, No. 2 (March/April 2004), p. 138.

28. Secretary of State Hillary Rodham Clinton, "Foreign Policy Address at the Council on Foreign Relations," U.S. State Department, Washington, DC (July 15, 2009), www .state.gov/secretary/rm/2009a/july/126071.htm.

29. Andrew F. Krepinevich Jr., "Strategy in a Time of Austerity: Why the Pentagon Should Focus on Assuring Access," *Foreign Affairs*, vol. 91, no. 6 (November/December 2012), pp. 58–69 at p. 63.

30. The concept of power makes sense only when the scope and domain of power (or influence attempt) are clearly specified. That is, a power relationship must identify power over whom and with respect to what. See Harold D. Lasswell and Abraham Kaplan, *Power and Society: A Framework for Political Inquiry* (New Haven, CT: Yale University Press, 1950); David A. Baldwin, "Power Analysis and World Politics: New Trends versus Old Tendencies," *World Politics*, vol. 31, no. 2 (January 1979), pp. 161–194, *Economic Statecraft* (Princeton, NJ: Princeton University Press, 1985), and *The Paradoxes of Power* (New York: Blackwell, 1989); and Stephen Lukes, *Power: A Radical View* (New York: Palgrave Macmillan, 2005).

31. For an informed argument that military resources are far more fungible than they have been typically portrayed, see Robert J. Art, "American Foreign Policy and the Fungibility of Force," *Security Studies*, vol. 5, no. 4 (Summer 1996), pp. 7–42.

32. Joseph S. Nye Jr., *The Paradox of American Power: Why the World's Only Superpower Cannot Go It Alone* (Oxford: Oxford University Press, 2002), p. 89.

33. See Gilpin, *War and Change*.

34. Nick Bilton, "Apple Denies Giving F.B.I. Device Information," *New York Times* (September 5, 2012), http://bits.blogs.nytimes.com/2012/09/05/apple-denies-giving-f-b-i -device-information/.

35. Robert Holton, "Globalization's Cultural Consequences," *Annals of the American Academy of Political and Social Science*, vol. 570 (July 2000), p. 150.

36. For hybridization, see Jan Nederveen Pieterse, *Globalization and Culture: Global Mélange* (Lanham, MD: Rowman & Littlefield, 2009).

37. Holton, "Globalization's Cultural Consequences," p. 142.

38. David Singh Grewal, *Network Power: The Social Dynamics of Globalization* (New Haven, CT: Yale University Press, 2008).

39. Ibid., p. 36.

40. Ibid., p. 6.

41. Ibid., p. 3.

CHAPTER FOUR: **The Role of Emerging Powers in the Age of Entropy**

1. See David A. Lake, "Beneath the Commerce of Nations: A Theory of International Economic, Structures," *International Studies Quarterly*, vol. 28, no. 2 (June 1984), pp. 143–170,

and Randall L. Schweller and Xiaoyu Pu, "After Unipolarity: China's Visions of International Order in an Era of U.S. Decline," *International Security*, vol. 36, no. 1 (Summer 2011), pp. 41–72 at p. 42. For a somewhat different but complementary list of strategies available to secondary powers, see Kristen P. Williams, Steven E. Lobell, and Neal G. Jesse, eds., *Beyond Great Powers and Hegemons: Why Secondary States Support, Follow, or Challenge* (Stanford, CA: Stanford University Press, 2012).

2. Power transition theory is a dyadic theory about a rising state that is on the verge of overtaking a stronger but declining one. The more systemic versions of this theory are called Hegemonic-War Cycle Theory or Power Preponderance Theory. Another version is called Long Cycle theory. See, for instance, Charles F. Doran and Wes Parsons, "War and the Cycle of Relative Power," *American Political Science Review*, vol. 74, no. 4 (December 1980), pp. 947–965, and George Modelski, "The Long Cycle of Global Politics and the Nation-State," *Comparative Studies in Security and History*, no. 20 (April 1978), pp. 214–238. These theories share an important feature: they do not consider alliances in their analyses of power and international politics, which makes for some very strange historical interpretations. Most notably, "long cycle" histories typically ignore Russia prior to 1945. Given that the Russian army defeated both Napoleonic France and Nazi Germany, this is a rather remarkable oversight.

3. See Robert Gilpin, *War and Change in World Politics* (New York: Cambridge University Press, 1981).

4. The theory assumes that the rising power is risk-acceptant with respect to gains, the declining hegemon is risk-acceptant to avoid losses, or both.

5. See Stewart Patrick, "Irresponsible Stakeholders?: The Difficulty of Integrating Rising Powers," *Foreign Affairs*, vol. 89, no. 6 (November/December 2010), pp. 44–53 at p. 46.

6. IISS, *The Military Balance 2012* (London: IISS, 2012).

7. Robert S. Ross, "The Problem with the Pivot: Obama's New Asia Policy Is Unnecessary and Counterproductive," *Foreign Affairs*, vol. 91, no. 6 (November/December 2012), pp. 70–82 at p. 73.

8. IISS, *The Military Balance 2012*.

9. Carla A. Hills and Dennis C. Blair, chairs, *U.S.–China Relations: An Affirmative Agenda, A Responsible Course* (New York: Council on Foreign Relations, 2007), p. 54.

10. Minxin Pei, "China's Not a Superpower," *The Diplomat.Com* (2010), http://apac2020.the-diplomat.com/feature/china<#213>s-not-a-superpower/.

11. C. Fred Bergsten, "A Partnership of Equals: How Washington Should Respond to China's Economic Challenge," *Foreign Affairs*, vol. 87, no. 4 (July/August 2008), pp. 57–69 at p. 58.

12. Current Account is the sum of the balance of trade (exports minus imports of goods and services), net factor income (such as interest and dividends), and net transfer payments (such as foreign aid). Though Beijing announced a more flexible exchange rate for the yuan in June 2010, it has allowed its currency to weaken this year amid slowing growth. Consequently, China reported a trade surplus of $31.7 billion in June 2012, a three-year high; its exports for the first six months of the year also climbed 9.2% to $954.38 billion. See "China Balance of Trade," *Trading Economics*, www.tradingeconomics.com/china/balance-of-trade; Eric Platt, "China's Trade Surplus Surges to $31.7 Billion,

A Three Year High," *Business Insider* (July 9, 2012), www.businessinsider.com/china-june
-trade-balance-2012-7; Zheng Lifei, "China's Import Growth Misses Estimates for June,"
Bloomberg News (July 10, 2012), www.bloomberg.com/news/2012-07-10/china-s-import
-growth-misses-estimates-for-june.html; and "China's Trade Surplus Up as Imports
Weaken," *Yahoo! Finance* (UK & Ireland) (July 10, 2012), http://uk.finance.yahoo.com/
news/surprise-jump-china-trade-surplus-072009885.html.

13. Bergsten, "A Partnership of Equals."

14. Ibid., p. 58.

15. Ibid., pp. 58, 63–64.

16. Yang Jiechi, "A Changing China in a Changing World," address to the Munich
Security Conference, Munich, Germany (February 5, 2010).

17. Question and answer session with Chinese foreign minister Yang Jiechi, Munich
Security Conference (February 5, 2010), http://np.china-embassy.org/eng/zgwj/t656702
.htm.

18. Quoted in Aude Genet, "Chinese TV Show Aims to Tell Africa's Real Story,"
Agence France-Presse (August 13, 2012), http://news.yahoo.com/cctv-africas-true-image
-chinas-strategic-vehicle-071857892.html.

19. Yu-Shan Wu quoted in ibid.

20. Quoted in ibid.

21. Responding to claims by Western analysts that China has been adopting a more
aggressively assertive policy in recent years, Fang Lexian, a researcher with the School of
International Studies, Renmin University of China, Beijing, writes:

> This is . . . baseless. China's assertiveness reflects only confidence in its position
> in the international community and is based on a more rational perception of its
> place in the world. It is also quite a normal response for a country trying to persist
> with its 'peaceful rise' precept. This gesture must not be construed as arro-
> gance. . . . As the world's largest developing country, China deeply cherishes its
> friendship and close cooperation with other developing nations, as they have had
> similar historical experiences and share a common development agenda. Based on
> the principle of equality and mutual benefit, China seeks to cement cooperation
> with, and is willing to jointly safeguard the legitimate rights and interests of, de-
> veloping countries. This policy has won for China trust and respect from others,
> and should not be viewed as efforts by the nation to become a 'self-proclaimed'
> leader of developing countries.

Fang Lexian, "Peaceful Rise Still Way Forward," *China Daily* (June 7, 2010), www
.chinadaily.com.cn/opinion/2010-06/07/content_9940870.htm.

22. Jagannath P. Panda, *China's New "Multilateralism" and the Rise of BRIC: A Realist
Interpretation of a "Multipolar" World Order*, Asia Paper (Stockholm: Institute for Security
and Development Policy, 2011), p. 6. In this work, Panda offers a compelling realist view
of the instrumental reasons behind China's association with BRICS.

23. Andrew J. Nathan and Andrew Scobell, "How China Sees America: The Sum of
Beijing's Fears," *Foreign Affairs*, vol. 91, no. 5 (September/October 2012), pp. 32–47 at p. 33.

24. Ibid., p. 35.

25. Ibid., p. 36.

26. Minxin Pei, *China's Trapped Transition: The Limits of Developmental Autocracy* (Cambridge, MA: Harvard University Press, 2006), p. 214.

27. Gordon Chang, "The Party's Over: China's Endgame," *World Affairs* (March/April 2010), www.worldaffairsjournal.org/article/partys-over-chinas-endgame.

28. Steven F. Jackson, "A Typology for Stability and Instability in China," introduction to David Shambaugh, ed., *Is China Unstable?: Assessing the Factors* (Armonk, NY: M. E. Sharpe, 2000), p. 5; David Shambaugh, preface to ibid., p. x.

29. Roger Irvine, "Primacy and Responsibility: China's Perception of Its International Future," *China Security*, vol. 6, no. 3 (2010), pp. 23–42 at p. 24.

30. Robert W. Merry, "The Revenge of Kaplan's Maps," *National Interest*, no. 121 (September/October 2012), pp. 62–72 at p. 69. Some analysts talk about China's "String of Pearls" strategy. According to Christopher Pehrson, the String of Pearls describes the manifestation of China's rising geopolitical influence through efforts to increase access to ports and airfields, develop special diplomatic relationships, and modernize military forces that extend from the coast of mainland China, through the littorals of the South China Sea, the Strait of Malacca, and the Indian Ocean, to the littorals of the Arabian Sea and the Persian Gulf. See Christopher J. Pehrson, *String of Pearls: Meeting the Challenge of China's Rising Power across the Asian Littoral* (Carlisle, PA: Strategic Studies Institute, U.S. Army War College, 2006).

31. Rahul Sagar, "State of Mind: What Kind of Power Will India Become?" *International Affairs*, vol. 85, no. 4 (July 2009), pp. 801–816.

32. "India as a Great Power: Know Your Own Strength," *Economist*, vol. 406, no. 8829 (March 30–April 5, 2013), pp. 27–30 at p. 28.

33. Sagar, "State of Mind."

34. Li Hongmei, "India's 'Look East Policy' Means 'Look to Encircle China'?" *People's Daily Online*, (October 27, 2010), http://english.peopledaily.com.cn/90002/96417/7179404.html.

35. The Editors, "Global Insider: India, South Korea Discover Common Strategic Interests," *World Politics Review* (June 25, 2012), www.worldpoliticsreview.com/trend-lines/12092/global-insider-india-south-korea-discover-common-strategic-interests.

36. Richard Weitz, "Global Insights: Russia Faces Challenges in India's Arms Market," *World Politics Review* (August 7, 2012), www.worldpoliticsreview.com/articles/12236/global-insights-russia-faces-challenges-in-indias-arms-market.

37. Juan de Onis, "Brazil's Big Moment: A South American Giant Wakes Up," *Foreign Affairs*, vol. 87, no. 6 (November/December 2008), pp. 110–122 at p. 110.

38. See Charles Lyons, "The Dam Boom in the Amazon," *New York Times* (July 1, 2012), Sunday Review, pp. 6–7.

39. Marcelo Ballvé, "Economic Slowdown Could Be End of Smooth Ride for Brazil's Rousseff," *World Policy Review* (June 13, 2012), www.worldpoliticsreview.com/articles/12051/economic-slowdown-could-be-end-of-smooth-ride-for-brazils-rousseff.

40. Goldman Sachs Global Economics Group, *BRICs and Beyond* (New York: Goldman Sachs Group, 2007).

41. Stephen M. Walt, "Alliances in a Unipolar World," *World Politics*, vol. 61, no. 1 (January 2009), p. 104.

42. Matias Spektor, "Brazilian Visions of Global Order," Memorandum for Discussion, U.S. National Intelligence Council Meeting, Washington, DC (November 12, 2010), p. 2.

43. President Lula said, "This is a crisis that was caused by people, white with blue eyes. And before the crisis they looked as if they knew everything about economics. . . . Once again the great part of the poor in the world that were still not yet [getting] their share of development that was caused by globalisation, they were the first ones to suffer. . . . Since I am not acquainted with any black bankers, I can only say that this part of humanity that is the major victim of the world crisis, these people should pay for the crisis? I cannot accept that. If the G20 becomes a meeting just to set another meeting, we'll be discredited and the crisis can deepen." Remarks by Brazilian President Luiz Inacio Lula da Silva at a Joint Press Conference with British Foreign Office Minister Lord Malloch-Brown, Brazilia, Brazil (March 25, 2009).

44. Peter Hakim, "A U.S.–Brazil Respect Deficit," *Los Angeles Times* (April 9, 2012), www.latimes.com/news/opinion/commentary/la-oe-hakim-brazil-policy-20120409,0, 6315636.story.

45. Brazilian foreign minister Celso Amorim quoted in Gus Lubin, "Brazil: Sorry Hillary, But We're Going to Side with Iran," *Business Insider* (March 4, 2010), www .businessinsider.com/brazil-sorry-but-were-going-to-keep-trading-with-iran-2010-3.

46. Simon Romero, "Brazil Gains Business and Influence as It Offers Aid and Loans in Africa," *New York Times* (August 7, 2012), p. A4.

47. Ibid.

48. See www.odebrecht.com/en/businesses-and-interests/international.

49. Romero, "Brazil Gains Business."

50. Nikolas K. Gvosdev, "BRIC Wall," *National Interest* (March 10, 2010), http:// nationalinterest.org/article/bric-wall-3402.

51. Chris Zambelis, "Egypt Gains Balance and Leverage in China," *Asia Times Online* (September 26, 2012), www.atimes.com/atimes/China/NI26Ad02.html.

52. Nikolas K. Gvosdev, "The Realist Prism: As Egypt Resets U.S. Ties, China Waits in the Wings," *World Politics Review* (September 28, 2012), www.worldpoliticsreview.com /articles/12379/the-realist-prism-as-egypt-resets-u-s-ties-china-waits-in-the-wings.

53. Ibid.

54. Randall L. Schweller, "Entropy and the Trajectory of World Politics: Why Polarity Has Become Less Meaningful," *Cambridge Review of International Affairs*, vol. 23, no. 1 (March 2010), pp. 145–163.

CHAPTER FIVE: **How Power Diffusion Works to a State's Advantage**

1. In some but not all ways, this situation resembles an orthodox liberal world, wherein international politics, like all politics, is a positive-sum game but remains quite competitive due to social and material scarcity. The concept of equilibrium is, by definition, a Pareto optimal condition, that is, one in which no actor has an interest in changing. See Alex Callinicos, "Does Capitalism Need the State System?" *Cambridge Review of International Affairs*, vol. 20, no. 4 (December 2007), pp. 533–549 at p. 546.

2. For the automatic balance of power, see Inis L. Claude Jr., *Power and International Relations* (New York: Random House, 1962).

3. Robert Gilpin, *Global Political Economy: Understanding the International Economic Order* (Princeton, NJ: Princeton University Press, 2001), p. 22.

4. "FM: 'No Power Shift Eastward,'" *China Daily* (August 2, 2010), www.chinadaily .com.cn/opinion/2010-08/02/content_11078582.htm.

5. See Jakub J. Grygiel, *Great Powers and Geopolitical Change* (Baltimore: Johns Hopkins University Press, 2006), chap. 7.

6. Catherine Cheney, "India, China Dial Back Tensions, but Problems Remain," *World Politics Review* (September 5, 2012), www.worldpoliticsreview.com/trend-lines /12306/india-china-dial-back-tensions-but-problems-remain.

7. See, for example, John Mueller, "War Has Almost Ceased to Exist: An Assessment," *Political Science Quarterly*, vol. 124, no. 2 (Summer 2009), pp. 297–321; Raimo Vayrynen, ed., *The Waning of Major Wars: Theories and Debates* (New York: Routledge, 2005); Christopher Fettweis, *Dangerous Times? The International Politics of Great Power Peace* (Washington, DC: Georgetown University Press, 2010); J. Joseph Hewitt, Jonathan Wilkenfeld, and Ted R. Gurr, *Peace and Conflict 2012* (Boulder, CO: Paradigm Publishers, 2009); World Bank, *World Development Report 2011: Conflict, Security, and Development* (Washington, DC: World Bank, 2011); Steven Pinker, *The Better Angels of Our Nature: Why Violence Has Declined* (New York: Viking, 2011); and Joshua Goldstein, *Winning the War on War: The Decline of Armed Conflict Worldwide* (New York: Dutton, 2011).

8. John J. Mearsheimer, *The Tragedy of Great Power Politics* (New York: W. W. Norton, 2001), pp. 43, 53.

9. Robert Jervis, "Cooperation under the Security Dilemma," *World Politics*, vol. 30, no. 2 (January 1978), p. 187.

10. Ibid., p. 167.

11. Ibid., p. 187. Also see Robert Jervis, "Was the Cold War a Security Dilemma?" *Journal of Cold War Studies*, vol. 3, no. 1 (Winter 2001), pp. 36–60.

12. See John Mueller, *The Remnants of War* (Ithaca, NY: Cornell University Press, 2004) and "Why Isn't There More Violence?" *Security Studies*, vol. 13, no. 3 (spring 2004), pp. 191–203.

13. Charles L. Glaser, *Rational Theory of International Politics: The Logic of Competition and Cooperation* (Princeton, NJ: Princeton University Press, 2010), p. 36.

14. Peter Liberman, *Does Conquest Pay? The Exploitation of Occupied Industrial Societies* (Princeton, NJ: Princeton University Press, 1996).

15. For a "domestic politics" explanation for the puzzle of under-aggression and under-expansion since 1945, see Randall L. Schweller, "Neoclassical Realism and State Mobilization: Expansionist Ideology in the Age of Mass Politics," in Steven E. Lobell, Norrin M. Ripsman, and Jeffrey W. Taliaferro, eds., *Neoclassical Realism, the State, and Foreign Policy* (Cambridge: Cambridge University Press, 2009), chap. 8.

16. Jeffrey Herbst, "War and the State in Africa," *International Security*, vol. 14, no. 4 (Spring 1990), p. 123.

17. K. J. Holsti, "International Relations Theory and Domestic War in the Third World: The Limits of Relevance," in Stephanie G. Neuman, ed., *International Relations Theory and the Third World* (New York: St. Martin's Press, 1998), p. 106.

18. They do fear terrorist attacks, however, and their fears are largely unwarranted and overblown. For the most recent and thorough discussion of this phenomenon, see

John Mueller and Mark Stewart, *Terrorism, Security, and Money: Balancing the Risks, Benefits, and Costs of Homeland Security* (New York: Oxford University Press, 2011).

19. See Robert Pape, "Empire Falls," *National Interest*, No. 99 (January/February 2009), pp. 21–34. For contrary views, see Stephen G. Brooks and William C. Wohlforth, *World Out of Balance* (Princeton, NJ: Princeton University Press, 2008), and, to a lesser extent, Fareed Zakaria, *The Post-American World* (New York: W. W. Norton, 2008).

20. For various views on the future status of the U.S. dollar, see Barry Eichengreen, *Exorbitant Privilege: The Decline of the Dollar and the Future of the International Monetary System* (New York: Oxford University Press, 2011) and "The Dollar Dilemma: The World's Top Currency Faces Competition," *Foreign Affairs*, vol. 88, no. 5 (September/October 2009), pp. 53–68; C. Fred Bergsten, "The Dollar and Deficits: How Washington Can Prevent the Next Crisis," *Foreign Affairs*, vol. 88, no. 6 (November/December 2009), pp. 20–38; and Roger C. Altman and Richard N. Haas, "American Profligacy and American Power: The Consequences of Fiscal Irresponsibility," *Foreign Affairs*, vol. 89, no. 6 (November/December 2010), pp. 25–34.

21. Referring to the annual meeting of westernized elites in Switzerland, Samuel P. Huntington coined the phrase "Davos culture," which comprises an elite group of highly educated people who operate in the rarefied domains of international finance, media, and diplomacy and share common beliefs about individualism, market economics, and democracy. See. Huntington, *The Clash of Civilizations and the Remaking of World Order* (New York: Touchstone, 1996), chap. 3.

CHAPTER SIX: **Rising Entropy at the Macro Level**

1. Geopolitics is the study of the relationship between politics and territory. As a method of foreign policy analysis, it uses geographical variables to explain and predict international political behavior and to prescribe foreign policies that exploit opportunities and guard against threats in the state's external environment.

2. See Robert D. Kaplan, *The Revenge of Geography: What the Map Tells Us about Coming Conflicts and the Battle against Fate* (New York: Random House, 2012).

3. Pankaj Ghemawat with Steven A. Altman, *DHL Global Connectedness Index 2011: Analyzing Global Flows and Their Power to Increase Prosperity* (Bonn: Deutsche Post DHL, 2011), pp. 17–21, quoted material appears on p. 21.

4. National Intelligence Council, *Mapping the Global Future: Report of the National Intelligence Council's 2020 Project* (Washington DC: US Government Printing Office, December 2004), p. 9, online at www/dni.gov/nic/NIC_2020_project.html.

5. For trenchant analysis of the Obama administration's drone program, see David Cole, "Drones and the CIA: 13 Questions for John O. Brennan," *New York Review of Books*, vol. 60, no. 3 (February 21, 2013), pp. 8 and 10.

6. Peter Andreas and Richard Price, "From War Fighting to Crime Fighting: Transforming the American National Security State," *International Studies Review*, vol. 3, no. 3 (Fall 2001), pp. 31–52 at p. 35.

7. Scott Shane, "Rise of the Predators: Targeted Killing Comes to Define War on Terror," *New York Times* (April 7, 2013), p. A1.

8. Richard K. Betts, "The Soft Underbelly of American Primacy: Tactical Advantages of Terror," *Political Science Quarterly*, vol. 117, no. 1 (Spring 2002), pp. 19–36.

9. William J. Lynn III, "Defending a New Domain: The Pentagon's Cyberstrategy," *Foreign Affairs*, vol. 89, no. 5 (September/October 2010), pp. 97–108.

10. Nicole Perlroth, "Virus Infects Computers across Middle East," *New York Times* (May 28, 2012), http://bits.blogs.nytimes.com/2012/05/28/new-computer-virus-looks-like -a-cyberweapon/.

11. See Kenneth Ryan, "The New Face of Global Espionage," *World Politics Review* (June 5, 2012), www.worldpoliticsreview.com/articles/12020/the-new-face-of-global -espionage?page=1.

12. Quoted in Nicole Perlroth and David E. Sanger, "Cyberattacks Seem Meant to Destroy, Not Just Disrupt," *New York Times* (March 29, 2013), pp. B1–B2 at B2.

13. Moisés Naím, "Five Wars of Globalization," *Foreign Policy* (January/February 2003), pp. 29–36 at pp. 29–30. See also Moisés Naím, *Illicit: How Smugglers, Traffickers, and Copycats Are Hijacking the Global Economy* (New York: Anchor Books, 2005).

14. John Arquilla and David Ronfeldt, "The Advent of Netwar (Revisited)," in John Arquilla and David Ronfeldt, eds., *Networks and Netwars: The Future of Terror, Crime, and Militancy* (Santa Monica, CA: RAND Corporation, 2001), p. 1.

15. Ibid., pp. 1–25; John Arquilla and David Ronfeldt, *Swarming and the Future of Conflict* (Santa Monica, CA: RAND Corporation, DB-311-OSD, 2000).

16. *U.S. National Security Strategy* (Washington, DC: U.S. Government Printing Office, May 2010), p. 19.

17. Johan Bergenas, "Defense, Security and Development in a Hybrid World," *World Politics Review* (September 11, 2012), www.worldpoliticsreview.com/articles/12324 /defense-security-and-development-in-a-hybrid-world?page=3.

18. See "Preparation of Government Stabilization Program Worldwide, Danish International Development Agency (DANIDA)," www.devex.com/en/projects/preparation -of-government-stabilisation-programme-worldwide.

19. See Johan Bergenas and Richard Sabatini, "Japan Takes the Lead in Coordinating Security and Development Aid," *World Politics Review* (August 1, 2012), www.world politicsreview.com/articles/12220/japan-takes-the-lead-in-coordinating-security-and -development-aid.

20. Mark Mazzetti and Eric Schmitt, "Murky Legacy of Army Hired to Fight Piracy: Stranded Soldiers Pose a Threat in Somalia," *New York Times* (October 5, 2012), p. A1.

21. Slaughter, "America's Edge."

22. George Hegel, *Philosophy of Right*, trans. T. M. Knox (1821; reprint, London: Oxford University Press, 1967), p. 76.

23. Mancur Olson, *The Rise and Decline of Nations: Economic Growth, Stagflation, and Social Rigidities* (New Haven, CT: Yale University Press, 1982).

24. Tanisha M. Fazal, *State Death: The Politics and Geography of Conquest, Occupation, and Annexation* (Princeton, NJ: Princeton University Press, 2008).

25. "Looking for India's Zuckerberg," *Economist*, vol. 406, no. 8827 (March 16–22, 2013), p. 16–17 at p. 16.

26. Vikas Bajaj, "As Grain Piles Up, India's Poor Still Go Hungry," *New York Times*, June 8, 2012, pp. A1 and A3.

27. Richard K. Betts, "The Delusion of Impartial Intervention," *Foreign Affairs*, Vol. 73, No. 6 (November/December 1994), pp. 20–33 at p. 31.

28. See Patrick, "Irresponsible Stakeholders?" and Kara C. McDonald and Stewart M. Patrick, *UN Security Council Enlargement and U.S. Interests*, Council Special Report no. 59 (New York: Council on Foreign Relations, 2010).

29. See Daniel W. Drezner, "The New New World Order," *Foreign Affairs*, vol. 86, no. 2 (March/April 2007), pp. 34–46; Benjamin J. Cohen, "The International Monetary System: Diffusion and Ambiguity," *International Affairs*, vol. 84, no. 3 (May 2008), pp. 455–470; and Scott Barrett, *Why Cooperate? The Incentive to Supply Global Public Goods* (New York: Oxford University Press, 2007).

30. Ian Bremmer, *Every Nation for Itself: Winners and Losers in a G-Zero World* (New York: Portfolio/Penguin, 2012).

31. See Michael Ignatieff, "We're So Exceptional," *New York Review of Books*, vol. 59, no. 6 (April 5, 2012), pp. 6, 8; David Scheffer, *All the Missing Souls: A Personal History of the War Crimes Tribunals* (Princeton, NJ: Princeton University Press, 2012); and Lydia Polgreen, "Global Courts, Uneven Justice: Arab Spring Highlights Flaws in the System," *New York Times* (July 8, 2012), pp. 1, 9.

32. David Brooks, "Where Obama Shines," *New York Times* (July 20, 2012), p. A19.

33. Gillian Wong, "China Touts Relations with Africa amid Grumbling," Associated Press (July 18, 2012), http://news.yahoo.com/china-touts-relations-africa-amid -grumbling-031631463—finance.html.

34. Ibid.

35. Ibid.

36. Jacob Zuma, address at the China-Africa Forum on Cooperation in Beijing (July 19, 2012), quoted in Jane Perlez, "With $20 Billion Loan Pledge, China Strengthens Ties to African Nations," *New York Times* (July 20, 2012), p. A6, and Leslie Hook, "Zuma Warns on Africa's Trade Ties to China," *Washington Post* (July 19, 2012), www.washington-post.com/world/asia_pacific/zuma-warns-on-africas-trade-ties-to-china/2012/07/19 /gJQAFgd7vW_story.html.

37. Ibid.

38. Quoted in Michael Martina, "China Aims to Rewrite Perceptions on Africa Investment Push-envoy," Reuters (July 18, 2012), http://news.yahoo.com/china-aims-re-write-perceptions-africa-investment-push-envoy-105554153—business.html.

39. Quoted in Perlez, "With $20 Billion Loan Pledge," p. A6.

40. Jane Perlez, "In Crisis with Japan, China Adjusts Strategy but Does Not Back Down," *New York Times* (September 30, 2012), p. 8.

41. Patrick Chovanec, "China-Japan Rare Earth Fracas Continues," *Forbes* (October 17, 2010), www.forbes.com/sites/china/2010/10/17/china-japan-rare-earth-fracas-continues/.

42. The following points are drawn from Herbert Lin, "Cyber Conflict and National Security," in Robert J. Art and Robert Jervis, eds., *International Politics: Enduring Concepts and Contemporary Issues*, 11th ed. (Upper Saddle River, NJ: Pearson Education, 2013), pp. 476–489 at p. 480.

43. William J. Lynn, III, "Defending a New Domain: The Pentagon's Cyberstrategy," *Foreign Affairs*, vol. 89, no. 5 (September/October 2010), pp. 97–108 at p. 99.

44. Lin, "Cyber Conflict and National Security," p. 478.

45. James W. Davis, "A Critical View of Global Governance," *Swiss Political Science Review*, vol. 18, no. 2 (June 2012), pp. 272–286 at p. 273.

46. John Gerard Ruggie, "Reconstituting the Global Public Domain—Issues, Actors, and Practices," *European Journal of International Relations*, vol. 10, no. 4 (December 2004), pp. 499–531 at p. 519.

47. Jeremy Rabkin, *Law without Nations? Why Constitutional Government Requires Sovereign States* (Princeton, NJ: Princeton University Press, 2005), p. 42.

48. Davis, "A Critical View of Global Governance," p. 276.

49. Margaret Chan, "Opening Remarks at the Fifth Global Meeting of Heads of WHO Country Offices," Geneva, Switzerland (November 2, 2009).

50. David A. Nadler, Robert B. Shaw, A. Elise Walton, and Associates, *Discontinuous Change: Leading Organizational Transformation* (San Francisco: Jossey-Bass, 1995), p. xiv.

CHAPTER SEVEN: **Rising Entropy at the Micro Level**

1. For a remarkably insightful and prescient book on the subject, see Orrin E Klapp, *Overload and Boredom: Essays on the Quality of Life in the Information Society* (New York: Greenwood Press, 1986).

2. Herbert A. Simon, "Designing Organizations for an Information-Rich World," in Martin Greenberger, ed., *Computers, Communication, and the Public Interest* (Baltimore: Johns Hopkins University Press, 1971), pp. 40–41.

3. Quoted in Hendrik Hertzberg, "Open Secrets," *New Yorker* (August 2, 2010), p. 18.

4. See Farhad Manjoo, *True Enough: Learning to Live in a Post-fact World* (Hoboken, NJ: John Wiley, 2008); David W. Moore, "Three in Four Americans Believe in Paranormal: Little Change from Similar Results in 2001," Gallup News Service (June 16, 2005), p. 12, www.gallup.com/poll/16915/Three-Four-Americans-Believe-Paranormal.aspx; and "Most Americans Believe in Ghosts: Survey Shows 1/3 Accept Astrology, 1/4 Reincarnation," *WorldNetDaily* (February 27, 2003), www.wnd.com/2003/02/17494/.

5. Quoted in Thomas L. Friedman, "Do You Want the Good News First?" *New York Times* (May 20, 2012), Sunday Review, p. 1.

6. Lymari Morales, "U.S. Distrust in Media Hits New High: Fewer Americans Closely Following Political News Now Than in Previous Election Years," *Gallup Politics* (September 21, 2012), at www.gallup.com/poll/157589/distrust-media-hits-new-high.aspx.

7. Josh Kron and J. David Goodman, "Online, a Distant Conflict Soars to Topic No. 1," *New York Times* (March 9, 2012), pp. A1 and A3.

8. Brian Stelter, "From Flash to Fizzle," *New York Times* (April 15, 2012), Sunday Review, p. 5. *Kony 2012* appeared in early March and rocketed at unheard of speeds across Twitter and Facebook by the middle of March only to flicker out by early April.

9. Edward Wong, "An Unlikely Jihadist, Denouncing Assad in Mandarin," *New York Times* (March 30, 2013), p. A7.

10. Tony Dokoupil, "Tweets. Texts. Email. Posts. Is the Onslaught Making Us Crazy?" *Newsweek* (July 16, 2012), pp. 24–30 at p. 26.

11. Ibid., p. 27.

12. Ibid.

13. Calling it the great American crack-up is a bit unfair, as these disorders have also been widely studied and reported in Britain, Korea, China, Taiwan, and Israel, among others places. It's a truly global phenomenon.

14. In fact, the relationship between cyberspace and democracy and freedom is far more complex. See Ian Bremmer, "Democracy in Cyberspace," *Foreign Affairs*, vol. 89, no. 6 (November/December 2010), pp. 86–92.

15. Eric Schmidt and Jared Cohen, "The Digital Disruption: Connectivity and the Diffusion of Power," *Foreign Affairs*, vol. 89, no. 6 (November/December 2010), pp. 75–85 at p. 75.

16. Larry Rosen as quoted in IB Times Staff Reporter, "Facebook May Cause Psychological Disorders, Study Says," *International Business Times* (August 9, 2011), www.ibtimes.com/facebook-may-cause-psychological-disorders-study-says-827739.

17. See, for instance, Nick Yee, Jeremy N. Bailenson, and Nicolas Ducheneaut, "The Proteus Effect: Implications of Transformed Digital Self-Representation on Online and Offline Behavior," *Communication Research*, vol. 36, no. 2 (April 2009), pp. 285–312.

18. Hing Keung Ma, "Internet Addiction and Antisocial Internet Behavior of Adolescents," *ScientificWorld Journal*, vol. 11 (2011), Article ID 308631, 10 pp, www.hindawi.com/journals/tswj/2011/308631/; R. A. Davis, "Cognitive-behavioral Model of Pathological Internet Use," *Computers in Human Behavior*, vol. 17, no. 2, (March 2001), pp. 187–195. Five diagnostic criteria have been advanced for a diagnosis of Internet addiction: the person (1) is preoccupied with the Internet (thinks about previous online activity or anticipates next online session); (2) needs to use the Internet for increased amounts of time in order to achieve satisfaction; (3) has made unsuccessful efforts to control, cut back, or stop Internet use; (4) is restless, moody, depressed, or irritable when attempting to cut down or stop Internet use; and (5) has stayed online longer than originally intended. In addition to these five symptoms, at least one of the following must be present: the person (1) has jeopardized or risked the loss of a significant relationship, job, educational, or career opportunity because of the Internet; (2) has lied to family members, therapist, or others to conceal the extent of involvement with the Internet; (3) uses the Internet as a way of escaping from problems or of relieving a dysphoric mood (e.g., feelings of helplessness, guilt, anxiety, depression). Hilarie Cash, Cosette D. Rae, Ann H. Steel, and Alexander Winkler, "Internet Addiction: A Brief Summary of Research and Practice," *Current Psychiatry Reviews*, vol. 8, no. 4 (November 2012), pp. 292–298 at p. 293.

19. Much of this section is drawn from Jennifer Mitzen and Randall L. Schweller, "Knowing the Unknown Unknowns: Misplaced Certainty and the Onset of War," *Security Studies*, vol. 20, no. 1 (January–March 2011), pp. 2–35.

20. The enduring work on the politics of "overselling" is Theodore Lowi, *The End of Liberalism* (New York: Norton, 1969), chap. 6.

21. Stephen Van Evera calls this phenomenon *blowback*, whereby elites and states become entrapped by their own myths. See Jack L. Snyder, *Myths of Empire: Domestic Politics and International Ambition* (Ithaca, NY: Cornell University Press, 1991), pp. 41–42.

22. Jeffrey W. Taliaferro, *Balancing Risks: Great Power Intervention in the Periphery* (Ithaca, NY: Cornell University Press, 2004), p. 32; George Quattrone and Amos Tversky, "Contrasting Rational and Psychological Analysis of Political Choice," *American Political Science Review*, vol. 82, no. 3 (September 1988), pp. 719–736 at p. 722.

23. Robert Jervis, *Why Intelligence Fails: Lessons from the Iranian Revolution and the Iraq War* (Ithaca, NY: Cornell University Press, 2010), p. 127.

24. Ibid., pp. 157–158.

25. Quoted in Walter Russell Mead, *Power, Terror, Peace, and War: America's Grand Strategy in a World at Risk* (New York: Alfred A. Knopf, 2004), p. 116.

26. Quoted in Thomas E. Ricks, *Fiasco: The American Military Adventure in Iraq* (New York: Penguin, 2006), p. 49.

27. For a discussion of how mutual overconfidence and positive illusions fueled this war, see Dominic D. P. Johnson, *Overconfidence and War: The Havoc and Glory of Positive Illusions* (Cambridge, MA: Harvard University Press, 2004), chap. 8.

28. One is tempted to say that in all stock transactions, either the buyer or seller is wrong about the future price of the stock. This is not true, however, for all stock trades. The seller and the buyer can agree about the future price of the stock, be correct, and still make the transaction. This is because it is possible that the seller, like the buyer, thinks that the stock will rise but chooses to sell anyway because, inter alia, he or she believes that another stock will rise even higher or faster or both than the one he or she is selling. A margin call can also explain agreement among traders about the future price of a stock.

29. Arie Kruglanski and Donna Webster, "Motivated Closing of the Mind: 'Seizing' and 'Freezing,'" *Psychological Review*, vol. 103, no. 2 (April 1996), pp. 263–283.

30. Here, *updating* refers to "Bayesian updating"—a method of inference in which Bayes' rule is used to update the probability estimate for a hypothesis as additional evidence is acquired. The logic of Bayesian updating is essentially that of inductive learning to make epistemological inferences. See Donald A. Sylvan, Thomas M. Ostrom, and Katherine Gannon, "Case-Based, Model-Based, and Explanation-Based Styles of Reasoning in Foreign Policy," *International Studies Quarterly*, vol. 38, no. 1 (March 1994), pp. 61–90. Another way to understand it would be as a mistaken image. See Richard K. Herrmann and Michael P. Fischerkeller, "Beyond the Enemy Image and Spiral Model: Cognitive-Strategic Research after the Cold War," *International Organization*, vol. 49, no. 3 (Summer 1995), pp. 415–450.

31. Robert Jervis, "Perceiving and Coping with Threat," in Robert Jervis, Richard Ned Lebow, and Janice Gross Stein, eds., *Psychology and Deterrence* (Baltimore: Johns Hopkins University Press, 1985), pp. 24–27.

32. While it does not necessarily result in "bad" outcomes—after all, people can be right for the wrong reasons—part of misplaced certainty's importance lies in its power to fuel the dynamics leading to war. Along these lines, Robert Jervis suspects that harmonious relations "are the product of routinized and highly constrained patterns of interaction more often than the result of accurate perceptions." Jervis, "War and Misperception," in Robert I. Rotberg and Theodore K. Rabb, eds., *The Origin and Prevention of Major Wars*, eds. (Cambridge: Cambridge University Press, 1989), p. 106.

33. See Edward Warner, "Douhet, Mitchell, Seversky: Theories of Air Warfare," in Edward Mead Earle, ed., *Makers of Modern Strategy* (Princeton: Princeton University Press, 1943), pp. 484–503; Arie Kruglanski and Uri Bar Joseph, "Intelligence Failure and Need for Cognitive Closure: On the Psychology of the Yom Kippur Surprise," *Political Psychology*, vol. 24, no. 1 (March 2003), pp. 75–99; Richard Ned Lebow, *Between Peace and War* (Baltimore: Johns Hopkins University Press, 1984); and Eliot Cohen and John Gooch, "Failure to Adapt: The British at Gallipoli, August 1915," in *Military Misfortunes: The Anatomy of Failure in War* (New York: Free Press, 1990), pp. 133–164.

34. Steven Sloman and Philip M. Fernbach, "I'm Right! (for Some Reason)," *New York Times* (October 21, 2012), Sunday Review, p. 12.

35. Quoted in Thomas Gilovich, *How We Know What Isn't So: The Fallibility of Human Reason in Everyday Life* (New York: Free Press, 1991), p. 1. Similarly, Mark Twain, who was greatly influenced by Artemus Ward, is widely quoted as having said, "The trouble with this world is not that people know too little, but that they know so many things that ain't so." It is unclear, however, if and where Twain actually said it.

36. The liberal radio host, Bill Press, as quoted in Brian Stelter, "After a New-Look Debate, a Harsh Light Falls on the Moderator," *New York Times*, October 5, 2012, p. A13.

37. Richard Kim as quoted in ibid.

CHAPTER EIGHT: **Maxwell's Demon and Angry Birds**

1. Crosbie Smith, *The Science of Energy* (London: University of Chicago Press, 1998), pp. 249–251.

2. James Clerk Maxwell as quoted in Ingo Müller and Wolf Weiss, *Entropy and Energy* (Berlin: Springer-Verlag, 2005), p. 236.

3. Henry Adams, *The Education of Henry Adams: An Autobiography* (Boston: Houghton & Mifflin, 1918), p. 451.

4. For a general discussion, see Kenneth Cukier and Viktor Mayer-Schoenberger, "The Rise of Big Data: How It's Changing the Way We Think about the World," *Foreign Affairs*, vol. 92, no. 3 (May/June 2013), pp. 28–40.

5. Nate Silver, *The Signal and the Noise: Why So Many Predictions Fail—but Some Don't* (New York: Penguin, 2012), p. 9; Andrew Hacker, "How He Got It Right," *New York Review of Books*, vol. 60, no.1 (January 10, 2013), pp. 16–20 at p. 16.

6. Cukier and Mayer-Schoenberger, "The Rise of Big Data," pp. 29, 34–35.

7. Ibid., p. 28.

8. Natasha Singer, "A Data Giant Is Mapping, and Sharing, the Consumer Genome," *New York Times* (June 17, 2012), Sunday Business, pp. 1 and 8.

9. Natasha Singer, "Your Attention, Bought in an Instant," *New York Times* (November 18, 2012), Sunday Business, pp. 1 and 5 at p. 5.

10. Natasha Singer, "When a Palm Reader Knows More Than Your Life Line," *New York Times* (November 11, 2012), Sunday Business, p. 3.

11. Gil Asakawa and Leland Rucker, *The Toy Book* (New York: Alfred A. Knopf, 1992), pp. 178–179; Sam Anderson, "Just One More Game . . . How Time-Wasting Video Games Escaped the Arcade, Jumped Into Our Pockets, and Took Over Our Lives," *New York Times Magazine* (April 8, 2012), pp. 28–33, and 55 at p. 28; Rick Polizzi and Fred Schaefer, *Spin Again: Board Games from the Fifties and Sixties* (San Francisco: Chronicle Books, 1991), pp. 116–117.

12. "Living: Let's Get Trivial," *Time*, vol. 122, no. 18 (October 24, 1983), p. 230.

13. Polizzi and Schaefer, *Spin Again*, pp. 116–117.

14. See the Wikipedia entry for Tetris at http://en.wikipedia.org/wiki/Tetris.

15. Anderson, "Just One More Game," p. 28.

16. For a readable history of information processing and technology, see James Gleick, *The Information* (New York: Pantheon, 2011), prologue.

17. Norbert Wiener, *I Am a Mathemetician: The Later Life of a Prodigy* (Cambridge, MA: MIT Press, 1964), p. 324.

18. Fernand Braudel, *On History*, trans. Sarah Matthews (Chicago: University of Chicago Press, 1980), p. 6.

19. See Andrew T. Price-Smith, *Contagion and Chaos: Disease, Ecology, and National Security in the Era of Globalization* (Cambridge, MA: MIT Press, 2009), introduction.

20. See Vaclav Smil, *Global Catastrophes and Trends: The Next Fifty Years* (Cambridge, MA: MIT Press, 2008).

21. Martin J. Rees, *Our Final Hour: A Scientist's Warning: How Terror, Error, and Environmental Disaster Threaten Humankind's Future in This Century—On Earth and Beyond* (New York: Basic Books, 2003), pp. 1–2.

22. This quantitative definition of global catastrophe is used in Nick Bostrom and Milan M. Ćirković, eds., *Global Catastrophic Risks* (New York: Oxford University Press, 2008).

23. In addition to Smil, *Global Catastrophes and Trends*; Rees, *Our Final Hour*; and Bostrom and Ćirković, *Global Catastrophic Risks*, see Richard A. Posner, *Catastrophe: Risk and Response* (New York: Oxford University Press, 2004); James Lovelock, *The Revenge of Gaia: Earth's Climate Crisis and the Fate of Humanity* (New York: Basic Books, 2006); James H. Kunstler, *The Long Emergency: Surviving the End of Oil, Climate Change, and Other Converging Catastrophes of the Twenty-First Century* (New York: Grove / Atlantic Monthly Press, 2005); and Jared Diamond, *Collapse: How Societies Choose to Fail or Succeed* (New York: Viking, 2004).

24. Quoted in Michael Specter, "Letter from Cameroon: The Doomsday Strain," *New Yorker* (December 20 & 27, 2010), pp. 50–63 at p. 56.

25. H. G. Wells, *The Discovery of the Future* (1913; reprint, London: Jonathan Cape, 1921), pp. 53–55.

26. Ibid., p. 55.

27. Rees, *Our Final Hour*, p. 13.

28. Price-Smith, *Contagion and Chaos*, p. 3. He goes on to say: "The profoundly destabilizing effects of contagion result from various manifestations of illness, including high levels of mortality and/or morbidity, the destruction of human capital, economic disruption, negative psychological effects, the consequent acrimony between affected social factions, and the deteriorating relations between the people and an often draconian state."

29. Jack S. Levy and William R. Thompson, *Causes of War* (West Sussex, UK: Wiley-Blackwell, 2010), p. 1.

30. Ibid., pp. 6–7.

31. Carl von Clausewitz, *On War* [1832], ed. and trans. Michael Howard and Peter Paret (Princeton, NJ: Princeton University Press, 1976), p. 87. For sophisticated works on civil-military relations, see Samuel P. Huntington, *The Soldier and the State: The Theory and Politics of Civil-Military Relations* (Cambridge, MA: The Belknap Press of Harvard University, 1957), and Eliot A. Cohen, *Supreme Command: Soldiers, Statesmen, and Leadership in Wartime* (New York: Free Press, 2002).

32. These examples of global public goods are drawn from Scott Barrett, *Why Cooperate?: The Incentive to Supply Global Public Goods* (Oxford: Oxford University Press, 2007).

33. Nonrivalry is also called *jointness*.

34. Ibid., pp. 13–18.

35. Duncan Snidal, "The Limits of Hegemonic Stability Theory," *International Organization*, vol. 39, no. 4 (Autumn 1985), pp. 579–614 at p. 581. The quote is somewhat misleading. Snidal is merely reiterating Charles Kindleberger's logic, which he borrowed from Mancur Olson and which Snidal himself disagrees with.

36. This is the so-called hegemon's dilemma. See Arthur Stein, "The Hegemon's Dilemma: Great Britain, the United States, and the International Economic Order," *International Organization*, vol. 38, no. 2 (Spring 1984), pp. 355–386. The core argument is that liberal trade regimes do not emerge from a hegemon alone; they are the result of asymmetric bargains between the hegemon and weaker powers that permit discrimination, especially against the hegemon itself. The price of hegemonic leadership is concessions to gain followers and make agreements.

37. Robert O. Keohane, "The Demand for International Regimes," *International Organization*, vol. 36, no. 2 (Spring 1982), pp. 325–355 at p. 331.

38. See Josef Joffe, "'Bismarck' or 'Britain'? Toward an American Grand Strategy after Bipolarity," *International Security*, vol. 19, no. 4 (Spring 1995), pp. 94–117, and *Überpower* (New York: W. W. Norton, 2006), chap. 5.

39. For various phases in the hegemonic cycle, see Robert Gilpin, *War and Change in World Politics* (New York: Cambridge University Press, 1981). Both Robert Gilpin and Stephen Krasner see hegemonic rule as more imperial and coercive than benevolent, though the hegemon does tend to overpay for the benefits it gains from global leadership. See Stephen Krasner, "State Power and the Structure of International Trade," *World Politics*, vol. 28, no. 3 (April 1976), pp. 317–347; and Robert Gilpin, *U.S. Power and the Multinational Corporation* (New York: Basic, 1975). In contrast, Robert Keohane and Charles Kindleberger theorize the hegemon as a benevolent leader that provides public goods at greater cost to itself than to everyone else. See Robert O. Keohane, *After Hegemony: Cooperation and Discord in the World Political Economy* (Princeton, NJ: Princeton University Press, 1984); and Kindleberger, "Systems of International Economic Organization," in David Calleo, ed., *Money and the Coming World Order* (New York: NYU Press, 1976). Both sides are partly correct. The hegemon provides benevolent leadership when it is far stronger than everyone else. As it declines, however, it becomes more like the Gilpin-Krasner "coercive" version of hegemony, demanding tribute and taxes for its services. For a discussion of the competing benevolent-coercive versions of hegemonic rule, see Snidal, "The Limits of Hegemonic Stability Theory," pp. 585–590.

40. Charles Kindleberger, *The World in Depression, 1929–1939* (Berkeley: University of California Press, 1974) and "Systems of International Economic Organization."

41. Though focused on the demand rather than the supply side, Keohane's argument essentially fits this logic. See Keohane, "The Demand for International Regimes" and *After Hegemony*.

42. Snidal, "The Limits of Hegemonic Stability Theory," pp. 598ff.

43. See Charles A. Kupchan, "The Democratic Malaise," *Foreign Affairs*, vol. 91, no. 1 (January/February 2012), pp. 86–89.

44. Charles A. Kupchan, *No One's World: The West, the Rising Rest, and the Coming Global Turn* (New York: Oxford University Press, 2012), pp. 144–145.

45. This argument is fully developed with respect to China's rise in Randall L. Schweller and Xiaoyu Pu, "After Unipolarity," *International Security*, vol. 36, no. 1 (Summer 2011), pp. 41–72.

46. Josef Joffe, "How America Does It," *Foreign Affairs*, vol. 76, no. 5 (September/October 1997), pp. 13–27 at p. 27.

47. Azar Gat, "The Return of Authoritarian Great Powers," *Foreign Affairs*, vol. 86, no. 4 (July/August 2007), pp. 59–69.

48. Robert Rycroft, "Self-Organizing Innovation Networks: Implications for Globalization," Occasional Paper Series (Washington, DC: George Washington University's Center for the Study of Globalization, 2003), www.gwu.edu/~cistp/assets/docs/research/articles/SelfOrganizing_RWR_2.24.03.pdf.

49. John A. Courtright, Gail T. Fairhurst, and L. Edna Rogers, "Interaction Patterns in Organic and Mechanistic Systems," *Academy of Management Journal*, vol. 32, no. 4 (December 1989), pp. 773–802; Richard L. Daft, *Essentials of Organization Theory and Design*, 2nd ed. (Mason, OH: Cengage Learning, 2007), chap. 4.

50. Gerald Zaltman, Robert Duncan, and Johnny Holbek, *Innovations and Organizations* (New York: Wiley, 1973), p. 131.

51. Rapid adaptability is key in an environment of extreme uncertainty and risk. The safest bet is a strategy of incremental change. Networks, for instance, prosper when they are able to deliver incremental improvements in performance, quality, and cost ahead of their competitors.

52. Jeffrey Herbst, *States and Power in Africa* (Princeton, NJ: Princeton University Press, 2000), p. 253.

53. Charles Tilly, "Reflections on the History of European State-Making," in Tilly, ed., *The Formation of National States in Western Europe* (Princeton, NJ: Princeton University Press, 1975), p. 42.

54. Samuel P. Huntington, *Political Order in Changing Societies* (New Haven, CT: Yale University Press, 1968), p. 123.

55. John Mueller, *The Remnants of War* (Ithaca, NY: Cornell University Press, 2004).

56. Jason K. Stearns, *Dancing in the Glory of Monsters: The Collapse of the Congo and the Great War of Africa* (New York: PublicAffairs, 2011), p. 329.

57. Ibid., p. 5.

58. Anjan Sundaram, "That Other War," *Foreign Policy* (November 20, 2012), www.foreignpolicy.com/articles/2012/11/20/that_other_war.

59. Ibid., emphasis added.

60. As the political scientist James Fearon avers, this latest episode in the war shows "just how easy it can be to take over some African states, or large parts of them. The post-independence historical record provides numerous examples where dozens or a few hundred armed men have done it." James Fearon, "The Unbelievable Lightness of Some African States," *The Monkey Cage* (November 23, 2012), http://themonkeycage.org/blog/2012/11/23/the-unbelievable-lightness-of-some-african-states/.

61. C. Fred Bergsten, "The Dollar and the Deficits: How Washington Can Prevent the Next Crisis," *Foreign Affairs*, vol. 88, no. 6 (November/December 2009), pp. 20–38 at p. 21.

62. "China's New Leadership," *Economist*, vol. 405, no. 8808 (October 27–November 2, 2012), p. 22.

63. Thane Gustafson, "Putin's Petroleum Problem: How Oil Is Holding Russia Back—and How It Could Save It," *Foreign Affairs*, vol. 91, no. 6 (November/December 2012), pp. 83–96.

64. Graham Denyer Willis, "What's Killing Brazil's Police?" *New York Times* (December 2, 2012), Sunday Review, p. 5.

65. "What Is Brazil's Army For?" *Economist* (September 9, 2010), www.economist. com/blogs/americasview/2010/09/brazils_military.

66. David D. Kirkpatrick, "Morsi Defends Wide Authority as Turmoil Rises," *New York Times* (December 7, 2012), p. A1.

67. Quoted in David D. Kirkpatrick, "Morsi Extends a Compromise to Opposition," *New York Times* (December 9, 2012), p. A1.

68. Amr Moussa as quoted in ibid., p. A12.

69. President Mohamed Morsi, as quoted in Richard Stengel, Bobby Ghosh and Karl Vick, "Transcript: TIME's Interview with Egyptian President Mohamed Morsi," *Time* (November 28, 2012), http://world.time.com/2012/11/28/transcript-times-interview-with -egyptian-president-mohamed-morsi/#ixzz2QM4219Pn.

70. Jacques Barzun, *From Dawn to Decadence: 500 Years of Western Cultural Life, 1500 to the Present* (New York: HarperCollins, 2000), p. xvi.

71. Albert Camus, *The Myth of Sisyphus and Other Essays* (1942; reprint, New York: Vintage International, 1991), p. 123.

72. R.E.M., "It's the End of the World as We Know It (And I Feel Fine)," music and lyrics by Bill Berry, Peter Buck, Mike Mills, and Michael Stipe, *Document* (IRS Records, 1987).

Index

Page numbers in *italics* refer to tables.